. . . for, lo, the eternal and sovereign luminous space,
where rule the unnumbered stars,
is the air we breathe in
and the air we breathe out.
And in the moment betwixt the breathing in
and the breathing out
is hidden all the mysteries
of the Infinite Garden.

— Essene Gospel of Peace

How to

*A Primer on the Life-Giving
Biointensive Method
of Organic Horticulture*

*than you ever thought possible

Grow More Vegetables*

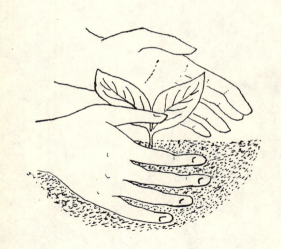

by John Jeavons

ECOLOGY ACTION of the MIDPENINSULA

1⊙ Ten Speed Press

on less land than you can imagine

Published by

TEN SPEED PRESS
P.O. Box 7123
Berkeley, California 94707

Library of Congress Cataloging in
    Publication Data

Jeavons, John.
    How to grow more vegetables than
you ever thought possible on less land
than you can imagine : a primer on the
life-giving biointensive method of
organic horticulture / by John Jeavons.
— Rev. ed.
            p.   cm.
    Includes bibliographical references.
    ISBN: 0-89815-415-4 (paperbound)
    1. Vegetable gardening. 2. Organic
gardening.   I. Title.
SB324.3.J43   1991
635—dc20   90-27896
                              CIP

Book and cover design by Brenton Beck,
    Fifth Street Design Associates
Cover and major illustrations by
    Pedro J. Gonzalez
Other illustrations by Betsy Jeavons
    Bruneau

Printed in the United States of America

      3   4   5 — 95 94 93 92

Drawing of Common Ground Garden provided by Landal Institute, Sausalito, CA

Contents

Preface / x

Introduction / vx

History and Philosophy / 2

Bed Preparation / 6

    Initial Preparation Chart
    Tools
    Double Digging Process

Fertilization / 21

    Soil Testing
    Fertilizers
    General Program

Compost / 34

    Simple Compost Recipe—46

Seed Propagation / 47

	Master Charts (Use Column H for spacings)
Seed Planting	
Flats	Vegetables—70
Transplanting	Grains—78
Moon Planting	Cover crops—82
Watering	Special Crops—86
Weeding	Tree and Vine Crops—90
Plant Seasons	Flowers and Herbs—100

Making the Garden Plan / 103

Simple Mini-Garden
One-Person Mini-Garden—Plans for Four Years
Family Garden

Companion Planting / 120

Health
Beneficial Herbs
Crop Rotation
Multi-Crop Planting
Physical Complementarity

Weed Control
Insect Control
Companion Vegetable Chart
Companion Herb Chart

A Balanced Natural Backyard Ecosystem and Insect Life / 134

An Ecosystem and Natural Predators
Simple Insect and Pest Control

Bibliography / 143

Plan your Own Mini-Course!

Animals
Arid
Bed Preparation
Companion Planting
Composting
Cover/Fodder/Organic
 Matter Crops
Development
Experiences
Fertilizer
Films and Video Tapes
Flowers
Food and Nutrition

General
Grains
Greenhouse Culture
Herbs
High-Altitude Food
 Raising
History and Philosophy
Homesteading
Income
Insect Life
Language and Travel
Learning/Teaching
Magazines

Other Crops
Seed Catalogs
Seed Propagation
Soil
Supply Catalogs
Terracing
Testing
Tools
Trees
Tropics/Groups
Tropics/Publications
Vegetables
Water

Who is Ecology Action? / 165

"The Method"—Made Simple

The preceding Table of Contents has special notations to make this book especially easy to use for the beginner. One of the advantages of *How to Grow More Vegetables* . . . is that it is a complete general approach to gardening. As one learns the basics of soil preparation, the simple joys of gardening grow in depth. This is because the bed preparation, fertilization, composting, seed propagation, transplanting, watering and weeding are performed essentially in the same way for *all* crops. Only the seedling flat and growing bed spacings are different from one crop to another and these are given in the *first* columns M and H of each section of the master charts beginning on page 70. So, once you know how to grow lettuce, you know most of the basics for growing onions, tomatoes, wheat, apple trees, and even cotton!

Remember to enjoy the gardening experience while you are working: the warmth of the sun, the touch of a breeze, the scent of a flower, the smell of freshly turned soil, the song of a bird, and the beauty of it all. Above all it should be fun!

One way to harvest the fullest enjoyment is to garden with your family or friends. Light conversations make the time pass quickly during even the most difficult tasks. Consider having a barbeque or picnic after double-digging, a neighborhood compost building party, and letting your children experience the joy of harvesting! And preserving the year's harvest is always a social occasion. Gardening together is a practical experience of learning and sharing for each of us, and it is at least half of the fun.

As a *beginning* gardener reads *How to Grow More Vegetables . . . ,* he or she will want to skip most of the tables except for the *first* column H in the master charts which list plant spacings. These charts begin on page 70. A beginner normally starts by growing vegetables and a few flowers and herbs and many of those crops could even be bought as seedlings from a local nursery. Starting your own seedlings is another level of skill that can be tried the second or third year.

As this book is reread, an *intermediate* gardener will begin to use more of the tables and charts and to grow some cover crops, grains, and fruit trees. The Bibliography will begin to be a source of additional learning on particular topics of interest as a skilled backyard mini-farmer begins to emerge.

Ten years in the garden will produce a fully experienced food grower. This person will draw on most of the information provided in the book as he or she works on growing most or all of the family's food at home, plants a mini-orchard in the front yard, or teaches others the skills already mastered.

How to Grow More Vegetables . . . , then, provides one with everything needed to create a garden symphony—from the basic techniques to a beautifully planted backyard homestead. What is exciting is that each of us will never know everything! Alan Chadwick, when he had been gardening for fifty years, often said, "I am still learning." And so are we all. There is a lifetime of growing before us and the living "canvas" we are "painting" will always be getting better!

Preface

The Common Ground Garden was started in 1972 to find the agricultural techniques that would make food-raising by small farmers and gardeners more efficient. We have come to call the result "mini-farming." Mini-farms can flourish in non-agricultural areas such as mountainous regions, arid areas, and in and around urban centers. Food can be produced where people live. With knowledge and skill, output per hour can be high without the expensive machinery that is the addiction of our current agriculture. Mini-farming is available to everyone.

So far we have concentrated on the exciting possibilities presented by the biointensive method—does this method really produce four times the yield, as its originator claimed? If so, does it take more water? Consume vast amounts of fertilizer and organic matter? Does it exhaust the soil? Or the people working? The only way to answer these questions was to plunge in and try it. We have mostly been working on the quantitative aspects, developing the tools and data to maximize yields within the framework of its life-giving approach. This has involved experimentation with and evaluation of plant spacings, fertilizer inputs, various watering methods, and other variables. The work has always been worthwhile despite ongoing difficulties attracting strong and sustaining support. The biggest single asset to this undertaking is John Jeavons's unfailing stamina and dedication. Over and over, when we all ask, "Can it work?" he answers, "How are we going to make it work?" It is becoming increasingly clear that use of "the method" will be an important part of the solution to starvation and malnutrition, dwindling energy supplies, unemployment, and exhaustion and loss of arable land, if the social and political barriers can be overcome.

After 10 years of testing, "the method" has produced amazing benefits, and a lot of work is still to be done. YIELDS can average 4–6 times those of U.S. agriculture and range on up to 31 times. The full potential has probably not yet been reached. We are still working to develop an optimally healthy soil system. GRAINS, BEANS, and COVER CROPS present the most challenges because they are crucial in meeting nutritional needs for people and the soil. Experiments include soybeans, alfalfa, fava beans, wheat, and comfrey. So far our yields are from one to five times the U.S. averages for these crops. WATER use is well below that of commercial agriculture per pound of food produced, and may be about 1/2 that of commercial techniques per unit of land area. ENERGY consumption, expressed in kilocalories of input, is 1/100 that used by commercial agriculture. The human body is still more efficient than any machine we have been able to invent. Several factors contradict the popular conception of this as a labor-intensive method. Using hand tools may seem to be more work, but the yields more than compensate. At 25¢ a pound *wholesale,* zucchini brings us $9.00 to $16.00 per hour depending on harvest size. Time spent in soil preparation is more than offset later in less need for weeding, thinning, cultivation, and other chores per unit of area and per unit of yield. Hand watering and harvesting appear to take the most time. Initial soil preparation may take up to 8 hours per 100-square-foot raised bed. Thereafter the time spent decreases dramatically. A new digging tool, the U-bar, has reduced subsequent bed preparation time to as little as 20 minutes when that is desirable. A new hand watering tool is also being developed which waters more quickly *and* more gently.

Nature has answered our original queries with an abundance even greater than expected and narrowed our search to the most important question that can be asked of any agricultural system. Is it sustainable? The biointensive method currently uses 1/2 or less the nitrogen fertilizer that commercial farmers use. Can we produce all fertilizer needs on site? Or is some outside input always necessary? We need to look more closely at other nutrients: phosphorus, potash, calcium, and trace minerals. Anyone can grow good crops on good soil, cashing in on Nature's accumulated riches. The biointensive method appears to allow anyone to take "the worst possible soil" (Alan Chadwick's appraisal of our research site) and turn it into a bountiful garden. The long-term question of soil sustainability is still to be answered. Preliminary monitoring of the soil-building process by a University of California soil scientist was probably the most important research performed at the garden. Continued monitoring may unlock new secrets and provide hope for people with marginal, worn-out or desertified soils. However, a complete answer will require at least 50 years of observation as the living soil system changes and grows!

Nine years of growing and testing in Ecology Action's

urban garden came to an end during 1980 due to the termination of our lease and the start of construction on that land. Like so much other agricultural land in the United States, our lovingly tended beds succumbed to the press of urbanization. The city garden has prepared us for a rural site. The "safety nets" of grocery store and electric lines will soon be removed to make room for open skies and room to grow more herbs, flowers, vegetables, beans, and grains than we ever imagined. We are especially looking forward to a permanent site where we can grow trees of all kinds, for food, fuel, and beauty. Other favored projects will be a self-fertilizing lawn composed of fragrant herbs and clovers, and a working "mini-farm." We estimate that a one-person small holding (1/8 to 1/2 acre) can grow crops bringing in a net income of $5,000 to $20,000 a year after 4 to 5 years. We hope to achieve this income from 1/8 acre set aside in a research area soon after a new site is established. Crops grown may include collards, chard, beets, spinach, green onions, garlic, radishes, romaine and Bibb lettuce, zucchini, patty pan squash, and cucumbers. Most importantly, we hope people will not look solely to Ecology Action for answers, but will dig in and try "the method" for themselves! The techniques are simple to use, as this book shows. No large capital expenses are necessary to get started. The techniques work in varied climates and soils. American farmers are "feeding the world," but mini-farming gives people the knowledge to feed themselves.

Posted on the wall of our local environmental center is a tongue-in-cheek guide called "50 Really Difficult Things You Can Do to Save the Earth." The first is "bury your car." The second is "grow all your own vegetables."

I had to chuckle. We moved up to our new mini-farm in Willits with a 5-Year Plan for food self-sufficiency. That was almost 9 years ago. Just last week we took a neighborly ribbing for racing down to the farmers' market where we go to buy sweet young corn, carrots, and strawberries to feed an extended family of staff, apprentices, visitors, and friends at the research farm.

After years of biointensive food-raising research, John Jeavons declared in the first edition of this book that the method used 1/4 the land, 1/3 the water, 1/2 or less the fertilizer, and 1/100 the energy to produce a pound of food. As a result of our many publications, individuals, families, and organizations now use this method of raising food with many notable projects in more than 100 countries, including Mexico, India, Kenya, and the Philippines. Now, after more years in a new research garden, we've learned that there are other, more complex reasons to grow a garden.

Of all the great ideas from the 1960's and 1970's, organic gardening is one that is still with us. Why? What keeps hundreds of thousands of people at something that is neither easy nor immediately rewarding?

Assistant garden manager Marion Cartwright gardens as a solution to excessive consumerism. "There is something impoverished about a life spent reaching over the counter for onions and potatoes," she says.

My first garden was a total failure. I planned, dug, and planted, but I hadn't really learned how to garden yet. Now my favorite class to teach is compost. I bring a glass jar of waste—a slimy brew of potato peels, coffee grounds, and last week's rotting roses. The other jar has compost—sweet smelling, earthy, and alive, and, by the way, nothing like the sifted and homogenized product sold at garden centers. These two jars remind me of the magical transformation of a garden: health from garbage, riches out of waste. I can "see" that magic in 30 seconds, though it may take me another 10 years to fully comprehend it!

Betsy Jeavons Bruneau, a senior staffperson of Ecology Action, has a special affinity for tiny life forms. She taught me to appreciate the infinitely variable lichens that cling to bare rock and fallen trees, creating soil for the larger life forms to follow. People used to bring insects into our store for identification. Betsy's first response was usually a hushed "how beautiful!" She still marvels at the intensely colorful tomato hornworms, the intricate markings on the shells of wise old snails, and the fact that earwigs are wonderful mothers.

We live in an age of consumerism, when we are constantly exhorted to measure ourselves by our possessions. Yet no matter how rich we manage to become, something human in us says our true worth is reflected by what we ourselves create. Why not make it full of life and beauty rather than pollution?

My neighbor Ellen spent all day putting up jars of string beans and piccalilli, then worked until midnight to finish up a batch of raspberries. Her note reads, "There is no rest for the gardener . . . but there is dessert!"

Gardening is not always easy, but the rewards are personal and fun. For most of us the environment is what is around us, separate from human activity. Gardening offers the chance to become partners with nature. The reward is not just the salad from the back step, or the gleaming jar of peaches. It is the process of digging the soil, starting small seeds, watching an apple tree grow. It is an education in observation, in harmony, honesty, and humility—in knowing and understanding our place in the world.

But the impact is also global. Alan Chadwick felt that gardening was the only way to prevent another world war—to bring a living, active peace on Earth by working with healthy, creative, positive life forces. In doing this, we become one with those life forces. The home-grown tomato requires no fuel in its transport, no packaging to be sent to the landfill, no political decisions about who will be allowed to work the fields or what level of pollutants will be tolerated in our groundwater.

We are beginning to realize that deserts may not be natural. They are usually the result of human activity. By the same token, nature is not always a Garden of Eden. Some partnership is required to bring out the best in both nature and people. "Give to Nature, and she will repay you in glorious abundance," was Chadwick's favorite line. Gardening gives us the opportunity to participate in the subtle transformation of the desert to dessert. All we need to do is to start with one growing bed and tend it well, and we've begun this exciting, expansive, giving process of enlivening and healing the Earth and ourselves.

Robin Leler Jeavons
January 1, 1991

Introduction

In September 1971, Larry White, Director of the Nature and Science Department for the City of Palo Alto, invited Stephen Kafka, Senior Apprentice at the University of California–Santa Cruz Student Garden, to give a 4-hour class on the biodynamic/French intensive method of gardening. Two years before, the City had made land available to the public for gardening and residents appeared eager to hear more about this method. Alan Chadwick had brought the method to Santa Cruz 5 years earlier, and with love, vision, and apparent magic, the master horticulturist had converted a barren slope into a Garden of Eden. Vegetables, flowers, and herbs flourished everywhere. The techniques of the method were primarily available through training in a 2-year apprentice program at Santa Cruz and through periodic classes given by Alan Chadwick or Stephen Kafka. However, neither detailed public classes nor vegetable yield research were being conducted regularly at Santa Cruz or in Palo Alto.

In January 1972, Ecology Action's Board of Directors approved a biointensive method research and education project. The purposes of the Ecology Action project were

- to teach regular classes
- to collect data on the reportedly fourfold yields produced by the environmentally sound horticultural method
- to make land available for gardening to additional mid-peninsula residents
- to publish information on the method's techniques.

In May, after a 5-month search for land, the Syntex Corporation offered 3-3/4 acres of their grounds in the Stanford Industrial Park at no cost and all the water needed for the project. Frank Koch, Syntex Public Affairs Director, told Dr.

Alejandro Zaffaroni of the Alza Corporation about the project and Dr. Zaffaroni subsequently contributed the first money to the project, $5,000 without which we never could have begun. Commitment by Frank Koch, Don Keppy, Chuck and Dian Missar, Ruth Edwards, Ibby Bagley, numerous individuals, several corporations, and the Point Foundation enabled the project to continue.

Alan Chadwick soon visited the garden site and gave us basic advice on how to proceed. We then attended a series of lectures given by Mr. Chadwick in Saratoga, California. Using the classes taught by Alan Chadwick and Stephen Kafka as a base, we began teaching our own classes in the spring of 1972.

Further study and experience in the garden have made it possible to increase the original class to a 5-week series which is continually "recycled." The series of classes led to the development of information sheets on topics such as vegetable spacings and composting techniques. Many people have asked for a book containing all the information we have gathered. Those who have been unable to attend our Saturday classes or have friends who live outside the area have been especially insistent. This book is the result. Robin Leler Jeavons, Betsy Jeavons Bruneau, Tom Walker, Craig Cook, Rip King, Bill Spencer, Claudette Paige, Kevin Raftery, Marion Cartwright, Paka, Phyllis Anderson, Wayne Miller, Paul Hwoschinsky, Dave Smith, Steve and Judi Rioch, Louisa Lenz, Bill Bruneau, Dean Nims, Tommy Derrick, members of Ecology Action, and friends have all made important contributions to its content and spirit.

I assume responsibility for any inaccuracies which may have been included—they are mine and not Alan Chadwick's or Stephen Kafka's. The book is not intended to be an exhaustive work on the subject, but rather one of simple completeness. We, ourselves, are only at a beginning to intermediate stage of knowledge. Its purpose is to "turn on" as many people as possible to a beautiful, dynamically alive method of horticulture and life. I had hoped that the great interest this book is stimulating would eventually encourage Alan to write an extensive work on the many sophisticated techniques which only he knew well. Because of his untimely death in 1980, this is no longer possible.

Our initial research seems to indicate that the method can produce an average of four times more vegetables per acre than the amount grown by farmers using mechanized and chemical agricultural techniques. The method also appears to use 1/8 the water, 1/2 to none of the purchased nitrogen fertilizer, and 1/100 the energy consumed by commercial agriculture, per pound of vegetable grown.[1] The flavor of the

1. Figures for yield and water and fertilizer consumption are based on data collected through 1979. The 1/100 energy consumption figure is from a November 2, 1973, letter from Richard Merrill, Director of the New Alchemy Institute–West, Pescadero, California.

vegetables is usually excellent and there are indications that their nutritive value can be higher than that of commercially grown vegetables. The method is exciting to me because each of us becomes important again as we find our place *in relation* to nature.

One person annually consumes in food the energy equivalent (in calories or British Thermal Units) of 32.6 gallons of gasoline.[2] In contrast, the best economy car available will use that much gas in a month or two of ordinary driving. Imagine the fuel consumed by a tractor or industrial machine each year! People are not only beautiful, they are very capable and efficient! At this point we believe "the method" can even produce more net income per acre than commercial agriculture. With "the method" we help provide for the needs of the plants instead of trying to dominate them. When we provide for these real needs, the plants bounteously provide more food. In striving for quality, a person will be able to provide a diet and income more than sufficient for his or her needs. The effort will produce a human renaissance and a cornucopia of food for all.

Our work grows out of a personal concern about worldwide starvation and malnutrition. If we could determine the smallest amount of land and resources needed for one person to supply all of his or her own needs in a *sustainable* way, we might have a *personal solution*. What if a person could, in a tiny area, easily raise the crops that would supply all food, clothes, building materials, compost materials, seeds, and income for an entire year?

We asked others if they knew the smallest area required to do this, and no one did—so we began our 20-year quest. If we could find these answers, we might help settle an ongoing problem and make possible a better quality of life.

Generally, the problem of world hunger is so overwhelming that we tend to look for big solutions, such as massive grain shipments, the breeding of high-yield miracle crops, or the establishment of infrastructures—bank loans, machinery and fertilizer purchases, markets, and roads. These solutions create long-term dependency. What is so exciting about a personal approach is that it seeks to answer the question, "How do we really enable ourselves to take care of our own needs?"

Once discovered, these personal solutions have as many varied applications as there are people, soils, climates, and

Energy Data were collected and evaluated by Mr. Merrill and Michael J. Perelman, Assistant Professor of Economics, California State University at Chico. The data are for a growing area with a proper humus content after a 5-year development period. The data are a qualitative projection and have been assembled during a 3-year period of tests performed on root and leaf crops (except brassicas) grown by hand cultivation in the Santa Barbara area with its 9-month growing season. (The 1/100 figure does not include the energy required to get the soil system to the point noted above and does not include unproductive plots which constituted 10% of the area under cultivation.)

2. Michael Perelman, "Efficiency in Agriculture: The Economics of Energy," in *Radical Agriculture,* edited by Richard Merrill, Harper and Row, New York, 1976, p. 86.

cultures. Our work is a beginning point from which others will develop the new combinations that will work best for them.

Most exciting to me are the universal scientific principles operating within sustainable biointensive mini-farming's biological systems. These are what we all need to learn more about and understand fully. The results change each time we modify the system. For example, the microbial life levels and yields differ depending on whether we prepare the soil 7 inches, 12 inches, or 24 inches deep. Why? We all get to explore this and many other variations to determine the answers. In the process, we will discover the principles underlying the changes, and a whole new world will unfold. Once we understand the principles we will be able to make changes to improve the health, fertility, effectiveness, and sustainability of the way we farm for an even better life on this planet.

Much new material is included in this latest revision: some improved soil preparation approaches, updated fertilizer and compost information, basic water consumption information for natural rainfall and drought growing, corrected and updated yield and planning data, added data for grain, fodder, cover, and tree crop growing, and a greatly expanded bibliography. In short, more information to add to your fun as you grow past the beginning stage of biointensive mini-farming in depth and breadth! This edition represents almost 2 decades of our working with plants, chickens, and goats. We hope it will make your path easier.

John Jeavons
January 1, 1991
Willits, California

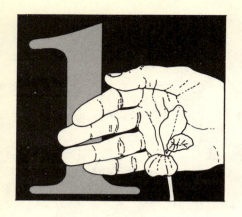

History and Philosophy

The biodynamic/French intensive method of horticulture is a quiet, vitally alive art of organic gardening which relinks people with the whole universe—a universe in which each of us is an interwoven part of the whole. People find their place by relating and cooperating in harmony with the sun, air, rain, soil, moon, insects, plants, and animals rather than by attempting to dominate them. All these elements will teach us their lessons and do the gardening for us if we will only watch and listen. We each become gentle shepherds providing the conditions for plant growth.

The biodynamic/French intensive method is a combination of two forms of horticulture begun in Europe during the late 1800's and early 1900's. French intensive techniques were developed in the 1890's outside Paris on 2 acres of land. Crops were grown on an 18-inch depth of horse manure, a fertilizer which was readily available. The crops were grown so close to each other that when the plants were mature their leaves would barely touch. The close spacing provided a *mini-climate* and a *living mulch* which reduced weed growth and helped hold moisture in the soil. During the winter glass jars were placed over seedlings to give them an early start. The gardeners grew up to nine crops each year and could even grow melon plants during the winter.

The biodynamic techniques were developed by Rudolf Steiner, an Austrian genius, philosopher, and educator in the early 1920's. Noting a decline in the nutritive value and yields of crops in Europe, Steiner traced the cause to the use of the newly introduced synthetic, chemical fertilizers and pesticides. An increase was also noticed in the number of crops affected by disease and insect problems. These fertilizers were not complete and vital meals for the plants, but single, physical nutrients in a soluble salt form. Initially, only nitrogen fertilizers were used to stimulate growth. Later phosphorus and

Winter lettuce growing in 1890's Cloche (Bell-Glass). Standard diameter 16-3/4 inches.

potash were added to strengthen the plants and to minimize disease and insect problems. Eventually, trace minerals were added to the chemical larder to round out the plants' diet. After breaking down nutrients into their component parts for plant food, people found it necessary to recombine them in mixtures approximating a balanced diet. This attempt might have been more successful if the fertilizers had not caused chemical changes in the soil which damaged its structure, killed beneficial microbiotic life, and greatly reduced its ability to make nutrients already in the air and soil available to plants.

Rudolf Steiner returned to the more gentle, diverse, and balanced diets of organic fertilizers as a cure for the ills brought on by synthetic, chemical fertilization. He stressed the holistic growing environment of plants: their rate of growth, the synergistic balance of their environments and nutrients, their proximity with other plants, and their various *companion* relationships. He initiated a movement to scientifically explore the relationship which plants have with each other. From centuries of farmer experience and from tests, it has been determined that certain flowers, herbs, weeds, and other plants can minimize insect attacks on plants. Many plants also benefit one another. Strawberries and green beans produce better when grown together. In contrast, onions stunt the growth of green beans. Tomatoes are narcissists—they prefer to be grown alone in compost made from tomato plants.

The biodynamic method also brought back raised planting beds. Two thousand years ago, the Greeks noticed that plant life thrives in landslides. The loose soil allows air, moisture,

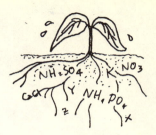

Artificial fertilization

Natural fertilization

French gardeners at lettuce beds —early 1900's.

(Left) Biodynamic/French intensive raised bed; (right) traditional rows.

Row plants are more susceptible to soil compaction.

warmth, nutrients[3] and roots to properly penetrate the soil. The curved surface area between the two edges of the landslide bed provides more surface area for the penetration and interaction of the natural elements than a flat surface. The simulated landslides or raised beds used by biodynamic gardeners are usually 3 to 6 feet wide and of varying lengths. In contrast, the planting rows usually made by gardeners and farmers today are only a few inches wide with wide spaces in between. The plants have difficulty growing in these rows due to the *extreme* penetration of air and the greater fluctuations in temperature and moisture content. During irrigation, water floods the rows, immerses the roots in water, and washes soil away from the rows and upper roots. Consequently, much of the beneficial microbiotic life around the roots and soil, which is so essential to disease prevention and to the transformation of nutrients into forms the plants can use, is destroyed and may even be replaced by harmful organisms. (About three-quarters of the beneficial microbiotic life inhabits the upper 6 inches of the soil.) After the water penetrates the soil, the upper layers dry out and microbial activity is severely curtailed. The rows are then more subject to wide temperature fluctuations. Finally, to cultivate and harvest, people and machines trundle down the troughs between the rows, compacting the soil and the roots which eat, drink, and breathe—a difficult task with someone or something standing on the equivalent of your mouth and nose!

These difficulties are also often experienced at the *edges* of biodynamic/French intensive raised beds prepared in clay soils during the first few seasons. Until the soil texture becomes friable, it is necessary to level the top of the raised bed to minimize erosion (see chapter on Bed Preparation) and the soil on the sides of the beds is sometimes too tight for easy planting. Increased exposure to the elements occurs on the sides and the tighter soil of the paths is nearby. The plants along the sides usually do not grow as vigorously as those further inside the bed. When raised beds are prepared in friable soil, the opposite is true. The top of the bed can now be curved and erosion will not be a problem. The soil is loose enough for plants to thrive along the sides. The mini-climate

3. Alan Chadwick used to call these *nutriments,* the things that "nourish or promote growth and repair the natural wastage of organic life." He used the term to distinguish them from *nutrients,* which are merely "nourishing substances or ingredients." He did this in particular to note the importance of multinutrient organic fertilizers, which break down over a long period of time and nourish microbial life growth. In contrast, chemical fertilizers generally break down rapidly and cause inefficient decomposition of organic matter. This organic matter is the microbial life's food source. In this book, *nutrient* has both meanings.

effect created by closely spaced plants is added to the edges of the beds and the water that runs from the middle of the bed provides the extra moisture which is needed.

During the time between the 1920's and the 1960's, Alan Chadwick, an Englishman, combined the biodynamic and French intensive techniques into the biodynamic/French intensive method. The United States was first exposed to the combination when Mr. Chadwick brought the method to the 4-acre organic Student Garden at the University of California's Santa Cruz campus in the 1960's. Alan Chadwick, a horticultural genius, had been gardening for half a century and was also an avid dramatist and artist. He studied under Rudolf Steiner, the French gardeners, and George Bernard Shaw, and worked as a gardener for the Union of South Africa. The site he developed at Santa Cruz was on the side of a hill with a poor, clayey soil. Not even "weeds" grew well there—except poison oak, which was removed with pickaxes. By hand, Alan Chadwick and his apprentices created a good soil in 2 to 3 years. From this soil and vision, a beautiful, wondrous, and real Garden of Eden was brought into existence. Barren soil was made *fertile* through extensive use of compost, with its life-giving humus. The humus produced a healthy soil that grew healthy plants less susceptible to disease and insect attacks. The many nuances of the biodynamic/French intensive method—such as transplanting seedlings into a better soil each time a plant is moved and sowing by the phases of the moon—were also used. The results were beautiful flowers with exquisite fragrances and tasty vegetables of high quality. As an added bonus for all the tender loving care they received, the vegetable plants produced yields four times greater than those produced by commercial agriculture.

Lush growing beds at Common Ground make optimal use of garden space.

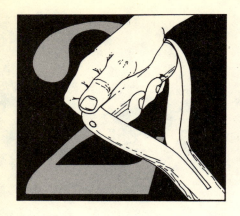

Bed Preparation

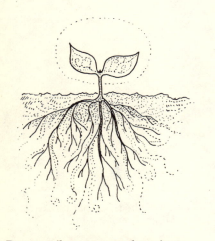

Proper soil structure and nutrients allow uninterrupted and healthy plant growth.

The preparation of the raised bed is the most important step in biodynamic/French intensive gardening (now called biointensive gardening by Ecology Action). The proper structure and nutrients allow uninterrupted and healthy plant growth. Loose soil with good nutrients enables roots to penetrate the soil easily and a steady stream of nutrients flows into the stem and leaves. How different from the usual situation when a plant is transferred from a flat with loose soil and proper nutrients into a hastily prepared backyard plot or a chemically stimulated field. Not only does the plant suffer from the shock of being uprooted, it is also placed in an environment where it is more difficult to grow. The growth is interrupted, the roots have difficulty getting through the soil and obtaining food, and the plant develops more carbohydrates and less protein than usual. Insects prefer the carbohydrates. The plant becomes more susceptible to insect attack and ultimately to disease. A debilitating cycle has begun which often ends in the use of pesticides that kill soil life and make the plants less healthy. More fertilizers are then used in an attempt to boost the health of the plants. Instead, the fertilizers kill more soil life, damage the structure of the soil further, and bring into being even sicker plants that attract more insects and need more toxic "medicines" in the form of pesticides and additional fertilizers. There are well-documented reports on a wide variety of commercial pesticides, which kill beneficial invertebrate predators while controlling pest populations. These pesticides exterminate earthworms and other invertebrates that are needed to maintain soil fertility. The pesticides also destroy microorganisms that provide symbiotic relationships between the soil and plant root systems. Why not strive for good health in the first place!

Unless you are lucky enough to have loose soil, preparing and planting a raised bed takes a lot of work—as much as 6 to

12 hours for a 100-square-foot bed 5 feet by 20 feet the first time. After the first crop, however, only 4 to 6 hours should be required because the soil will have better texture. Once the beds are planted, only about 5–10 minutes a day are required to maintain a 100-square-foot area—an area large enough to provide one person with vegetables 12 months a year in an area with a 4–6 month growing season.[4] Even less time per day and only a 50-square-foot area are required in an area with an 8- to 12-month growing season. Beginning gardeners may require a 200-square-foot area for the same yield, but we recommend a new gardener only use 100 square feet and allow his or her improving skills and soil to gradually produce more food. It is much easier.

The square footage required to provide the vegetable supply for one person is approximate since the exact amount varies depending on whether the individual likes corn (which takes up a lot of space per pound of edible vegetable grown) or a lot of carrots, beets, potatoes, and tomatoes (which require much less area per pound of food produced). Using the tables in the Planning chapter (based on yields produced by the method for all vegetable crops), the homeowner or farmer can determine the actual amount of area that should be allowed for each crop. Be patient in this soil-building process. It takes 5 to 10 years to build up a good soil and one's skill. Actually, this is very rapid. Nature often requires a period of 2,000 years or more to build a soil!

An Instruction Chart for the first preparation of a 100-square-foot bed in a heavy clay, very sandy, or good soil is given below. A chart for the repreparation of a bed each season is also given. After the soil has been initially prepared you will find the biointensive method requires less work than the gardening technique you presently use. The Irish call this the "lazy bed" method of food raising. In addition, you will receive good-tasting vegetables and an average of four times as many vegetables to eat! Or, if you wish to raise only the same amount of food as last year, 1/4 the area will have to be dug, weeded, and watered.

4. 100 square feet can yield over 300 pounds of vegetables and soft fruits in a 4- to 6-month growing season. The average person in the United States consumes about 322 pounds of vegetables and soft fruits annually.

INITIAL PREPARATION PER 100 SQUARE FEET

Perform a Soil Test (see soil test section in the chapter on Fertilization).

1. Soak area to be dug for *2 hours* with a sprinkler (for hard, dry clays).

2. Let soil dry out partially for *2 days*.

3. Loosen soil 12 inches deep with spading fork and remove weeds: *1–2 hours*.

4. Water gently by hand for *5 minutes,* and let soil rest for *1 day.* If your soil has particularly large clods, wait several extra days and let nature help do the work. The warm sun, cool nights, wind, and water will help break down the clods. Water the bed lightly each day to aid the process.

5. At this time sand may be added to a bed with clayey soil, or clay to a bed with sandy soil, to improve texture. Normally you should not add more than a 1-inch layer (8 cubic feet) of sand or clay. (More sand may allow the water-soluble fertilizers to percolate down too rapidly.) Mix the sand or clay thoroughly into the upper 12 inches with a spading fork: *1 hour.*

6. A 1-inch layer (8 cubic feet) of compost may be added to the surface of a bed with good soil. (You may add up to a 2-inch layer [1 cubic yard or 27 cubic feet per 100 square feet] of compost [preferably] or aged manure[5] to soil with poor [very sandy or very clayey] texture one time only.)

7. Water gently by hand for *5 minutes,* and let soil rest for *1 day.*

8. Remove 7 5-gallon buckets of soil from the upper level of the first trench. Use 6 to make compost and 1 to make flat soil. (These will eventually be returned to the growing beds in the form of added compost.) There will be enough soil at the end of the double-dig process to fill in the last trench, due to the expansion of the soil's volume as air is incorporated into the soil during the dig.

9. Double-dig the soil with a flat spade and spading fork. Be sure to use a digging board to avoid unnecessary compaction of the soil (see pages 10–17 for double-digging instructions): *2–4 hours.* Be sure to dig trenches across the *width* of the bed. It helps to level the soil with a rake after every 3–4 trenches during the digging process.

10. Level and shape bed: *1 hour.*

11. Water gently by hand for *3–5 minutes* and let soil rest for *1 day* (for heavy soil) or less (for medium or light soil).

12. Sprinkle organic nitrogen, phosphorus, potash, calcium, and trace mineral fertilizers (such as blood, fish, hoof and horn, alfalfa, bone and kelp meals, wood ash, and eggshells) indicated by the soil test evenly over surface of bed after leveling and shaping bed. Also include desirable levels of pH modifiers (such as leaf/pine needle compost to make the soil less alkaline, or lime to make the soil less acid) indicated by the soil test. Sift in fertilizers and pH modifiers only 4–6 inches deep with spading fork. Reshape bed if needed. Tamp down with the digging board by placing it on various sections of the bed and then standing on it. This removes excess air from the upper few inches of the bed: *1–2 hours.*

13. Plant or transplant: *1–2 hours.*

TOTAL: 7–12 hours

5. Two-year-old steer or cow manure, or 2-year-old horse manure which originally contained a lot of sawdust, or 2-*month*-old horse or chicken manure not containing much sawdust.

The proper tools will make the
work easier and more productive.

FOR SEED PROPAGATION

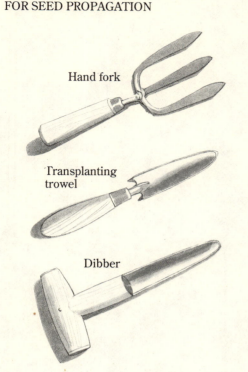

Hand fork

Transplanting
trowel

Dibber

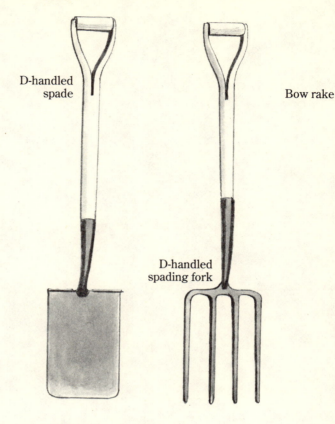

D-handled
spade

Bow rake

D-handled
spading fork

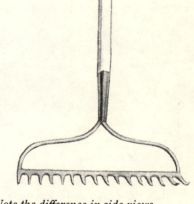

Note the difference in side views
of shovels.

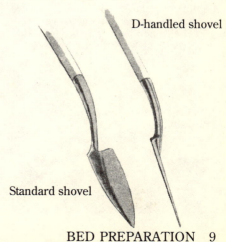

D-handled shovel

Standard shovel

ONGOING PREPARATION FOR REPLANTING PER 100 SQUARE FEET—BEFORE EACH NEW CROP

1. Remove 7 5-gallon buckets of soil from the upper level of the first trench. Use 6 to make compost and 1 to make flat soil. They will eventually be returned to the growing bed in the form of added compost.

2. Remove remaining vegetation and then double-dig the soil: *2–3 hours.*

3. Shape bed: *1/2 hour.*

4. Water gently by hand for *3–5 minutes.* If soil is still heavy, let rest for *1 day.*

5. Add a 1-inch layer (8 cubic feet) of compost per 4-month growing season to the top of the bed, and add any fertilizers and pH modifiers indicated by soil test and a 1/4-inch layer (2 cubic feet) of aged manure to the surface.[6] Sift in materials 4–6 inches deep with spading fork: *1/2–1 hour.* (Adding the compost *after* the double-dig for *ongoing* soil preparations minimizes problems caused by more rapid water-soluble nitrogen leaching in increasingly loose soil.)

6. Plant or transplant: *1–2 hours.*

TOTAL: 4–6-1/2 hours

6. Generally our practice *for autumn compost crops* is to only single-dig and to add no compost or fertilizers.

The Initial Double-dig Process

Step by Step

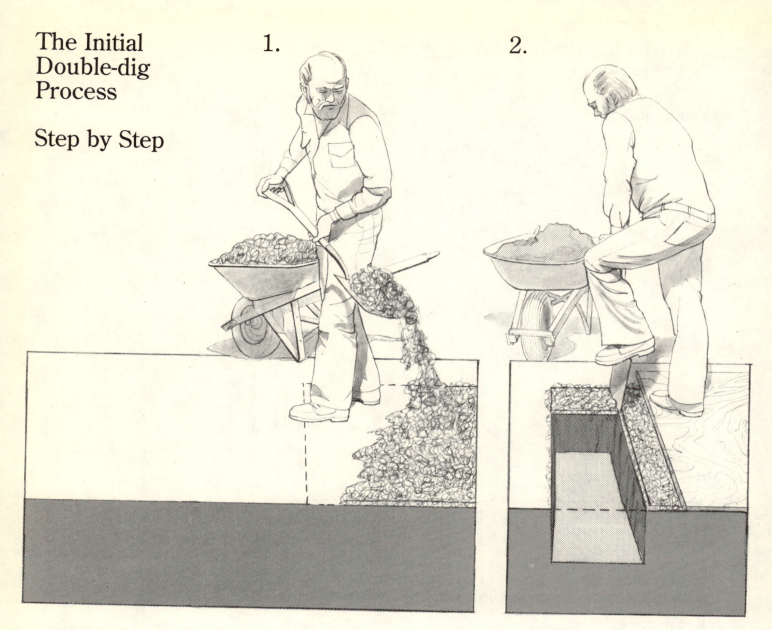

1.

2.

1. Spread a layer of compost over entire area to be dug.

2. Using a spade, remove soil from a trench 1 foot deep and 1 foot wide across the width of the bed. Remove 7 5-gallon buckets of soil from the upper level of the first trench for use in making compost and flat soil. (The trench being dug is across the *width* of the bed.)

Sides of bed should be dug outward into path.

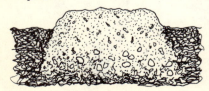

The goal of double-digging is to loosen the soil to a depth of 24 inches below the surface. The first year you may only be able to reach 15 to 18 inches with reasonable effort. Be satisfied with this result. Do not strain yourself or your tools. More important than perfection the first day or year or two is going in the right direction. Nature, the loose soil, worms, and the plant roots will further loosen the soil with each crop so that each year digging will be easier and the depth will increase 3 to 6 inches. This is easier on you and your tools!

For all-around ease, D-handled flat spades and D-handled spading forks of good temper are usually used for bed preparation. (Poor tools will wear out rapidly while the garden area is being prepared.) D-handles allow the gardener to stand straight with the tool directly in front. A long-handled tool must frequently be held to the side of the gardener. This position does not allow for simple, direct posture and leverage. When digging for long periods of time, many people find the

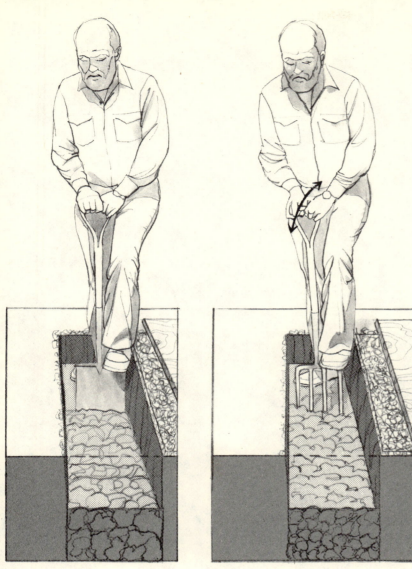

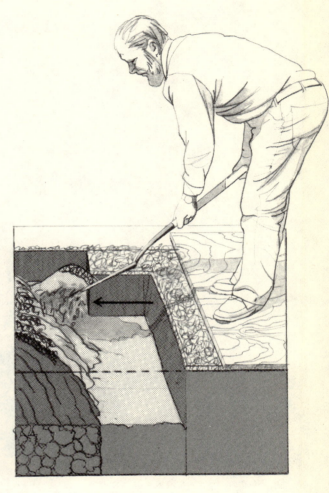

use of a D-handled tool less tiring (though it will probably take the digging of 3 beds to get used to!). However, people with back problems may need long-handled tools. In fact, people with back problems and those not in good health should check with their physician before proceeding with the physically active process of double-digging.

The flat spade has a particular advantage in that it digs equally deep all along its edge rather than along a pointed "V" pattern. This is especially important in the double-dig when all points in the bed should be dug to an equal depth. The blade of the flat spade also goes into the soil at less of an angle and without the curve of the usual shovel. This means the sides of the bed can be dug perpendicular or even diagonally outward into the path, a plus for root penetration and water flow.

Digging should only be performed when the soil is evenly moist. It is easier and better for the soil. Digging a hard, dry soil breaks down the structure and it is difficult to penetrate.

3. *In good soil:* While standing in trench, loosen soil an additional 12 inches with a spade by digging into its full depth, lifting soil out on spade pan, and then tipping pan downward so that the loosened, aerated soil slides back into trench. Mix up soil layers as little as possible.

4. *Alternate for moderately compacted soil:* Loosen soil an additional 12 inches with a spading fork by digging tool into its full depth and then pushing tool handle downward so fork tines will lever through soil, loosening and aerating it.

5. Dig out upper part of second trench 1 foot deep and 1 foot wide. Move each spadeful of dirt forward (into the first trench) mixing the soil layers as little as possible.

6a. *Alternate for compacted soil:* While standing in trench, loosen soil an additional 12 inches with a spading fork by digging in the tool to its full depth and lifting out a tight soil section on the fork pan.

6b. Then, by moving your arms upward in a small jerk, cause the soil to break apart as it falls downward, hits the fork tines, and falls into the hole below.

Wet soil is heavy and easily compacted. Compaction destroys a friable structure and minimizes aeration. These conditions kill microbiotic life. The main reason for drying-out periods after watering the soil is to allow the proper moisture level to be reached and to make digging enjoyable and beneficial. Soil is too dry for digging when it is loose and will not hold its shape after being squeezed in the palm of your hand (in the case of sands or loams) or when it is hard and dry and cannot easily be penetrated by a spade (in the case of clays). Soil is too wet when it sticks to the spade as you dig.

Double-digging is the term used for the process of preparing the soil two spades deep (about 24 inches). To begin, mark out a bed 3–5 feet wide and at least 3 feet long. Most people prefer a bed 5, 10, or 20 feet long, but the maximum is up to you. To double-dig, remove the soil from a trench 1 foot deep and 1 foot wide across the width of one end of the bed. Use a 5/8-inch-thick plywood board, 2–3 feet long by 3–5 feet wide, to stand on. Place it on top of the compost layer you spread over the bed and advance it along the bed 1 foot at a time as you prepare to dig each new trench. Move 7 5-gallon buckets of the soil from the first trench to a soil storage area for use in making compost and flat soil. Make as few motions as possible in the process. This will conserve your energy and involve less work. You can move the soil by hand with the shovel or by wheelbarrow. (When you are through double-digging, you will have enough soil in the bed to fill in the last trench at the back of the bed.) Next, standing in the trench, dig down another 12 inches (if possible) with a spading fork, a few inches at a time if the soil is tight. Leave the fork as deep as it has penetrated and loosen the subsoil layer by pushing the fork handle down and levering the tines through the soil. If the soil is not loose enough for this process, lift the chunk of soil out of the trench on the fork tines. Then throw the chunk slightly upward and allow it to fall back on the tines so it will break apart. If this does not work, use the points of the fork tines to break the soil apart. Work from one end of the trench to the other in this manner.

Next, dig another trench behind the first one, moving each spadeful of soil forward into the first trench. Sometimes you will have to go over a trench a second or third time to remove all the soil and obtain the proper trench size. Repeat the subsoil loosening process in the second trench. Dig a third trench and so on until the entire bed has been double-dug. It helps to level the soil with a rake after every 3–4 trenches during the digging process.

When you are throwing the soil forward from one trench into another, notice two things. First, some of the compost layer you have added to the surface of the bed before beginning to dig slides 3 to 6 inches down into the trench along the small mound of soil or landslide. This approximates the way nature adds leaves, flower bodies, and other decaying vegetation to the top of the soil, where they break down and where their essences can percolate into the soil. Second, the *upper* layer should not be turned over during the double-dig and succeeding double-digs. Most of the microbiotic life lives in the upper 6 inches of the soil. Also, the natural layering of the soil which is caused by rainfall and leaching, leaf litter, water, temperature, gravity, and other natural forces is less disturbed when the soil is not generally mixed, even though the soil is loosened up and mixed a little. Thus, there is a balance between nature's natural stratification and man's shepherding landslide loosening. As a goal, strive not to mix the soil layers. The goal is important even though it will never be reached and significant mixing sometimes occurs. Without the goal, however, excessive disruption of the soil layers will occur.

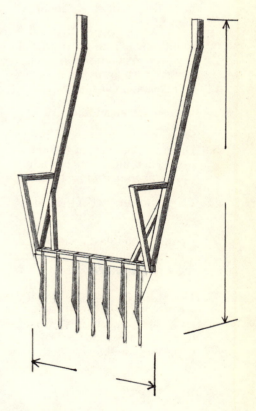

The U-bar

TYPES OF DEEP SOIL PREPARATIONS

Simplified Side Views

Ecology Action uses four basic types of deep soil preparation processes: the initial double-dig, the ongoing double-dig, the complete texturizing double-dig, and the U-bar dig. Following are simplified side views of these processes for easy reference. The first two are described in the text. The complete texturizing double-dig was developed to improve soil quality more rapidly and is used one time only. It is used usually in

THE *INITIAL* DOUBLE-DIG

1. After soil is lightly moist, pre-loosen entire area to be dug 12 inches deep with spading fork and remove weeds.

2. Spread a 1-inch to 2-inch layer of compost over entire area to be dug (after mixing in a 1-inch layer of sand—optional—12 inches deep).

3. Remove soil from upper part of first trench and place in a soil storage area for use in making compost and flat soil.

4. Loosen soil an additional 12 inches.

5. Dig out upper part of second trench and move forward into upper, open part of first trench.

6. Loosen lower part of second trench.

7. Continue double-digging process (repeating steps 3 and 4) for remaining trenches.

8. Shape bed by raking. Then spread any fertilizers needed evenly over entire area and sift in 4–6 inches deep with a spading fork: the completed double-dug bed.

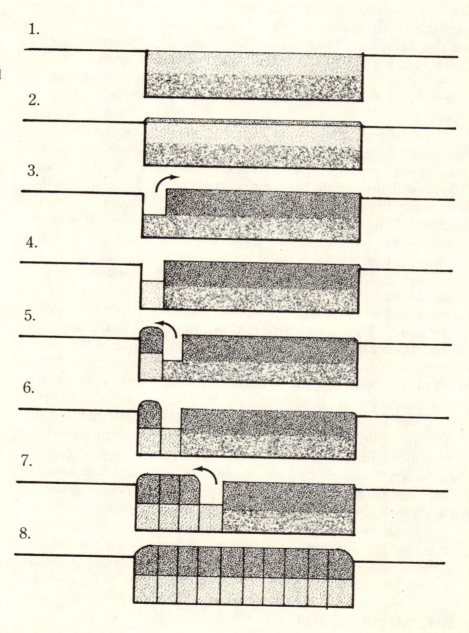

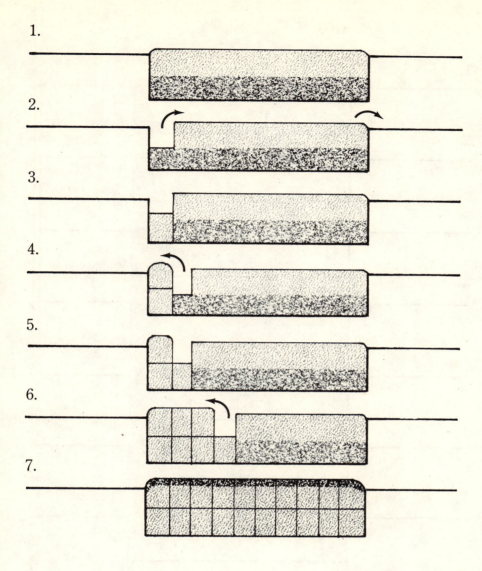

1. Bed shown after harvest with slightly raised mound of partially recompacted soil and residual compost. After soil is lightly moist, preloosen entire area to be dug 12 inches deep with a spading fork and remove weeds.

2. Remove soil from upper part of first trench and place in a soil storage area for use in making compost and flat soil.

3. Loosen soil an additional 12 inches. (See NOTE below.)

4. Dig out upper part of second trench and move forward into upper, open part of first trench.

5. Loosen lower part of second trench.

6. Continue double-digging process (repeating steps 4 and 5) for remaining trenches.

7. Shape bed by raking. Spread 1-inch layer of compost and any fertilizers needed evenly over entire area. Sift in compost and any fertilizers 4–6 inches deep with a spading fork.

NOTE: After the lower trench has been loosened, "Irish" potatoes may be placed on its surface on 9-inch centers using offset spacing. The soil from the next trench's upper level may then be moved forward onto them. This is the easiest way we have found to plant potatoes. (Mark the location of the potatoes with stones or sticks in the outside paths before covering them with soil. This will indicate where potatoes should be placed on the surface of each succeeding lower trench.)

place of the initial double-dig, but can be used at a later point in time. We have found this soil preparation process greatly improves plant health and yields immediately in poor soil. It is often worth the extra digging time involved. The U-bar dig can be used as a substitute for the ongoing double-dig in soil which is in reasonably good shape. This usually means after one normal double-dig or more. The 18-inch-long U-bar tines do not prepare the soil as deeply, but compaction in the lower 12 inches of the growing bed is much slower than in the upper 12 inches. Also, the U-bar appears to have the advantage of mixing up the soil strata much less than double-digging with a spade and a spading fork. It aerates the soil less, however. This is an advantage in looser, sandier soil and can be a problem in tighter clays. If you use a U-bar regularly, do a normal double-dig as often as increased compaction indicates.

THE COMPLETE TEXTURIZING DOUBLE-DIG

1. After soil is lightly moist, pre-loosen entire area to be dug 12 inches deep with a spading fork and remove weeds.

2. Spread 1-1/2- to 2-inch layer of compost over entire area to be dug (after mixing in a 1-inch layer of sand—optional—12 inches deep).

3. Thoroughly mix in compost 12 inches deep.

4. Remove soil from upper part of first trench and place in a soil storage area for use in making compost and flat soil.

5. Loosen soil an additional 12 inches.

6. Spread 1-1/2- to 2-inch layer of compost on top of loosened soil in lower first trench.

7. Thoroughly mix in compost on top of lower first trench 12 inches deep.

8. Dig out upper part of second trench and move forward into upper, open part of first trench.

9. Loosen lower part of second trench.

10. Spread 1-1/2- to 2-inch layer of compost on top of loosened soil in lower second trench.

11. Thoroughly mix in compost on top of lower second trench 12 inches deep.

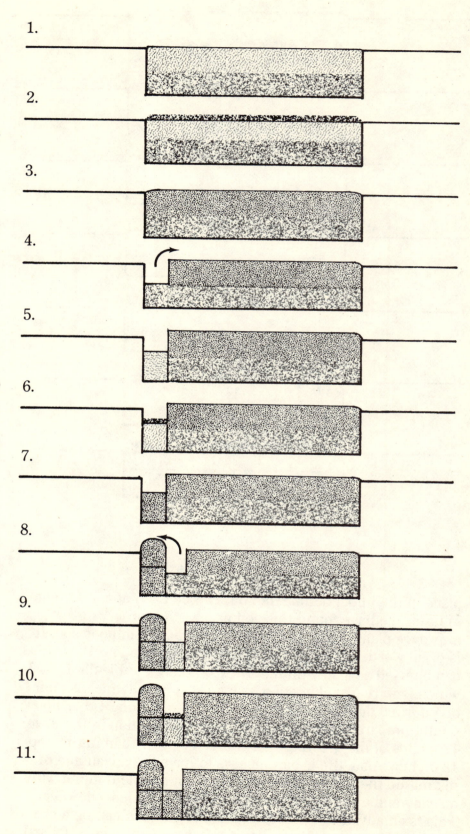

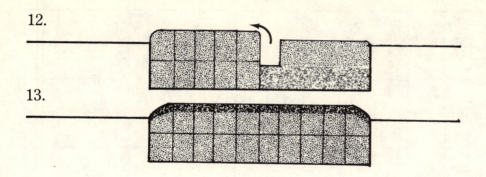

12.

13.

12. Continue complete texturizing double-digging process (repeat steps 8 through 11) for remaining trenches.

13. Shape bed by raking. Then spread any fertilizers needed evenly over entire area and sift in 4–6 inches deep with a spading fork: the completed "complete texturizing double-dug" bed.

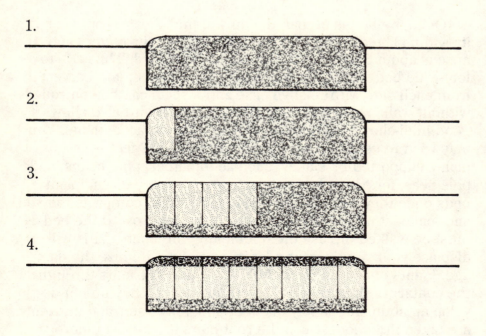

1.

2.

3.

4.

THE U-BAR DIG

1. After harvest, if necessary, weed entire slightly raised bed.

2. After soil is lightly moist, begin U-barring soil along length of bed. No digging board is used. Soil will be loosened 3/4 as deep as in double-dig.

3. Continue U-barring until bed is complete. Two or three U-barrings along the length of the bed may be necessary depending on the width of the bed. The U-bar is 2 feet wide and loosens the soil 2 to 2-1/2 feet wide. See photo on page 172.

4. Break up any remaining large clumps with a spading fork. Shape bed by raking. Then spread compost and any fertilizers needed evenly over entire area and sift in 4–6 inches deep with a spading fork.

NOTE: See *Backyard Homestead, Mini-Farm and Garden Log Book* on the proper techniques for using a U-bar.

U-barring is quicker and easier, though some knowledge of how your soil is improving, or not improving, is lost with the decreased personal contact with the soil. (For detailed plans on how to build a U-bar, see Ecology Action's *Backyard Homestead, Mini-Farm and Garden Log Book.*) We, ourselves, prefer to double-dig, as we learn more from it and stay in touch with the soil.

SELECTED VEGETABLE ROOT SYSTEMS SHOWN IN SCALE

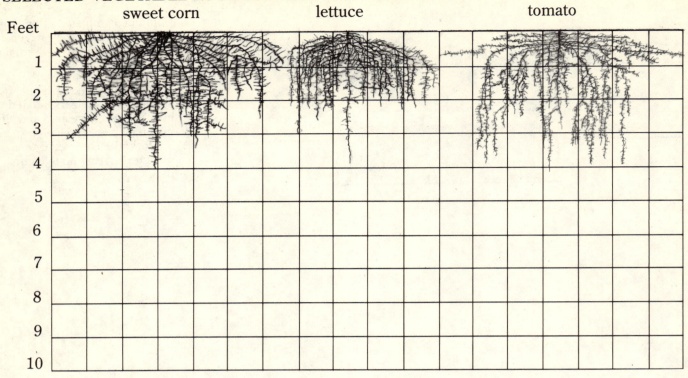

sweet corn   lettuce   tomato

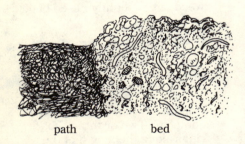

path   bed

Soil in path is subject to compaction; soil in bed remains loose.

The loosened soil of the planting bed makes weeding easier. The entire weed root usually comes out intact.

Once the bed is prepared, you will find great advantages in its width. The distance between the tips of your fingers and nose is about 3 feet when your arm is extended. Thus a 3- to 5-foot-wide bed can be fertilized, planted, weeded, and harvested from each side with relative ease and insects can be controlled without walking on the beds. A 3- to 5-foot width also allows a good mini-climate to develop under closely spaced plants. You may wish to use a narrower bed 1-1/2 to 2-1/2 feet wide for plants supported by stakes, such as tomatoes, pole beans, and pole peas, for easier harvesting. Try not to step on the plant beds once they have been prepared. To do so compacts the soil and makes it more difficult for the plants to grow. If the bed must be walked on, use the double-digging board. This will displace your weight over a large area and minimize the damage. Plants obtain much of their water and nutrients through the contact of their root hairs with the soil. If they do not develop an abundant supply of root hairs, less water and nutrients are taken in. In looser soil the root hairs are more numerous and vigorous, so keep your soil loose!

When weeding, note that the entire weed root usually comes up out of loosened raised bed soil. This is a welcome change to the weeding process—and, if you get all the root, you will not have to weed as often. Also, you do not need to cultivate the soil of raised beds as much. The *living mulch* shade cover provided by mature plants helps to keep the soil surface loose. If the soil compacts between young plants before the mini-climate takes effect, you should cultivate.

Once this beautifully alive bed is prepared, it should be kept

carrot   cauliflower   beet

evenly moist until and after planting so the microbiotic life and plants will stay alive. It should be planted as soon as is convenient, so the plants can take advantage of the new surge of life made possible by the bringing together of the soil, compost, air, water, sun, and fertilizers.

A good growing bed will normally be 2–10 inches higher than the original surface of the soil. A good soil contains 50% air space. (In fact, adequate air is one of the missing ingredients in most soil preparation processes.) Increased air space allows for increased diffusion of oxygen (which the roots and microbes depend on) into the soil, and of carbon dioxide (which the leaves depend on) out of the soil. The increased "breathing" ability of a double-dug bed is a key to improved plant health.

Thus, the prepared depth will be as much as 34 inches in clayey soil. A sandy soil will probably not raise as high as clayey soil at first. If the bed raises higher than 10 inches as you are double-digging, be sure to level it out with a rake as you go along. Otherwise you will find a very wide and deep trench at the end of the bed. Then you will have to move a large amount of soil from one end of the bed to the other to even it out when you are tired. This would also cause a disproportionate misplacing of topsoil into the subsoil area. Whenever you re-dig a bed (after each crop or season), the 24-inch depth of the bed should be measured from the top of the bed, rather than from the path surface. We currently reprepare the soil after each crop, except for autumn compost crops. Some people prefer to do this only once each year. As your soil

The biointensive method raised bed. A balance between nature's natural stratification and man's shepherding landslide loosening.

improves, and the large clods disappear, your bed may not raise as high as initially. Do not worry about this. It is just a sign that you and your soil are being successful. The goal of double-digging is not in the height of the bed, but in the looseness and good structure of the soil.

The soil's *texture* is determined by its basic ingredients: silt, clay, and sand particles. Its *structure* is the way its ingredients hold together. With the assistance of the gardener, "threads" exuded by microbial life and "glue" exuded by plant roots help in this process. The goal is to create a sumptuous "living sponge cake." Bon appétit!

Fertilization

T he *first* goal of adding fertilizers to your soil is to build nutrients up to their proper levels and balances for the soil type, rainfall, climate, exposure to the sun, altitude, and cation-exchange capacity. The *second* goal is to keep those nutrients in your food-raising area by composting properly and recycling all wastes. A *third* goal is to use *enough* nutrients, water, and compost in your growing area.

During a drought years ago, several women in India grew food using biointensive methods. Their production was double that of others who used single-dug row cropping practices. One woman got even higher yields than other biointensive gardeners by using her one unit of water, fertilizers, and seed on *one* growing area. Hoping for higher yields, the others had spread their single units of resources over seven to fifteen units of growing area. The woman with the best results got more total production in one-seventh to one-fifteenth the area. She had benefited by Alan Chadwick's observation, "Begin with one bed and tend it well! Then expand your growing area."

Over the years we have seen gardeners in many countries obtain excellent, good, and fair yields using biointensive techniques, depending on the care taken with the resources and on what results individuals believed they would obtain. A good level and balance of nutrients in your soil will help your garden flourish and make it most healthy and productive.

Our ultimate goal is to design a *living soil test kit* of plants grown in a small area that can be "read" to determine existing nutrient levels in the soil of that area. Until about 100 years ago, this is how farmers determined soil nutrient needs. It will take many years to fully rediscover and develop all the information. In the meantime, a professional soil test performed by a laboratory will provide you with the most complete evaluation. Unfortunately, because of variations in soil types, climates,

Taking a soil sampling

The La Motte soil test kit

SOIL TEST

Date Performed:_____

Performed by:_____

Test	Results	Recommendations Per 100 Square Feet
Nitrogen		
Phosphorus		
Potash		
pH (6.5 or slightly acid is optimum)		
Remarks (including texture)		

NITROGEN (N), PHOSPHORUS (P), AND POTASH (K)

Pounds of fertilizer to add per 100 square feet. Pounds of *pure* nutrients added given in parentheses.
NOTE: The goal is to build up nutrient deficiencies in the soil slowly over time. (If you add large amounts of readily available nutrients all at once, nutrients not in short supply in the soil may become unavailable.)

Test Rating	Nitrogen (N)	Phosphorus (P)	Potash (K)
Very High[7]	**(.1)** .75 lb. blood meal or 1.25 lbs. alfalfa meal or 1 lb. fish meal or .75 lb. hoof and horn meal	**(.2)** 1 lb. bone or 2 lbs. phosphate rock or soft phosphate	**(.15)** 1.5 lbs. wood ashes[8] and 1.5 lbs. crushed granite[9]
High[7]	**(.2)** 1.5 lbs. blood meal or 2.5 lbs. alfalfa meal or 2 lbs. fish meal or 1.5 lbs. hoof and horn meal	**(.3)** 1.5 lbs. bone or 3 lbs. phosphate rock	**(.2)** 1.5 lbs. wood ashes and 2.5 lbs. crushed granite
Medium High	**(.25)** 2 lbs. blood meal or 3.125 lbs. alfalfa meal or 2.5 lbs. fish meal or 2 lbs. hoof and horn meal	**(.35)** 1.75 lbs. bone or 3.5 lbs. phosphate rock	**(.25)** 1.5 lbs. wood ashes and 3.5 lbs. crushed granite
Medium	**(.3)** 2.25 lbs. blood meal or 3.75 lbs. alfalfa meal or 3 lbs. fish meal or 2.25 lbs. hoof and horn meal	**(.4)** 2 lbs. bone or 4 lbs. phosphate rock	**(.3)** 1.5 lbs. wood ashes and 4.5 lbs. crushed granite
Medium Low	**(.35)** 2.75 lbs. blood meal or 4.375 lbs. alfalfa meal or 3.5 lbs. fish meal or 2.75 lbs. hoof and horn meal	**(.45)** 2.25 lbs. bone or 4.5 lbs. phosphate rock	**(.35)** 1.5 lbs. wood ashes and 5.5 lbs. crushed granite
Low	**(.4)** 3 lbs. blood meal or 5 lbs. alfalfa meal or 4 lbs. fish meal or 3 lbs. hoof and horn meal	**(.5)** 2.5 lbs. bone or 5 lbs. phosphate rock	**(.4)** 1.5 lbs. wood ashes and 6.5 lbs. crushed granite
Very Low	**(.5)** 4 lbs. blood meal or 6.25 lbs. alfalfa meal or 5 lbs. fish meal or 4 lbs. hoof and horn meal	**(.6)** 3 lbs. bone or 6 lbs. phosphate rock	**(.5)** 1.5 lbs. wood ashes and 8.5 lbs. crushed granite

7. Addition of nutrients at these levels is optional.
8. Wood ash application is not recommended for soils with a pH above 6.5.
9. Finely ground.

cultivation practices, rainfall, altitude, exposure to the sun, drainage conditions, the types of crops grown, and cation-exchange capacity, no standard added nutrient formula will work in all situations.

If you can, test your soil for major nutrients and trace minerals, including pH (the acidity or alkalinity level of your soil), before choosing fertilizers. The major minerals, those that plants utilize in relatively large amounts, include nitrogen, phosphorus, potassium, sulfur, magnesium, and calcium. Trace minerals are important elements such as zinc, boron, and sulfur that are required in very small quantities. For professional soil testing, we use the *Timberleaf* soil testing service.[10] It specializes in testing for organic farmers and gardeners, with an emphasis on biointensive fertility. The service analyzes all soil and plant minerals and the soil's physical characteristics and can provide follow-up review and advice on your year's experience in the garden. If you are unable to arrange a professional soil test, purchase a home test kit. The best such kit is the *La Motte kit.*[11] With the home kit you will be limited to testing nitrogen, phosphorus and potassium content and pH.

To take a soil sample from your yard, use a nonferrous trowel or a stainless steel spoon to dig a vertical soil slice from the 0- to 6-inch level below the surface. Take samples from 6 to 8 representative areas and mix them together well in a plastic bucket. Make sure you do not include residues, such as roots and surface organic litter, in the composite sample. Also, do not sample for 30 days after adding any fertilizers, manure, or compost to the area. The samples should normally be taken at the end of a growing season or just before one. You will need a total soil volume of 1 pound for professional testing or 4 heaping tablespoons for the home test kit. Remember that soil tests can save you a lot of money, since they will guard against overapplication of fertilizers, allow you to account for nutrients already available in your soil for good plant growth, and increase yields.

To use the *Timberleaf* service, ship your composite sample as instructed in its soil test packet without drying the soil. For a home test kit, let samples dry in a small paper bag in indirect sunlight—*not* in the sun or an oven. When you are ready to begin testing, use the easy-to-understand instructions included with the kit. Record home test results on a photocopy of the chart on page 22.

Once you have completed the test, use the information beginning on page 23 to determine a general fertilization plan for your garden.

10. 5569 State Street, Albany, OH 45710.

11. La Motte Chemical Products, Box 329, Chestertown, MD 21620: Model STH.

ANALYSIS OF RECOMMENDED ORGANIC
SOIL AMENDMENTS

N, P, and K refer to three of the major nutrients plants need. According to law any product sold as a fertilizer must provide an analysis upon request for these three minerals. NITROGEN contains proteins, is a food source in compost piles, and causes green growth. PHOSPHORUS gives plants energy and is necessary for the growth of flowers and seeds. POTASH aids in protein synthesis and the translocation of carbohydrates to build strong stems. Plants also need a good supply of ORGANIC MATTER to give them additional nitrogen, phosphorus, sulfur, copper, zinc, boron, and molybdenum, and they need eight other nutrients. Only under *ideal conditions* do native soil minerals provide these nutrients naturally. Nature needs a full meal of nutrients, and as good stewards of the soil we are responsible for providing them. Be aware that laboratory analysis to determine fertilizer amendments does not always show *all* of the actual needs of the soil plant system.

NITROGEN

Alfalfa Meal
8.4% N, .7% P, 2.25% K. Lasts 3–4 months. Use up to 6.25 lbs./100 sq. ft. A quick-acting source of nitrogen and some potash.

Blood Meal (Steamed)
12.5% N, 1.3% P, .7% K. Lasts 3–4 months. Use up to 4 lbs./100 sq. ft. A quick-acting source of nitrogen; good for slow compost piles. Can burn plants if more than 3 lbs. per 100 sq. ft. are used. If using higher amounts, wait 2 weeks to plant. Blood meal can burn the plants during this time because it releases nitrogen rapidly at first.

Hoof and Horn Meal
14% N, 2% P, 0% K. Lasts 12 months. Use up to 4 lbs./100 sq. ft. Highest nitrogen source. Slow releasing: no noticeable results for 4–6 weeks.

Fish Meal
10.5% N, 6% P, 0% K. Lasts 6–8 months. Use up to 5 lbs./100 sq. ft. Good combined nitrogen and phosphorus source.

PHOSPHORUS

Bone Meal
3% N, 20% P, 0% K. Lasts 6 months to 1 year. Use up to 3 lbs./100 sq. ft. Excellent source of phosphorus. Especially good on roses, around bulbs, and around fruit trees and flower beds.

Phosphate Rock
33% P. Lasts 3–5 years. Use up to 6 lbs./100 sq. ft. Very slow releasing.

Soft Phosphate (colloidal)
18% P. Lasts 2–3 years. Use up to 6 lbs./100 sq. ft. Clay base makes it more available to plants than the phosphorus in phosphate rock, though the two are used interchangeably.

Remember that too much nitrogen in your soil can cause the soil's all-important organic matter to break down too quickly.

POTASH

Wood Ashes
1–10% K. Lasts 6 months. Use up to 1.5 lbs./100 sq. ft. Ashes from wood are high in potash and help repel root maggots. Ashes also have an alkaline effect on the soil, so use them with care if your soil pH is above 6.5. Black wood ash is best.

Crushed Granite (Finely Ground)
3–5% K. Lasts up to 10 years. Use up to 8.5 lbs./100 sq. ft. A slow-releasing source of potash and trace minerals.

SOIL MODIFIERS

Dolomitic Lime
A good source of calcium and magnesium to be used when both are needed. Do not use lime to "sweeten" the compost pile as doing so will result in a serious loss of nitrogen. A layer of soil will discourage flies and reduce odors.

High Calcium Lime (Calcite)
A good source of calcium when magnesium levels are too high for applying dolomitic lime. Oyster shell flour lime is a good substitute.

Gypsum (Calcium Sulfate)
Used to correct excess levels of exchangeable sodium. Apply only on the recommendation of a professional soil test.

Crushed Eggshells
High in calcium. Especially good for cabbage family crops. Eggshells help break up clay and release nutrients tied up in alkaline soils. Use up to 2 lbs./100 sq. ft.

Manure (All Types)
A good source of organic matter in the garden. The nutrient levels in each manure will depend on proper management of the curing process and on the amount of straw or sawdust in the manure. Optimally, do not use more than 4 cubic feet of aged manure per year (about 136 lbs., or a 1/2-inch layer). It is best to use manure that contains little undecomposed sawdust. Approximately 2 cubic feet of manure (50 lbs. dry weight) applied per 100 square feet can lower the pH *one* point.

Manures—Solids
(Approximate)

Chicken—Fresh	1.5% N	1.0% P	.5% K
Chicken—Dry	4.5% N	3.5% P	2.0% K
Dairy Cow	.56% N	.23% P	.6% K
Horse	.69% N	.24% P	.72% K
Pig—Fresh	.5% N	.32% P	.46% K
Sheep	1.4% N	.48% P	1.2% K
Steer	.7% N	.55% P	.72% K

Compost
Good compost is the most important part of the garden. It aerates soil, breaks up clay, binds together sand, improves drainage, prevents erosion, neutralizes toxins, holds precious moisture, releases essential nutrients,

and feeds the microbiotic life of the soil, creating healthy conditions for natural antibiotics, worms, and beneficial fungi. Use an inch of compost each year (8 cu. ft./100 sq. ft.) or up to 3 inches in a first-year garden. (One cubic yard equals 27 cubic feet. One cubic yard will cover 100 square feet 3 inches deep. Eight cubic feet will cover 100 square feet 1 inch deep. Two cubic feet will cover 100 square feet 1/4 inch deep.) Manure may be substituted for compost the first year if you do not have a ready supply of compost.

What a Home Soil Test Will Not Tell You

A *professional soil test* is an excellent tool for analyzing deficiencies, excesses, and the relative balance of all plant nutrients. A *home test kit,* however, is very limited and only points out pH level and deficiencies of nitrogen, phosphorus, and potassium. If you have difficulty growing healthy plants in your garden, a home test kit may not provide the solution. Plants grown in soil lacking any of the major or trace minerals show their deficiency in yellowed leaves, stunted growth, purple veins, or any number of other ways.

When seeds fail to germinate, or plants hardly grow at all after germination, some common causes are:

1. Use of redwood compost. This compost is widely available as a mulch or soil conditioner but contains growth inhibitors that can keep seeds from germinating or plants from growing well. (This is how redwood trees reduce competition.)

2. Planting too early or too late in the season. Seeds and seedlings wait for the right temperature and length of day to start and continue growth.

3. Use of weed killers or soil sterilants. Many weed killers are short-lived, but they can limit growth in a garden long after they are supposed to degrade. Soil sterilants can last for 2 years. Some people use them to minimize or eliminate yard care, but they can continue to have an effect after the users move away and you move in. There is never any reason to use these poisons in your yard. Also, dumping used motor oil can destroy valuable growing areas. Take it to a service station for recycling.

4. Use of old seeds. Check your source.

5. Planting in soil that is too wet. Wet soil restricts oxygen, which is required for root growth. Plants can die in fertile soils when soil oxygen is too low to sustain growth.

pH

A pH reading tells you the relative acidity/alkalinity of the soil water, generally called the soil solution. Nutrient availability for vegetable plants, soil microbial activity, and soil struc-

SOIL pH SCALE

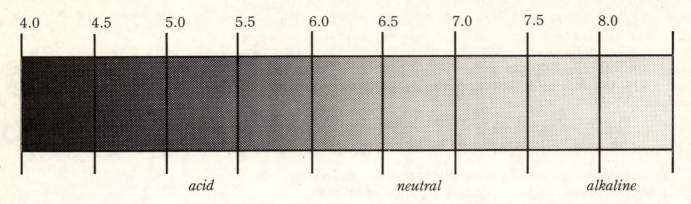

4.0 4.5 5.0 5.5 6.0 6.5 7.0 7.5 8.0

acid   *neutral*   *alkaline*

ture are all affected by pH. Most vegetables grow best in a slightly acidic soil with a pH of 6.8. A range of 6.0 to 7.0 is fine for most crops.

More important than the actual pH reading is the quality of the pH represented by this number. This is determined by testing for the amount of plant-available potassium, magnesium, calcium, and sodium in your soil. Only a professional soil test can determine the mineral balance. You will want to know this information before you apply pH modifiers to the soil. For instance, limestone is a common pH modifier; however, all limestones do not have the same mineral composition. An application of a dolomitic instead of a calcitic lime to a soil with a high magnesium content could disrupt your soil balance and adversely affect plant growth.

Soil-applied organic matter and manure can alter the pH over time. When adequate organic matter is used, we find crops will tolerate a wider pH range. Leaf mold, pine needles, and sawdust can produce an acidic compost that can lower the pH. Manures may be alkaline and raise the pH. Compost can be either acidic or alkaline. Using the proper limestone with the correct mineral balance is the least expensive and most practical way to increase pH. Mined sulfur, a soil nutrient deficient in many soils, is an excellent amendment to lower the pH. Although you can use organic matter to alter pH, you will need to know your soil mineral structure, the existing soil pH, and the pH of the applied material in order to apply it accurately and in an effective amount.

The Analysis of Recommended Organic Soil Amendments, beginning on page 25, gives the mineral nutrient content of many commonly used organic fertilizers. This information will help you determine the amounts of each fertilizer to add if you are using a home test kit and are unable to have a professional soil test performed. In your calculations, it is not necessary to *subtract* the nutrients added to the soil in the form of manure and compost. Be careful about adding manure. Much aged or composted manure actually contains little nitrogen and may have a substantial amount of nitrogen-demanding sawdust. If you use a lot of manure containing large amounts of sawdust as a soil texturizer, you may want to add about 1 extra pound of blood, fish, or hoof and horn meal per 100 square feet. Notice that the release times are different for each fertilizer. Sometimes we use a combination of blood meal (which releases over a 3- to 4-month period), fish meal (which releases over a 6- to 8-month period), and hoof and horn meal (which releases over a 12-month period). This spreads the nitrogen release over a longer period of time. For example, if a soil test indicates that we need 0.4 pounds of pure nitrogen per 100 square feet, we might add:

1 pound blood meal	&	1 pound fish meal	&	1 pound hoof and horn meal
.125 pounds N (12.5%)		.105 pounds N (10.5%)		.140 pounds N (14%)

.125
.105
.140

.370 pounds N or approximately the .4 pounds N needed

More Sustainable Fertilization

It should be the goal of each gardener over time to use less and less fertilizer that is brought in from outside his or her own garden area. This will be especially true as such amendments become more scarce when divided among the increased number of people using them. There are at least four ways to create a "closed system" garden:

1.   Use most of the food you grow *at home,* so that all the residues can be returned to your soil. "Export" as little as possible of your valuable soil resources.

2.   Grow some trees. Their deep root systems will bring up nutrients from deep down in the subsoil, and even further, into the tree leaves. These materials would not otherwise become available for use as plant food.

3.   "Grow" your own fertilizers by raising plants strictly for making compost, which concentrates the nutrients required in a form the plants can use. For beginning information on plants to use, see Ecology Action's Self-Teaching Mini-Series Booklet No. 12, *Growing and Gathering Your Own Fertilizers* (see Ecology Action Publications, page 171) and Bargyla and Gylver Rateaver's *Organic Method Primer* and Joseph A. Cocannouer's *Weeds and What They Tell* (see General and Companion Planting sections of the Bibliography, respectively). If everyone were to use organic fertilizers, there would be a worldwide shortage;

eventually the key will be growing our own and recycling *all* wastes. Deep-rooting alfalfa (as deep as 125 feet) and comfrey (up to 8 feet) also help bring up leached out and newly released nutrients from the soil strata and rocks below.

4. Maintain at least a 4–6% organic-matter level in at least the upper 6 inches of soil. This will encourage microbial life growth, which can keep nutrients from leaching out of the soil.

The bed should be shaped before the fertilizers are added. If your soil is in good condition, use a rake to shape the bed into a mound. The soil will not easily wash off or erode from beds shaped in this manner, once the structure of the soil is improved. While you are still improving the structure of heavy clay soils, you may want to form a *flat-topped bed* with a small lip on the outer edges of the bed instead. This will minimize watering-caused erosion. It is also desirable to provide the sides of the beds with about a 30-degree slope. A sharper angle will encourage erosion. When the bed has been shaped, tamp the soil down before planting by placing the digging board on all parts of the bed and walking across the board. If a lip is added to the bed, it is done after the soil is tamped down.

Add the fertilizers and other additives one at a time. Avoid windy days and hold fertilizer close to the bed surface when spreading. Use the different colors to help you. The soil is darkish, so sprinkle a light-colored fertilizer (such as bone meal) on first, then a dark one (such as blood meal) and so on.

(Left) Raking soil outward from the inside for lip, (right) raking the soil up from the side for lip.

It is better to under-apply the fertilizers because you can go back over the bed afterwards to spread any left over but it is difficult to pick up fertilizer if too much falls in one place. Aim for even distribution. After all are applied, sift in the fertilizers and other additives by inserting a spading fork 4–6 inches deep and lifting it upwards with a slight jiggling motion.

Several things should be noted about the special nature of the nutrients added in the upper 4–6 inches of soil. (1) The nutrients are added to the upper soil layer as in nature. (2) The nutrients are relocated through the soil strata by the movement of larger soil organisms and by the downward flow of water. (3) Organic fertilizers break down more slowly than most chemical fertilizers. By utilizing natural nutrient cycles, they release plant-available minerals over an extended period of time.

The bone meal often used in the upper layer provides quality growth-producing phosphorus and calcium to the plants plus an important animal essence. Wood ash (preferably black wood ash) provides strength and plant essence, aids in insect control, and is a flavor enhancer for vegetables, especially lettuce and tomatoes. Black wood ash is produced from a controlled, soil-covered, slow-burning fire built during a soft drizzle or rain. This ash is higher in potash and other minerals because they do not readily escape into the atmosphere as the wood is consumed by fire. Wood ashes should be stored in a tight container until they are used. Exposure to air will destroy much of their nutrient value. Ashes from a fireplace may be used if they are from wood and not from colored or slick paper.

(Left) Casting fertilizer onto bed surface; (right) sifting in fertilizers with spading fork. (A "twist dig" is now being used to sift in fertilizers as well. It is easier on the back and does not require bending over as far. This method requires three motions at once: [1] a slight up-and-down motion with the left hand, [2] a twist back and forth holding onto the D-handle with the right hand, and [3] a slight pushing in and out of the handle through the left hand with the right hand. Develop this skill by practicing.) Do not rake the bed to smooth it out after sifting in fertilizers, as this usually creates irregular concentrations of fertilizers that were previously spread evenly.

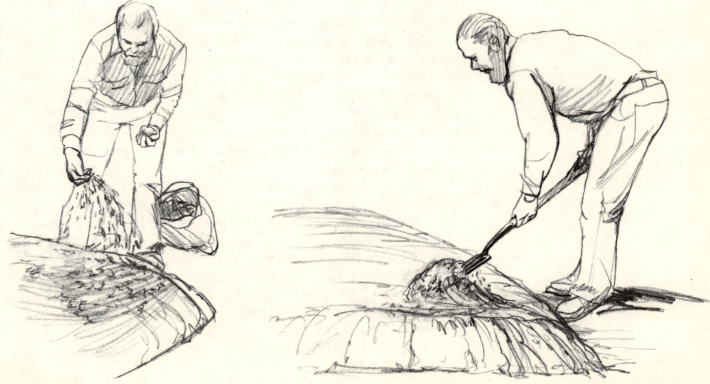

Manure is a microbial life stimulant and an animal and plant essence that has been "composted" both inside the animal and outside in a curing pile. Avoid using too much manure because manures that do not contain much sawdust or straw can contain excess salt and imbalanced ratios of nitrogen, phosphorus and potash. The biointensive method uses as much (or more) phosphorus and potash as nitrogen. This results in stronger, healthier plants. It is one difference between this method and the French intensive approach, which depended heavily on the use of horse manure, which is about 3 parts nitrogen to 1 part phosphorus to 3 parts potash. This is an unbalanced ratio in favor of nitrogen, which in time results in weak and rank plant growth more susceptible to disease and insect attack. A ratio of 1 part nitrogen to 1 part phosphorus to 1 part potash is better. The use of a large amount of composted or aged manure is recommended as an alternative to compost only when compost is not available.

The heavy emphasis which the biointensive method places on compost should be noted. The demand for most organic fertilizers is increasing while the supply available to each person in the world is decreasing. Soon, few fertilizers will be available at reasonable prices. Also, the materials used for the production of chemical fertilizers are becoming less available. Materials for biointensive method compost, on the other hand, are plants, animals, and earth which can be produced in a sustained way by *living* soils. These compostable materials can be produced indefinitely if we take care of our soils and do not exhaust them. In fact, 96% of the total amount of nutrients needed for plant growth processes are obtained as plants use the sun's energy to work on elements already in the air and water.[12] Soil and compost provide the rest.

The biodynamic/French intensive method has roots 5,000 years into the past in Chinese intensive agriculture, 2,000 years into the past in the Greek use of raised beds, and, more recently, in European farming. Similar practices are still used today in the native agriculture of many countries, such as Guatemala. "The method" will extend its roots into a future where environmentally balanced resource usage is of the utmost importance.

Compost made according to "the method" (the process will be discussed in the chapter on Compost) is usually high in the majority of major and trace minerals. It also contains a small amount of nitrogen and, when made with nitrogen-fixing cover crops, can be high in nitrogen. Additional nitrogen may also be obtained from the thin layer of manure added during the fertilization stage. Lastly, nitrogen is obtained for the garden system by the periodic growing of legumes such as peas,

12. Joseph A. Cocannouer, *Farming with Nature,* University of Oklahoma Press, Norman, Oklahoma, 1954, p. 50.

beans, clover, alfalfa, and vetch in the planting beds. The nitrogen that they fix from the air is released in the decomposition of their roots, stems, and leaves. Compost, bone meal, manure, wood ash, nitrogen from legumes, and nutrients from the growth of certain kinds of weeds in the beds (which is discussed in the chapter on Companion Planting) make up the 4% of the plant diet not provided by the air.

The Balanced Eco-system. Nothing happens in living nature that is not in relation to the whole. —Goethe

Compost

In nature, living things die and their death allows life to be reborn. Both animals and plants die on forest floors and in meadows to be composted by time, water, microorganisms, sun, and air to produce a soil improved in structure and nutrients. Organic plant growing follows nature's example. Leaves, grass, weeds, prunings, spiders, birds, trees, and plants should be returned to the soil and reused—not thrown away. Composting is an important way to recycle such elements as carbon, nitrogen, magnesium, sulfur, calcium, phosphorus, potash, and trace minerals. These elements are all necessary to maintain the biological cycles of life that exist in nature. All too often we participate instead in agricultural stripmining.

Composting in nature occurs in at least three ways: (1) In the form of manures, which are plant and animal foods composted inside the body of an animal (including earthworms) and then further aged outside the animal by the heat of fermentation. Earthworms are especially good composters. Their castings are 5 times richer in nitrogen, 2 times richer in exchangeable calcium, 7 times richer in available phosphorus, and 11 times richer in available potassium than the soil they inhabit. (2) In the form of animal and plant bodies which decay on top of and within the soil in nature and in compost piles. (3) In the form of roots, root hairs, and microbial life which remain and decay beneath the surface of the soil after harvesting. It is estimated that one rye plant in good soil grows 3 miles of roots a day, 387 miles of roots in a season, and 6,603 miles of root hairs each season![13]

Compost has a dual function. It improves the structure of the soil. This means the soil will be easier to work, will have good aeration and water retention characteristics, and will be resistant to erosion. Compost also provides *nutrients* for plant

13. Helen Philbrick and Richard B. Gregg, *Companion Plants and How to Use Them,* Devin-Adair Company, Old Greenwich, Connecticut, 1966, pp. 75-76.

A CROSS SECTION OF THE FOREST FLOOR

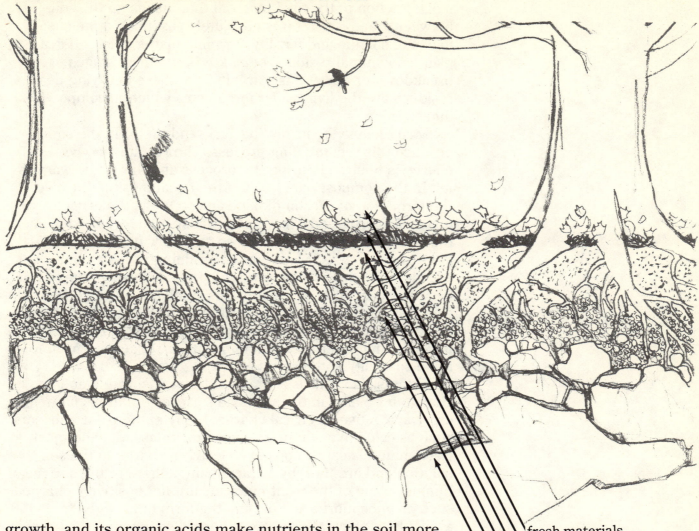

fresh materials

breaking down materials

topsoil

fine rock particles

larger rock pieces

rock

growth, and its organic acids make nutrients in the soil more available to plants. Fewer nutrients leach out in a soil with adequate organic matter.

Improved structure and nourishment produce a healthy soil. A healthy soil produces healthy plants better able to resist insect and disease attacks. Most insects look for sick plants to eat. The best way to control insects and diseases in plants is with a living, healthy soil rather than with poisons which kill this beneficial soil life.

Compost keeps soil at maximum health with a minimum of expense. Generally, it is unnecessary to buy fertilizers in order to be able to grow plants with nature. At first, organic fertilizers may have to be purchased so that the soil can be brought to a satisfactory level of fertility in a short period of time. Once this has been done, the health of the soil can be maintained with compost, crop rotation, and small amounts of manure, bone meal, and wood ash.

Compost is created from the decomposition and recombining of various forms of plant and animal life, such as leaves, grass, wood, garbage, natural fiber clothes, hair, and bones. These materials are *organic matter*. Organic matter is only a small fraction of the total material that makes up the soil—between 1 and 8%. Yet it is absolutely essential to the sustenance of soil life and fertility. Organic matter refers to dead plant and animal residues of *all* kinds and in *all* stages of breakdown or decay. Inseparable from these decaying dead residues are the living microorganisms which decompose, or digest, them.

Microscopic life forms (bacteria and fungi) in the soil produce this recombining process. The result is *humus.* Heat energy is liberated during the process and this is the warmth felt in the compost pile. Most of the decomposition involves the formation of carbon dioxide and water as the organic material is broken down. As the available energy is consumed, the microbial activity slows down and their numbers diminish—the pile cools. Most of the remaining organic matter is in the form of *humus compounds.* As humus is formed, nitrogen becomes part of its structure. This stabilizes nitrogen in the soil, because the humus compounds are resistant to decomposition. They are worked on slowly by soil organisms, but the nitrogen and other essential nutrients are protected from too rapid solubility and dissipation.

Humus also acts as a site of nutrient adsorption and exchange for plants in the soil. The surfaces of humus particles carry a negative electrical charge. Many of the plant nutrients, such as calcium, sodium, magnesium, potassium, and most trace minerals carry a positive electrical charge in the soil solution and are thereby attracted and adhere to the surface of humus. Some of the plant nutrients are not positively charged, such as phosphorus, sulfur, and the form of nitrogen that is available to plants. Fortunately, a good supply of these nutrients becomes available to the plants through biological transformations in the compost pile and soil.

As plant roots grow through the soil in search of nutrients, they feed off of the humus. Each plant root is surrounded by a "halo" of hydrogen ions which are a by-product of the roots' respiration. These hydrogen ions also carry a positive electrical charge. The root actually "bargains" with the humus, exchanging some of its positively charged hydrogen ions for positively charged nutrient ions stuck on to the surface of the humus. An active exchange is set up between humus and roots, the plants "choosing" which nutrients they need to balance their own inner chemistry.

Therefore, humus is the most reliable plant food, as the plants pull off whatever combinations of nutrients they "choose" from its surface. Biointensive practices rely on a natural, continual, slow-releasing biological process for nutrient release to the plants, rather than making available all the season's nutrients chemically at one time.

The beauty of humus is that it feeds the plants with nutrients it picks up on its surface, and also safely stores nutrients in forms which are not readily leached. In the center of the humus is much of the remainder of the original nitrogen that was put in the compost pile in the form of grass, kitchen wastes, and so on. The humus was formed by the resynthesizing activity of numerous species of microorganisms feeding off that original "garbage."

The microorganisms in the soil then continue to feed on the humus after the finished compost pile is spread on the soil. As they feed, the core nutrients are released in forms available to plant roots. Thus, the microorganisms are an integral part of the humus, as one cannot be found without the other. The only other component of the soil that holds onto and exchanges with plant roots is clay, but humus can hold onto and exchange a far greater amount of these nutrients.

It is also important to add soil to your compost pile. The soil contains a good starter supply of microorganisms. The organisms help in several ways. Some break down complex compounds into simpler ones the plants can utilize. There are many species of free-living bacteria which fix nitrogen from the air in a form available to plants. Many microorganisms tie up nitrogen surpluses. The surpluses are released gradually as the plants need nitrogen. An excessive concentration of available nitrogen in the soil (which makes plants susceptible to disease) is therefore avoided. There are predaceous fungi which attack and devour nematodes, but these fungi are only found in large amounts in a soil with adequate humus.

The microbial life provides a living pulsation in the soil which preserves its vitality for the plants. The microbes tie up essential nutrients in their own body tissues as they grow, and then release them slowly as they die and decompose. In this way, they help stabilize food release to the plants. These organisms are also continuously excreting a whole range of organic compounds into the soil. Sometimes described as "soil glue," these excretions contribute to the building of the soil structure. The organic compounds also contain disease-curing antibiotics and health-producing vitamins and enzymes that are integral parts of biochemical reactions in a healthy soil.

It is important to note the difference between *fertilization* and *fertility*. There can be plenty of fertilizer in the soil and plants still may not grow well. Add compost to the soil and the organic acids it contains will release the hidden nutrients in a form available to the plants. This was the source of the amazing fertility of Alan Chadwick's garden at Santa Cruz.

The recipe for a biointensive method compost is, **by weight:** 1/3 *dry vegetation,* 1/3 *green vegetation* (including *kitchen wastes*) and 1/3 *soil*—though we have found with our heavy clay soil that less soil produces better results. This 1/3 to 1/3 to 1/3 recipe will give you a carbon-nitrogen ratio in your built compost pile of about 25 to 1, and will produce a quality compost high in humified carbon. The ground under-

KEY ORGANIC MATTER FUNCTIONS

1. Organic matter feeds plants through nutrient exchange and nutrient release upon its decomposition.

2. It is a continual slow-release source of nutrients for plants.

3. Organic acids in humus help dissolve minerals in the soil, making the mineral nutrients available to plants. Organic acids also increase the permeability of plant root membranes and therefore promote the uptake of water and nutrients by plant roots.

4. Organic matter is the energy source for the soil's microbial life forms, which are an integral part of soil health. In one gram of humus-rich soil there are several *billion* bacteria, one million fungi, ten to twenty million actinomycetes and 800,000 algae.

5. The microbes which feed on organic matter in the soil temporarily bind the soil particles together. The fungi with their *thread-like* mycelia are especially important. They quite literally sew the soil together. The microbes secrete compounds into the soil as they live, metabolize, and ultimately decompose. Their secretions are a bacterial *glue* (polysaccharides) which holds soil particles, thus improving the structure. Structure is vital to soil productivity because it insures good aeration, good drainage, good water retention and erosion resistance.

6. Organic matter is the key to soil structure, keeping it safe from severe erosion and keeping it in an open, porous condition for good water and air penetration.

Microbial life forms thrive and greatly increase in activity when the nighttime air temperature reaches a minimum of 60°F. The next time you go out in the morning early in the season and notice that your garden has grown a foot overnight and is a darker, lush green, check the previous night's temperature. You will be surprised!

neath the pile should be loosened to a depth of 12 inches to provide good drainage. The materials should optimally be added to the pile in 1- to 2-inch layers with the dry vegetation on the bottom, the green vegetation and kitchen wastes second, and the soil third (a 1/4- to 1/2-inch layer). You can, however, build a pile spontaneously, adding materials daily or so, as they become available. This kind of pile will usually take a little longer to cure, but can be built more easily. Be sure to always cover kitchen wastes and fresh manures with soil to avoid flies and odors!

Green vegetation is 95 percent more effective than dry vegetation as a "starter" because its higher nitrogen content helps start and maintain the fermentation process. Dry vegetation is high in carbon content. It is difficult for the microbes in the compost pile to digest carbon without sufficient amounts of nitrogen. Unless you have a large household it may be necessary to save your kitchen scraps in a tight-lidded unbreakable container for several days to get enough material for the kitchen waste layer. You may want to hold your breath when you dump them because the stronger-smelling *anaerobic* form of the decomposition process has been taking place in the closed container. The smell will disappear within a few hours

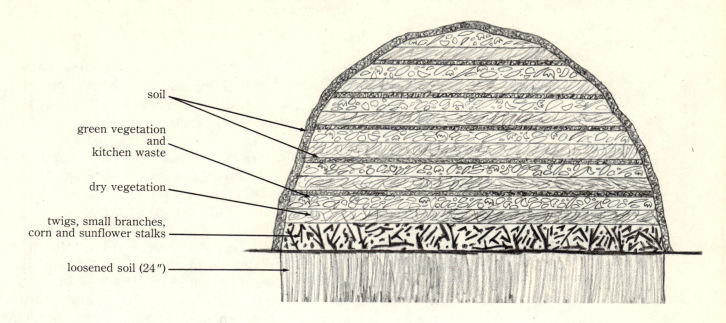

soil

green vegetation
and
kitchen waste

dry vegetation

twigs, small branches,
corn and sunflower stalks

loosened soil (24″)

after reintroduction to air. All kitchen scraps may be added except meats and sizable amounts of oily salad scraps. Be sure to include bones, tea leaves, coffee grounds, eggshells, and citrus rinds.

Add the soil layer immediately after the kitchen waste. It contains microorganisms which speed decomposition, keeps the smell down to a minor level, and prevents flies from laying eggs in the garbage. The smell will be difficult to eliminate entirely when waste from members of the cabbage family is added. In a few days, however, even this soil-minimized odor will disappear. As each layer is added, water it lightly so the pile is *evenly* moist—like a wrung-out damp sponge that does not give out excess water when squeezed. Sufficient water is necessary for the proper heating and decomposition of the materials. Too little water results in decreased biological activity and too much simply drowns the aerobic microbial life. Water the pile when necessary as you water the garden. The particles in the pile should glisten. During the rainy season some shelter or covering may be needed to prevent over-watering and the less optimal anaerobic decomposition that occurs in a waterlogged pile. (The conditions needed for proper functioning of a compost pile and those required for good plant growth in raised beds are similar. In both cases the proper mixture of air, soil nutrients, structure, microorganisms, and water is essential.)

Compost piles can be built in a pit in the ground or in a pile above the ground. The latter is preferable, since during rainy

Soil is added to compost pile after green vegetation and kitchen waste layer.

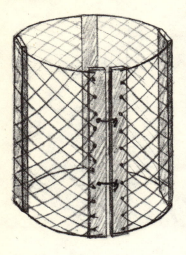

The least expensive type of compost container

periods a pit can fill up with water. A pile can be made with or without a container. We build our compost piles without using containers. They are unnecessary and use wood and metal resources.

For those who wish to use them, containers can help shape a pile and keep the materials looking neat. The least expensive container is made of 12-foot-long, 3-foot-wide, 1-inch mesh chicken wire with five 3-foot-long, 1-inch-by-2-inch boards and two sets of small hooks and eyes. The boards are nailed along the two 3-foot ends of the wire and at 3-foot intervals along the length of the wire (see illustration). The hooks and eyes are attached to the two end boards near the top and bottom. The unit is then placed as a circle on the ground, the hooks attached to the eyes, and the compost materials placed inside. The materials hold up the circle. After the pile is built, the wire enclosure may be removed and the materials will stay in place. You may now use the enclosure to build another pile, or you may use it later to turn the first pile into, if you decide to turn it to speed the decomposition process. We rarely try to acceler-

Four kinds of compost piles

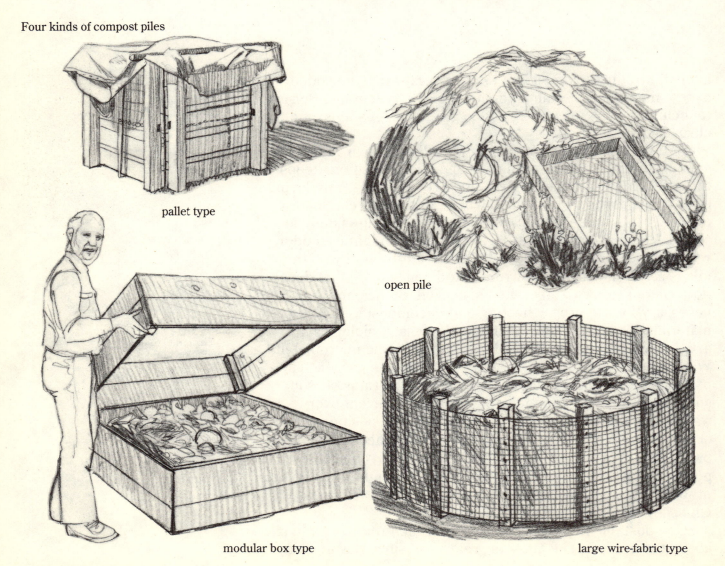

pallet type

open pile

modular box type

large wire-fabric type

ate its natural process, which results in the highest quality product.

There are three ways to speed up the decomposition rate in a compost pile—though they will leave you with a much lower quality product, a good topsoil or a mineralized compost rather than the life-enhancing compost you most seek. One way is to *increase the amount of nitrogen*. The ratio of carbon to nitrogen is critical for the breakdown rate. Materials with a high carbon to nitrogen ratio, such as wood, take a long time to decompose alone since they lack sufficient nitrogen-bearing materials upon which the bacteria depend for food. Such materials are sawdust, dry leaves, wood shavings, grainstubble, and straw. To boost the rate of decay in carbonaceous materials, add nitrogen-rich materials such as newly cut grass, fresh manure, vegetable wastes, green vegetation, or a fertilizer such as blood or fish meal. Three to five pounds of blood or fish meal per cubic yard of compost is probably a good amount of fertilizer with which to fortify a compost pile which has a high carbon content. These fertilizers are lightly sprinkled on each layer as the pile is built.

A second method is to *increase the amount of air* (aeration). Beneficial aerobic bacteria thrive in a well-aerated pile. Proper layering and periodic turning of the pile will accomplish this.

Third, the *surface area of the materials may be increased*. The smaller the size of the materials, the greater the amount of their exposed surface area. Broken up twigs will decompose more rapidly than twigs that are left whole. We discourage the use of power shredders because nature will do the job in a relatively short time and everyone has sufficient access to materials which will compost rapidly without resorting to a shredder. The noise from these machines is quite disturbing and spoils the peace and quiet of a garden. They also consume increasingly scarce fuel.

Note that at least *three different materials of three different textures* are used in the biointensive method compost recipe and in many other recipes. The varied texture will allow good drainage and aeration in the pile. The compost will also have a more diverse nutrient content. A pile made primarily of leaves or grass cuttings makes the passage of water and air through the pile difficult without frequent turning because both tend to mat. Good air and water penetration are both required for proper decomposition. The layering of the materials further promotes a mixture of textures and nutrients and helps insure even decomposition.

A minimum pile size of 3 feet by 3 feet by 3 feet (1 cubic yard of lightly moist, cured compost, weighing about 1,000 pounds) is recommended. (In colder climates a minimum pile size of 4 feet by 4 feet by 4 feet will be needed to properly insulate the heat of the composting process.) Smaller piles fail to provide the insulation necessary for proper heating (up to

An abundant garden starts with good compost made of "waste products" such as vegetable peelings, weeds, and manures. With some knowledge and planning, the garden can produce all its needed fertilizer and organic matter.

140 F degrees) and allow the penetration of too much air. It is all right to build up piles slowly to this size as materials become available, though it is best to build an entire pile at one time. A pile will cure to 1/2 to 1/3 its original size, depending on the materials used. A large pile size might be 5 feet high, 10 feet wide, and 12 feet long.

The best time to prepare compost is in the *spring or autumn* when biological activity is highest. (Too much heat or cold slows down and even kills the microbial life in the pile.) The two high activity periods conveniently coincide with the maximum availability of materials in the spring, as grass and other plants begin to grow rapidly, and in the autumn, as leaves fall and other plant life begins to die. The pile should optimally be built under a deciduous oak tree. This tree's nature provides the conditions for the development of excellent soil underneath it. And compost is a kind of soil. The second best place is under any other kind of deciduous tree (with the exceptions of walnut and eucalyptus). As a last resort, evergreen trees or any shady place in your backyard may be used. The shade and windbreak provided by the trees help keep the pile at an even moisture level. (The pile should be placed 6 feet away from the tree's trunk so it will not provide a haven for potentially harmful insects.)

Compost is ready to use when it is dark and rich-looking. You should not be able to discern the original source of the materials from the texture, and the compost should crumble in your hands. Mature compost even smells good—like water in a forest spring! A biointensive pile should be ready to use in 2-1/2 to 3 months. Usually, one turning is needed to adjust the moisture level and make the materials homogeneous for complete breakdown. This should be done at 6–8 weeks, when the *temperature* of the compost pile *peaks and begins to decrease.* A *decrease in moisture* usually occurs at the same time, the *color* begins to change to *brownish* from the original green and yellow, and the compost's *odor* begins to change from musty to an *earthy, freshly plowed soil aroma.* The compost will then normally be ready about 1 month later. We make separate compost piles of small tree branches, since they can take 2 years to decompose. Compost for use in flats should be passed through a sieve of 1/4-inch or 1/8-inch wire fabric. In the garden a *minimum* maintenance dressing of 1/2 pound of compost per square foot should be added to the soil before each crop. Guidelines for *general* maintenance dressings are a 1-inch layer of compost, or 8 cubic feet of compost per 100 square feet (about 3 pounds per square foot).[14]

The biointensive method of compost making differs in

14. Current research indicates that this amount may eventually be significantly reduced with the use of a high-quality compost containing higher concentrations of carbon and nutrients than are obtained in many composting processes. (See Ecology Action's Self-Teaching Mini-Series Booklet No. 23, *Biointensive Composting,* for more details.)

particular from the biodynamic method in that it is simpler to prepare, normally uses no manure, and usually uses no herbal solutions to stimulate microorganism growth.[15] Manure, used continually and in large amounts, is an imbalanced fertilizer, although it is a good texturizing agent because of its usual decomposed sawdust content. Rather than herbal solutions, weeds, such as stinging nettle, and plants, such as fava beans, are sometimes added in the preparation of special piles. Special mixtures are created to meet particular pH, structure, and nutrient requirements.

The biointensive method of making compost differs from the Rodale compost method in the use of little or no manure and usually no rock powder fertilizers or nitrogen supplements.[16] Fertilizers do not need to be added to the pile, since successful compost can be made from a mixture of ingredients. The nitrogen supplements do, however, speed up the decomposition process. Both the biodynamic and Rodale methods are good ones, proven by use over a long period of time. Chadwick's biointensive recipe seems simpler to use and equally effective.

Some people use *sheet composting* (a process of spreading uncomposted organic materials over the soil and then digging them into the soil where they decompose). The disadvantage of this method is that the soil should not be planted for 3 months or so until decomposition has occurred. Soil bacteria tie up the nitrogen during the decomposition process, thereby making it unavailable to the plants. Sheet composting is beneficial if it is used during the winter in cold areas, because the tie-up prevents the nitrogen from leaching out during winter rains.

Other people use *green manure composting* (the growing of cover crops such as vetch, clover, alfalfa, beans, peas, or other legumes until just before maturity when the plants are dug into the soil). This is an excellent way to bring unworked soil into a reasonable condition. These cover crops are rich in nitrogen, so they boost the nutrient level of the soil without one's having to resort to the purchase of fertilizers. Their stems and leaves contain a lot of nitrogen and their roots support nitrogen-fixing bacteria. These bacteria take nitrogen from the air and fix it in nodules on the roots, which you can see when you pull the plants up. They also help you dig. Their roots loosen the soil and eventually turn into humus beneath the earth. Fava beans are exceptionally good for green manuring if you plan to plant tomatoes, because their decomposed bodies help eradicate tomato wilt organisms from the soil.

15. For the biodynamic method of compost preparation, see pages 37 to 51 in *The Pfeiffer Garden Book,* edited by Alice Heckel, Biodynamic Farming and Gardening Association, Inc., Stroudsburg, Pennsylvania, 1967.

16. For the Rodale method of compost preparation, see pages 59 to 86 in *The Basic Book of Organic Gardening,* edited by Robert Rodale, Ballantine Books, New York, 1971.

Due to their high nitrogen content, cover crops decompose rapidly. Planting can usually follow 1 month after the plants are dug into the soil. The disadvantage of the green manuring process is that the land is out of production during the period of cover crop growth and the shorter 1-month period of decomposition. In some areas, the long-term improvement in the soil's nutritive content and structure compensates for this limitation.

The advantage of the small-scale biointensive method is that backyard composting is easily feasible. Even if you decide to use cover crop produce and not to dig the crop residues in, the growing process will put nitrogen into the soil and will make it possible to grow plants such as corn and tomatoes, which are heavy nitrogen feeders. (See Companion Planting chapter.) And the plant residues may be used in the compost pile.

Some materials should not be used in the preparation of compost:

☐ Plants infected with a disease or a severe insect attack where eggs could be preserved or where the insects themselves could survive in spite of the compost pile's heat.

☐ Poisonous plants, such as oleander, hemlock, and castor bean, which harm soil life.

☐ Plants which take too long to break down, such as magnolia leaves.

☐ Plants which have acids toxic to other plants and microbial life, such as eucalyptus, California bay laurel, walnut, juniper, acacia, and cypress.

☐ Plants which may be too acidic or contain substances that interfere with the decomposition process, such as pine needles. Pine needles are extremely acidic and contain a form of kerosene. (Special compost piles are often made of acidic materials, such as pine needles and leaves, however. This compost will lower the soil's pH and stimulate acid-loving plants like strawberries.)

☐ Ivy and succulents, which may not be killed in the heat of the decomposition process and can regrow when the compost is placed in a planting bed.

☐ Pernicious weeds such as wild morning glory and Bermuda grass, which will probably not be killed in the decomposition process and which will choke out other plants when they resprout after the compost is placed in a planting bed.

☐ Cat and dog manures, which can contain pathogens harmful to infants. These pathogens are not always killed in the heat of the compost pile.

Plants infected with disease or insects and pernicious weeds should be burned to be properly destroyed. Their ash then becomes a good fertilizer. The ash will also help control harmful soil insects, such as carrot worms, which shy away from the alkalinity of ashes.

Parts of a regular compost pile which have not broken down completely by the end of the composting period should be placed at the bottom of a new pile. This is especially true for twigs and small branches which can use the extra protection of the pile's height to speed their decomposition in a situation of increased warmth and moisture.

FUNCTIONS OF HUMUS/COMPOST IN SOIL

Improved Structure—breaks up clay and clods, and binds together sandy soil. Helps make proper aeration in clayey and sandy soil possible.

Moisture Retention—holds 6 times its own weight in water. A soil with good organic matter content soaks up rain like a sponge and regulates the supply to plants. A soil stripped of organic matter resists water penetration, thus leading to crusting, erosion, and flooding.

Aeration—plants can obtain 96% of the nutrients they need from the *air, sun, and water*. A loose, healthy soil assists in the diffusion of air into the soil and in the exchange of nutrients and moisture. Carbon dioxide released by organic matter decomposition diffuses out of the soil and is absorbed by the canopy of leaves above in a raised bed mini-climate created by closely spaced plants.

Fertilization—compost contains some nitrogen, phosphorus, potassium, magnesium, and sulfur but is especially important for trace elements. The important principle is to return to the earth, by the use of plant residues and manures, all that has been taken out.

Nitrogen Storage—the compost pile is a storehouse for nitrogen. Because it is tied up in the compost breakdown process, water-soluble nitrogen does not leach out or oxidize into the air for a period of 3 to 6 months or more—depending on how the pile is built and maintained.

pH Buffer—a good percentage of compost in the soil helps plants to resist changes in the soil pH.

Soil Toxin Neutralizer—important recent studies show that plants grown in organically composted soils take up less lead, heavy metals, and other urban pollutants.

Nutrient Release—organic acids dissolve soil minerals and make them available to plants. As organic matter decomposes, it releases nutrients for plant uptake and for the soil microbial population.

Food for Microbial Life—good compost creates healthy conditions for soil organisms that live in the soil. Compost harbors earthworms and beneficial fungi that fight nematodes and other soil pests.

The Ultimate in Recycling—the earth provides us food, clothing, and shelter, and we close the cycle in offering fertility, health, and life through the shepherding of materials.

We sometimes build a compost pile on an unused growing bed so that the next crop grown in that bed will pick up and utilize any nutrients leached out from the pile into the soil. The next season we build compost on another unused growing bed.

BUILDING A COMPOST PILE STEP BY STEP

1. Loosen soil under the pile area 12 inches deep with a spading fork.

2. Lay down *roughage* (brush, corn stalks, or other material) 3 inches thick for air circulation, if it is available.

3. Put down a 4-inch layer of *dry vegetation*—dry weeds, leaves, straw, grass clippings, hay, and old garden wastes.

4. Put down a 2-inch layer of *green vegetation and kitchen waste*—fresh weeds, grass clippings, hedge trimmings, green cover crops, and kitchen waste you have saved. Cover lightly with a 1-inch layer of *soil* to prevent flies and odors.

5. Add new layers of dry vegetation, green vegetation, kitchen waste, and soil as materials become available until pile is 3 to 5 feet high.

6. Let completed pile cure 3 to 6 months while building a new pile. Turn once for faster decomposition.

7. Water completed pile regularly until ready for use. For planning purposes, remember that a 5-foot-high compost pile will be only 1-2/3 to 2-1/2 feet high when it is ready to use.

NOTE: Materials with a high carbon content, such as leaves, dry weeds and grass clippings, sawdust, and wood chips, are very slow to decompose, taking 6 months to 3 years. To hasten decomposition, keep moist and add materials high in nitrogen such as fresh manure or blood meal. Green weeds, fresh grass clippings, and juicy kitchen waste are quick to decompose. Alone, these highly nitrogenous materials can break down in as little as 2 weeks, BUT they can attract flies and cause offensive odors unless mixed with high-carbon materials.

Seed Propagation

Now that we know a little about the body and soul of our Earth, we are ready to witness the birth of seedlings. For a minute close your eyes, pretend you are the seed of your favorite plant, tree, vegetable, fruit, flower, or herb. You are all alone. You can do nothing in this state. Slowly you begin to hear sounds around you. The wind, perhaps. You feel warmth from the sun—the ground underneath you. What things do you need in relation to you for good growth? Think like a seed and ask yourself what a seed needs in nature—air, warmth, moisture, soil, nutrients, microorganisms. You need these things, at least, along with other plants, birds, insects, spiders, frogs, and chickens. You need an entire microcosm of the world.

Generally the first elements fall into two categories: the terrestrial (soil and nutrients) and celestial (air, warmth, moisture). These elements cannot be completely categorized, however, since air, warmth, and moisture come from the heavens to circulate through the soil and gases can be taken into plants through their roots as well as their leaves. Nutrients, on the other hand, can be borne upon the air currents. In fact, the important trace mineral zinc is taken in more readily by citrus tree leaves than by their roots. The parts that other elements in the plant and animal worlds play—the parts of other plants and insects, for example—will be discussed in the chapter on Companion Planting.

Seed Planting

Seeds should be planted as deep as the thin vertical dimension of each seed. Lima and fava beans may be planted on their sides. The root system, which emerges from the eye, will still be able to grow straight down. Preferably, the seed should be covered with sifted compost, which is similar to decomposed plant matter found over germinating seeds in nature. This

The depth to which a seed is planted is equal to its vertical dimension.

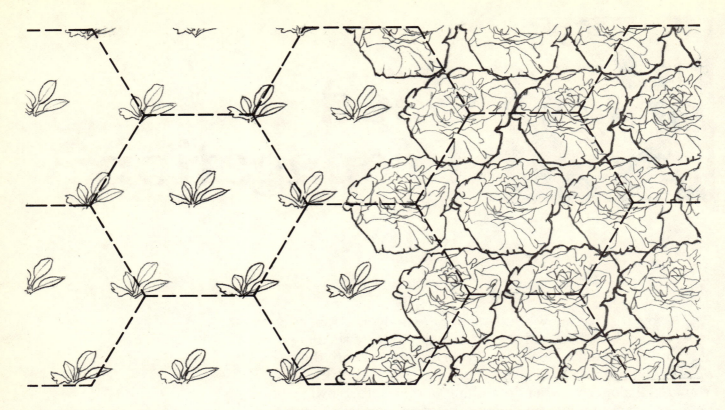

HEXAGONAL SPACING
Leaf lettuce—8-inch centers

compost stimulates the germination process.

The seeds, whether they are planted in beds or flats, should be planted in a diagonally offset or hexagonal spacing pattern with each seed the same distance from all the seeds nearest it. The spacings given in the chart later in this section show how far to place different plants from each other, so that when the plants are mature in the flats or the planting beds their leaves will barely touch and provide the living mulch mini-climate under the leaves so essential to balanced, uninterrupted growth. In general, the plant spacings for vegetables, flowers, and herbs are the "within the row" spacings listed on the back of seed packets or sometimes 3/4 of this distance. *Disregard* the "between rows" spacings. Spacing for plants normally grown on hills has to be determined by experimentation. Our best spacings to date for these are given in the spacing charts. Plants spaced accordingly form a *living mulch,* which retards weed growth and aids in the retention of soil moisture by shading the soil. When spacing seeds in flats, place the seeds so far apart that the seedlings' leaves will barely touch when the seedlings are transplanting size. Try 1-inch to 2-inch spacings depending on the size of the seedling at its transplanting stage (see spacing chart at the end of this chapter).

To make the placement of seeds in the planting beds or flats easier, use frames with 1-inch and 2-inch mesh chicken wire stretched across them. The mesh is built on a hexagonal pattern, so the seeds can be dropped in the center of a hexagon and be on the proper center. Or, if a center greater than 1

Spacing frame for placing seeds in flats.
Place seed in center of each space.

inch is involved and you only have 1-inch mesh, just count past the proper number of hexagons before dropping the next seed. When transplanting or planting seeds on spacings of 3 inches or more, try using measuring sticks cut to the required length to determine where the plant should be located. Drop a seed at each point of the triangulation process.

Once you have gotten the feel for plant spacing, you may want to practice broadcasting seeds by hand and eventually graduate to this method of sowing. Broadcasting is the method used by Alan Chadwick and his apprentices in both flats and growing beds. When you reach this stage, seeds should end up 1/4 to 1/2 inch apart in the first flat. This way the seeds can take advantage of complete mini-climate growth stimulation and health earlier in their life. It does require more time to do several transplantings though. When these seedlings' leaves are barely touching, they should be transplanted into other flats on 1/2- to 1-inch centers. Approximately four flats will be filled by one flat of these broadcasted seeds. Or you can broadcast the seeds on 1/2- to 1-inch spacings initially and thin the areas where plants are too close together. Sometimes little thinning is needed. Broadcasting on wider centers and thinning can also eventually be done in the growing beds. Thinning will probably take the same amount of time (or more) as placing seeds on their proper centers in the first place, but the health of plants from broadcast seeds will probably be better because of an earlier-established mini-climate. You will also eventually learn to transplant with reasonable accuracy without measuring!

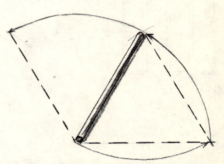

Spacing stick for placing seeds in beds.
3-inch to 36-inch sizes used according to crop planted. Triangulation is the way we plant most seeds and transplant seedlings.

Triangular spacing template for placing seeds in beds

Use your digging board as a planting board to minimize compaction, and as you move it along the bed, reloosen the soil underneath with a hand fork or a spading fork.

Seedling flat construction
Sides and bottom are of bender board.

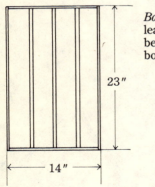

Bottom view: leave 1/16″ between bender board pieces.

23″

14″

Ends are of 1″ × 3″, 1″ × 6″, and 1″ × 10″ redwood.

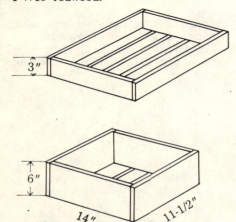

3″

6″

14″   11-1/2″

Deeper flat half as long to insure manageable weight

Cover the seeds in flats with a layer of the flat soil mixture described below. Seeds in a planting bed should normally be covered with soil taken from the bed itself *after* the double-digging has been completed and *before* the shaping and fertilization steps are begun. Or, large seeds may be poked into the soil to the proper depth with your index finger. The hole may then be filled by pushing soil into it with your thumb and index finger.

Flats

If you build your own flats, the standard flat size is 3 inches deep by 14 inches wide by 23 inches long. The depth is critical since too shallow a depth allows the seedling roots to touch the bottom too soon. When this occurs, the plants believe they have reached the limit of their growth and they enter a state of "premature senility." In this state the plants begin to flower and fruit even though they are only transplanting size. We have experienced this with broccoli and dwarf marigolds. The broccoli heads were the size of a little fingernail. The length and width of the flat are not as critical. Their size should not become too large, however, if the flat is to be easy to carry in weight and size. If plants must remain in the container more than 4 to 6 weeks, a container 6 inches or more in depth should be used.

When planting seeds or seedlings, remember that the most important areas for the plant are the 2 inches above and the 2 inches below the surface of the flat or the planting bed. This is because of the mini-climate created under the plants' leaves and because of the important protection of the upper roots in the flat or the bed by the soil. Without proper protection, the plants will develop tough necks at the point where the stem emerges from the soil. A toughened neck slows the flow of plant juices and interrupts and weakens plant growth. These areas are also important because in a very real sense the roots are *leaves in the soil* and the leaves are *roots in the air*. The explanation for this dualism lies in the fact that the roots "breathe" in (absorb) gases in significant amounts as if they were leaves and that the leaves absorb moisture and nutrients from the air. Also, plant life activity varies above and below the ground according to monthly cycles. Root growth is stimulated more during the third quarter of each 28-day period and leaf growth is stimulated more during the second quarter, in accordance with the phases of the moon. (See pages 54–55.)

The exact critical distance above and below the surface of the planting bed is not necessarily 2 inches. Obviously it will be different for radishes than for corn, since their leaves begin at different heights from the soil surface and because they have different depths to their root systems. Generally speaking, though, the 2-inch/2-inch guideline helps us develop a sensitivity to the plants' needs above and below ground. (The need for proper conditions above and below ground was also noted in the comparison between the normal use of rows in gardening and farming and the use of raised beds for growing plants on pages 3 and 4.) In particular, the mini-climate protects the feeder roots and the microbial life, which are both concentrated in the upper soil.

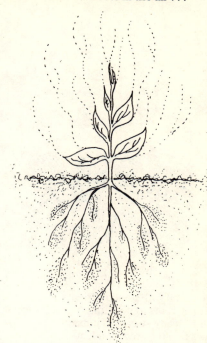

The leaves are roots in the air . . .

roots are leaves in the ground . . .

Flat Soil

You are now ready to prepare the soil in which to grow these versatile plants. A good planting mixture to use for

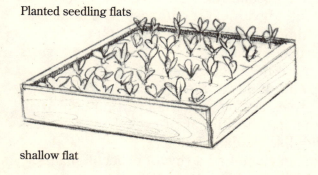

Planted seedling flats

shallow flat

deep flat

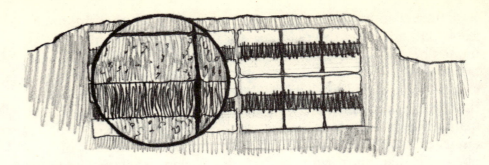

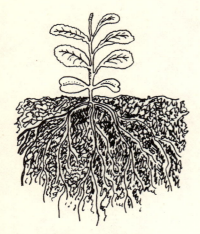

Loose soil with good nutrients enables roots to penetrate the soil easily and a steady stream of nutrients flows into the stem and leaves.

Hold seedling by leaves.

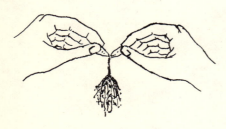

The hand fork

starting seeds in flats is 1/3 each *by weight* compost, sharp (gritty) sand, and turf loam. The three ingredients provide a fertile, loose-textured mixture. These elements should be mixed thoroughly together and placed in the flat on top of a 1/8-inch layer of oak leaf mold (partially decayed oak leaves) or compost, which lines the bottom of the flat for drainage and additional nutrients. Crushed eggshells may also be placed above the oak leaf mold for calcium-loving plants such as carnations and members of the cabbage family. The eggshells should be lightly sprinkled so 1/4 of the total surface area will be covered. Turf loam is made by composting sections of turf grass grown in good soil. The sections are composted with the grass side of the sections together and the soil sections together within the pile. Good garden soil can be substituted for the turf loam.

Transplanting

The biointensive method continually seeks to foster uninterrupted plant growth. Part of this technique is embodied in the "Breakfast-Lunch-Dinner!" concept stressed by Alan Chadwick. Frequently, seedlings are raised in a very good soil—in terms of nutrients and texture—only to be transplanted into an area which has few nutrients and a poor texture. The plant suffers root shock when it is uprooted from the flat and then encounters nutrient deficiency and physical impediment to growth in poor soil. Better results occur when seedlings are transplanted from a flat with a good planting-mixture "breakfast" into a second flat with a "lunch" consisting of a similar mixture fortified with extra compost. The plant will forget its trauma in tasting the delectable new lunch treats in the second flat. This process minimizes shock and even fosters growth. In the biointensive method, transplanting stimulates growth rather than slowing it down. Finally, a splendid biointensive "dinner" greets the plant in the growing bed! With this kind care and stimulated healthy plant growth there is less likelihood of insect and disease damage.

A biodynamic gardener once had a row of broccoli plants. Only two had aphids on them, and both were quite infested. The two plants were dug up and the gardener discovered the plants had experienced root damage during transplanting. The healthy broccoli, which had experienced uninterrupted growth, went untouched by the insects, while nature eliminated the unhealthy plants.

When transplanting, it is important to handle the seedlings gently, and to touch them as little as possible. Plants do not like their bodies to be handled, though they do like to have human companionship and to have dead leaves removed from their stems. You should hold them only by the tips of their leaves (if the plant must be touched) or by the soil around their roots. If the seedlings have been grown in flats, use a hand fork to gently separate a 4-square-inch section of soil and plants from the rest. Using the fork, gently lift the section from the flat and place it on the ground. Then carefully pull away one plant at a time from the section for transplanting. If it is particularly dry, hot, or windy, the section should be placed on a wet towel and three of its sides should be protected from exposure by the towel. Always keep as much soil around the roots as possible. If the seedling has been grown in a pot, turn the pot upside down, letting the plant stem pass between your second and third fingers, and tap firmly on the bottom of the pot with your other hand. Or tap the lip of the pot on something solid. Optimally, transplanting should be done in the early evening, so the seedling will be more able to overcome transplanting shock at a time of more moderate climatic conditions. If transplanting is performed at other times, some temporary shading may be needed.

In all cases, if the plants are root bound (roots so tightly grown together that with the soil they constitute a tight mass), gently spread the roots out in all directions. This process is important, because the plant would spend critical growth energy in sending out a new, wide-ranging root system for eating and drinking, when a good root system has already been produced. How much better if the energy goes into the natural flow of continuous growth rather than into the correction of an abnormal situation. In spreading the roots out, we physically minimize a problem which has occurred when the plant was kept in a starting flat or pot too long.

Be sure to place the seedling into a large enough hole so that the plant can be buried up to its first set of true leaves. This way, as the soil is packed down under the pressure of watering, the final soil level will remain high enough to cover the upper roots. Press the soil firmly around the seedling, but not too tightly. Tight packing will damage the roots and will not allow the proper penetration of water, nutrients, and air. Too loose a soil will allow air and moisture to concentrate around the roots. This will cause root burn and decay. Firm contact of the plant's roots with the soil is necessary for the proper absorption of water and nutrients by the plant through the roots. Water the seedlings after transplanting to help settle the soil around the roots, to eliminate excess air spaces, and to

The correct way to unpot a seedling.

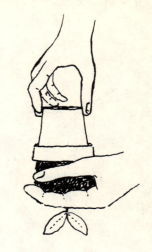

Spread root-bound plant roots out before transplanting into bed.

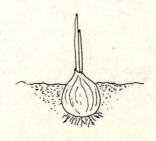

Most vegetables should be transplanted up to their first two leaves.

proper

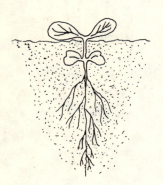

improper

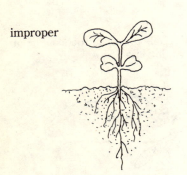

result

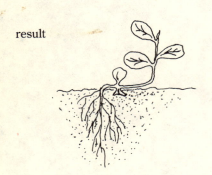

provide an adequate amount of water for growth.

A second reason for transplanting seedlings up to their first two leaves is to prevent them from becoming top-heavy and bending over during the early growth period. (This is especially true for members of the cabbage family.) If the plant bends over, it will upright itself, but a very tough neck will be created that will reduce the quality and size of the plant and vegetable. Onions and garlic, however, do better if the bulb does not have so much soil weight to push up against.

Transplanting should be used whenever possible. Space and water are conserved in this way, because seedlings in flats require less of both (as little as 1/2 gallon of water per day for one flat, compared to 10 to 20-plus gallons for a 100-square-foot growing bed). More importantly, transplanting is a way to improve plant health. Beds become compacted as they are watered from day to day. Thus, if a seed is planted directly in the bed, some compaction will have occurred by the time it is a "child" a month later and, in some cases, so much so after 2 months, when it is likely to be an "adolescent," that its "adulthood" may be seriously affected. If, instead, you transplant the 1-month-old "child" into the growing bed, a strong adult root system can develop during the next 2 months and a good adult life is likely. In fact, a study at the University of California at Berkeley in the 1950's indicated that a 2–4% increase in root health can increase yields 2 to 4 times.[17]

Planting by the Phases of the Moon

One of the most controversial aspects of the biointensive method is the planting of seeds and the transplanting of seedlings by phases of the moon. *Short- and extra-long-germinating seeds* are planted *2 days before the new moon,* when the first significant magnetic forces occur, and up to 7 days after the

17. Charles Morrow Wilson, *Roots: Miracles Below—The Web of Life Beneath Our Feet,* Doubleday and Company, Garden City, New York, 1968, p. 105.

PLANTING BY THE PHASES OF THE MOON

2 days before New Moon   *First 7 days*   *Second 7 days*

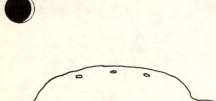

Plant short- and extra-long-germinating seeds (most vegetables and herbs) in flats and/or beds

Balanced increase in rate of root and leaf growth

Moonlight +
Lunar Gravity –

Increased leaf growth rate

Moonlight +
Lunar Gravity +

new moon. *Long-germinating seeds* are planted *at the full moon* and up to 7 days afterward. *Seedlings* are *transplanted at the same time.* Both planting periods take advantage of the full sum of the forces of nature, including gravity, light, and magnetism. The greatest sum of increasing forces occurs at the new moon. The lunar gravitational pull which produces high tides in the oceans and water tides in the soil is very high. And the moon, which is dark, gets progressively lighter. (See drawing.) The importance of the time of the month in planting seeds and transplanting is not so much in the exact day on which you perform the task, but rather in generally taking advantage of the impetus provided by nature.

When you place short-germinating seeds in the ground 2 days before the lunar tide forces are greatest, the seed has time to absorb water. The force exerted on the water in the seed helps create a "tide" that helps burst the seed coat in conjunction with the forces produced by the swelling of the seed. No doubt you have wondered why one time beet seeds come up almost immediately and another time the germinating process takes 2 weeks in the same bed under similar conditions. Temperature and moisture differences, pH changes, and humus levels may influence the seeds in each case, but the next time you note marked difference in germination time, check your calendar to determine the phase the moon was in when the seeds were sown. You may be surprised to find the moon had an influence.

Looking at the drawing, you can see that there are both increasing and decreasing lunar gravitational and light force influences that recur periodically during the lunar month. Sometimes the forces work against each other and sometimes they reinforce one another. When the lunar gravitational pull decreases and the amount of moonlight increases during *the first 7 days,* plants undergo a period of balanced growth. The decreasing lunar gravity (and the corresponding relative increase in Earth's gravity) *stimulates root growth.* At the same time, the increasing amount of moonlight *stimulates leaf growth.*

When broadcasting seeds onto a growing bed is desirable, gently "chop" them in afterward with a bow rake to a depth equal to their diameter (when they are lying flat on a surface). Be sure to chop the rake only up and down; do not pull it toward you. If you pull, seeds, fertilizers, and compost will usually concentrate irregularly over the bed rather than remain evenly spread.

KEY:

● New Moon
◐ First Quarter
○ Full Moon
◑ Fourth Quarter
+ = Increasing
− = Decreasing

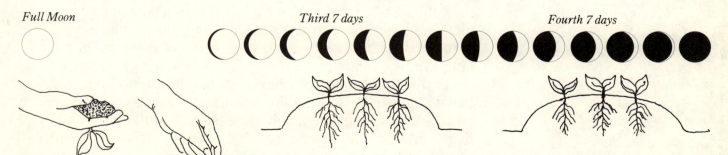

Full Moon

Transplant seedlings from flat into beds and plant long-germinating seeds (most flowers) in flats and/or beds

Third 7 days

Increased root growth rate
Moonlight −
Lunar Gravity −

Fourth 7 days

Balanced decrease in rate of root and leaf growth (resting period)
Moonlight −
Lunar Gravity +

During *the second 7 days,* the lunar gravitational force reverses its relative direction and increases. This pull *slows down the root growth* as Earth's relative gravitational pull is lessened. The moonlight, on the other hand, continues to a peak and *leaf growth is especially stimulated.* If root growth has been sufficient during previous periods, then the proper amounts of nutrients and water will be conveyed to the above-ground part of the plant and balanced, uninterrupted growth will occur. In this time of increasing gravitational, moonlight, and magnetic forces, seeds which have not yet germinated receive a special boost from nature. If they did not germinate at the time of the new moon, they should do so by the full moon. It is during this period that Alan Chadwick says seeds cannot resist coming up and mushrooms suddenly appear overnight.

During *the third 7 days,* the amount of moonlight decreases along with the lunar gravitational pull. As the moonlight decreases, the above-ground *leaf growth slows down.* The *root growth is stimulated* again, however, as the lunar gravitational pull decreases. This is a good time to transplant, since the root growth is active. The activity enables the plant to better overcome root shock and promotes the development of a good root system while leaf growth has been slowed down. Then, 21 days later, when leaf growth is at a maximum, there will be a developed root system that can provide the plant with sufficient nutrients and water. It is also the time to plant long-germinating seeds. Seeds which take approximately 2 weeks to germinate will then be ready to take advantage of the boost from the high gravitational pull of the new moon.

During *the last 7 days,* the lunar gravitational force increases and *root growth slows down.* The amount of moonlight decreases and also *slows down leaf growth.* This period is one of a balanced decrease in growth or a period of rest, just as the first 7 days in the lunar month is a period of a balanced increase in growth. The last 7 days, then, is a rest period which comes before the bursting forth of a period of new life. Short- and extra-long-germinating seeds are planted 2 days before the new moon so they will be able to take advantage of this time of new life. (The extra-long-germinating seeds take approximately 1 month to germinate.) The short-, long-, and extra-long-germinating seed varieties are given in the large chart later in this chapter.

In time, a planted seed bursts its seed coat around the twenty-eighth day of the lunar month and proceeds into a period of slow, balanced, and increasing growth above and below ground, passes into a period of stimulated leaf growth, then goes into a period of stimulated root growth (getting ready for the next period of stimulated leaf growth), and then goes into a time of rest. This plant growth cycle repeats itself monthly. Plants are transplanted at the full moon, so they may begin their life in the growth bed during a time of stimulated root growth. The stimulation is important to the plant because root shock occurs during transplanting. It is also important for the plant's root system to be well developed so it can later provide the leaves, flowers, and vegetables with water and nutrients. The transplanted plant then enters into a time of rest before beginning another monthly cycle. The workings of nature are beautiful.

(It should be noted that planting by the phases of the moon is a nuance which improves the health and quality of plants. If you do not follow the moon cycles, your plants will still grow satisfactorily. However, as your soil improves and as you gain experience, the nuances will become more important and will have a greater effect. Try it and see.)

Watering

The watering of beds and flats in the biointensive method is performed in a way which approximates rainfall as much as possible. The fine rain absorbs beneficial airborne nutrients, as well as air, which help the growth process. For seeds and seedlings in flats, a special English Haws sprinkling can is used, which has fine holes in the sprinkler's "rose."[18] The "rose" points up so that when you water, the shower first goes up into the air, where much of the pressure built up when the water is forced through the rose is dissipated. The water then falls on the plants from above like rain, with only the force of gravity pulling the water down. When watering planting beds, the same method of spraying the water into the air and letting it fall back down may be used, using a water gun unit with a fan spray nozzle attached.[19] Or the fan may be used without the water gun. (If a water gun is used, a heavy duty hose will be required to contain the water pressure.) This method of spraying water into the air in a relatively fine rain means that the soil in the bed will pack down less and that the plants will not be hit and damaged by a hard water spray. If you choose to point the fan downward, stand as far away from the plants as possible and/or keep the water pressure adjusted to a low point so soil compaction and water damage problems will be minimized.

Daily watering washes the dust, grime, and insects from plant leaves and creates a deliciously moist atmosphere conducive to good plant growth and thriving microbial life.

Some plants, such as those of the cabbage family, like to have wet leaves. It is all right, and in fact beneficial, to water these plants from overhead. Other plants, such as tomatoes, peas, and members of the squash and melon families, can suffer from wilt, mildew, and the rotting of their fruit when their leaves are wet, especially in foggy or humid climates.

18. Available by mail order from Walter F. Nicke, Box 667G, Hudson, NY 12534.

19. A Ross No. 20 from your local hardware store is the best one.

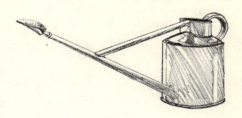

Haws watering can

Close-up of special upward-pointing Haws watering rose

Ross watering fan attached to a variable water pressure gun

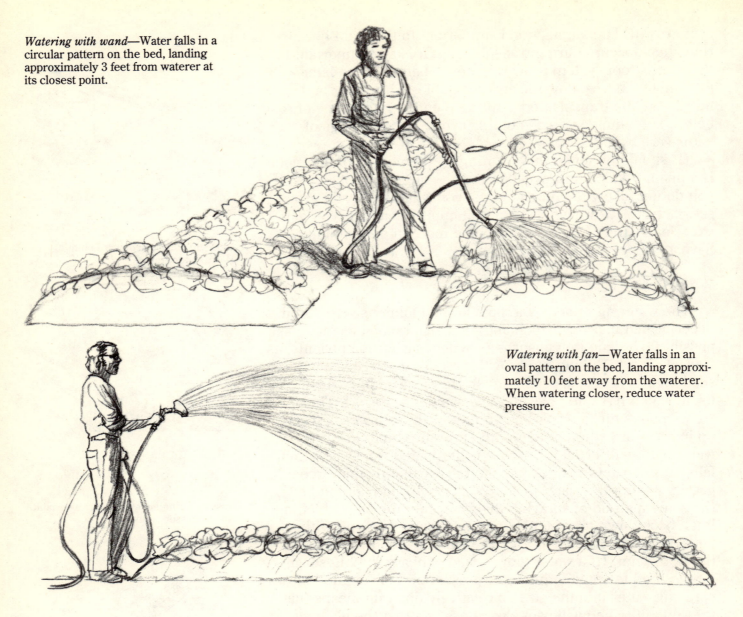

Watering with wand—Water falls in a circular pattern on the bed, landing approximately 3 feet from waterer at its closest point.

Watering with fan—Water falls in an oval pattern on the bed, landing approximately 10 feet away from the waterer. When watering closer, reduce water pressure.

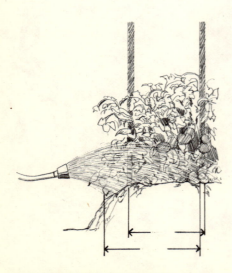

Technique for watering tomato plants using wand

Care should normally be taken, when watering these plants, to water only the soil whenever possible. (In drier climates it will probably not matter.) To avoid spraying the leaves, the fan should be held just above the soil and be pointed sideways. A better method is to use a watering wand which will allow you to more easily place water under the plant's leaves.

The beds are watered lightly each day to keep them evenly moist. (Watering may be more or less frequent when the weather is warmer or cooler than normal.)

Mature plants in beds should be watered when the heat of the day first subsides. This is about 2 hours before sunset during the summer and earlier during the winter. However, weather conditions, especially cloud cover, may necessitate earlier watering. The cool water is warmed by the warm soil and the water temperature is modified by the time it reaches the plant roots. The roots suffer less shock and the soil and plants have more time to absorb water during the cooler, less

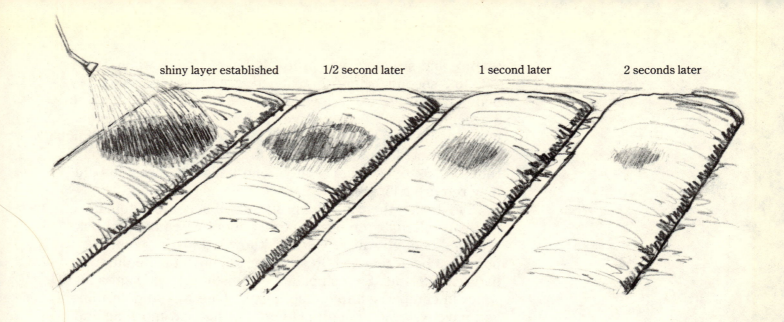

shiny layer established   1/2 second later   1 second later   2 seconds later

A newly prepared bed is properly watered when the *shiny layer* of excess water disappears within 1/2 to 3 seconds after watering stops.

windy night. The availability of moisture is critical, since plants do a significant amount of their growing at night. If you water early in the morning, much of the water will be lost in evaporation caused by the sun and wind and the watering will be less effective. The loss will be even greater if you water at midday. If you water in the evening, the plants will be more susceptible to mildew and rust problems due to unevaporated water left on their leaves. By watering primarily in the late afternoon, you allow the water to percolate into the soil for 12 hours or more before the sun and wind reappear in strength. When they do, the bed will be a good reservoir of water from which the plants can draw.

Seeds and seedlings in flats and seeds and immature plants in the growing beds may have to be watered in the morning and at noon as well as late in the afternoon. Until the living mulch effect occurs, the flats and beds need more watering because they dry out more rapidly. As the leaves grow closer together, less watering will be required.

To determine how much water to give a bed each day, strive for a 1/2- to 15-second "shiny."[20] When you first begin to water, a *shiny layer* of excess water will appear on top of the soil. If you stop watering immediately, the shiny layer will disappear quickly. You should water, then, until the shiny layer remains for 1/2 to 15 seconds after you have stopped watering. The actual time involved will differ depending on the texture of your soil. The more clayey the texture, the longer the time will be. A newly prepared bed with good

20. Another simple way to estimate the amount of water a bed is receiving is to first measure the gallons delivered per minute. Turn the hose on and point the spray into a 1-gallon jar or 4-quart watering can. If, for example, it takes 15 seconds to fill the jar, then you know you are delivering 4 gallons per minute to the bed. Currently, in our moderately heavy clay, we find each 5' × 20' bed will take anywhere from 5 to 20 gallons daily (10 gallons on the average), depending on the weather, the size of the plants, the type of plant, and the tightness of the soil.

texture and structure will probably have enough water when a 1/2- to 3-second "shiny" is reached. A newly prepared clayey bed may indicate enough watering has been done with a 3- to 5-second "shiny," since a clayey soil both retains more moisture *and* lets the water in less rapidly. A month-old bed (which has compacted somewhat due to the watering process) may require a 5- to 8-second "shiny," and beds 2 to 3 months old may require a longer one.

Eventually, the watering process will become automatic and you will not even have to think about when the bed has received enough water. You will know intuitively when the point has been reached. Remember to allow for the different natures of plants. Squash plants, for instance, will want a lot of water in comparison to tomato plants. One way to determine if you have watered enough is to go out the next morning and poke your finger into the bed. If the soil is evenly moist for the first 2 inches and continues to be moist below this level, you are watering properly. If the soil is dry for part or all of the first 2 inches, you need more "shiny." If the soil is soggy in part or all of the upper 2 inches, you need less "shiny."

Remember also to adjust your watering according to the weather. A bed may lose more moisture on a cloudy, windy, *dry* day than on a hot, clear, *humid,* and still one. And there are times when the flats and beds need no water or watering twice a day. It is important to note these differences and to become sensitive to the needs of the plants. You should water for good fruit, flower, and vegetable production, not just so the plant will stay alive. Be sure to water the sides and edges of the planting beds more. These areas, which many people miss or under-emphasize, are critical because they are subject to more evaporation than the middle of the bed. Pay special attention to older beds. The soil tends to compact in older beds, so two light waterings may be required to get the proper penetration. Similarly, newly dug but still unplanted beds should be watered daily so they will not lose their moisture content. A transplant in a bed which has a low moisture level (except in the recently watered upper 2 inches or so) will have difficulty growing well because of the dry pan below. If you wait until plants are wilting and drooping to water, the plants will revive but they will have suffered some permanent damage—an open invitation for pests and diseases. Slight drooping, however, is not usually a sign you should water. Plants are just minimizing the water loss (due to transpiration) when they droop on a hot day and watering them at this time will increase water loss rather than lessen it. It will also weaken the plant through too much pampering.

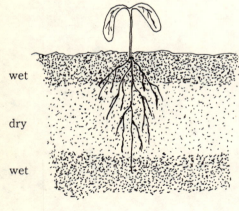

wet

dry

wet

Dry pan

KEY WATERING FACTORS

The biointensive method is especially important for areas with scarce water. We have discovered that much more experimentation is needed in this area. Using the information below should assist you.

☐ Seventy-five percent of the Earth's land surface where food is generally grown receives 10 inches of rainfall or more per year.

☐ About *one-half* this rainfall can be retained in properly prepared soil for plant use.

☐ The biointensive method uses an average of 10 gallons (a 5- to 20-gallon range) per 100 square feet while producing four times the food from that area in comparison with commercial agricultural practices. (Commercial food-raising consumes about 20 gallons per day on the average for the same area.)

☐ Research by academic institutions has shown that soil which has living compost as 2% of its volume in the upper 11 inches of soil can *reduce* the rainfall or *irrigation* required for poor soils *by as much as 75%.* (Poor soils contain about 1/2 of 1% living compost in their upper soil area. "The method" utilizes an even higher amount of compost than the 2% amount.)

☐ Even under arid conditions, soil which is shaded can *reduce evaporation up to 63%* depending on soil type. The *mini-climate* from closely spaced plants provides good shading.

☐ *Transpiration* of water by the plant can be *reduced as much as 75%* in soils which contain good quantities of nutrients in the soil water. The biointensive method prepares the soil in a manner which provides for a high level of fertility.

☐ If you combine the last three factors above together, you find that water consumption can sometimes be reduced to 1/32 the level (1/4 × 1/2 × 1/4) normally experienced. We have found water consumption on the average to be 1/8 that of normal methods per pound of vegetable produced and about 1/3 that of normal methods per pound of grain produced once the soil is in reasonable shape.

☐ Native peoples in some parts of Africa have been using a similar deep bed approach successfully with grains. They triple-dig(!) the soil, incorporating a lot of organic matter into it just before the seasonal rains. Immediately after the rains stop, seeds are planted. No more rain falls, yet crops are harvested at the end of the season. Others in the area

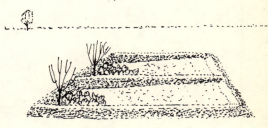

Sloped beds on flat ground—side view

Indian diamond beds

are reportedly unable to grow crops well during this season.

☐ People using biointensive techniques, we feel, should be able to grow at least four times the yield under natural rainfall conditions (when not irrigating) that would be obtained under the same conditions with commercial natural rainfall techniques. Let us know what works for you.

☐ American Indians in the southwestern United States have used a number of approaches to grow food in limited rainfall areas. One is to make the growing area into large square-shaped diamonds on a slight slope with one point each being at the top and the bottom of the slope. Crops are planted in the bottom 1/4 to 1/2 of the square—depending on how much rainfall there is. (More water per unit of soil area has been concentrated in the bottom part of the square.)

☐ To determine how much of the above square to plant, use the following information: Approximately 10 inches of water per unit of area needs to be retained in the soil to grow one complete crop in well-prepared soil (623 gallons per 100 square feet) during a 4-month growing season. To have this amount of water retained in the soil, about 20 inches of rainfall must occur (1,246 gallons per 100 square feet). If only 10 inches fall, you would have only 1/2 the water needed and so would plant only the bottom 1/2 of each diamond. If you had only 5 inches of rain, you would only have 1/4 the water needed for a crop and so would only plant the bottom 1/4 of the square (more or less). Experimentation will be required before you have optimum success. Be careful not to overplant. A soil with all water removed does not rewet or absorb water easily. This will lead to erosion. To be on the safe side, start with a small area and plant 1/4 less crop than the 1/2 and 1/4 crop areas noted above to insure some moisture is retained in the soil. Once you are successful, the area under cultivation can be increased. Please share your experiences with us and others so this approach can be better understood.

☐ Be sure to realize that you are watering *the soil,* not the plant. Keeping the soil *alive* will retain water best and minimize the water consumed!

☐ See John A. Widtsoe, *Dry Farming,* under "Water" in the Bibliography for more dry farming information.

Weeding

Weeding intensively planted raised beds is not required as often as in other gardening methods due to the living mulch provided by the plants. Usually, weeding needs to be performed only once, about a month after the bed is planted. A bed prepared in a new area may have to be weeded more often at first, however, since many dormant seeds will be raised to a place in the soil where they can germinate readily. Over a period of time, as the soil becomes richer and more alive, you will probably have fewer weeds, since they tend to thrive more in poor and deficient soils rather than in healthy ones.

There really is no such thing as a "weed." A weed is just a plant which is growing in an area where you, the gardener, do not want it to grow. In fact, many so-called weeds, such as stinging nettle, are quite beneficial to the soil and other plants. (This will be discussed in more detail in the chapter on Companion Planting.) Instead of weeding indiscriminately, the natures and uses of the different weeds should be learned so you will be able to identify and leave some of the most beneficial ones in the growing beds. The weeds taken out should be placed in the compost pile. They are rich in trace minerals and other nutrients, and will help grow good crops in the next season. And until taken out, the weeds help establish a more quickly nourishing mini-climate for your current crops.

Correct posture for easy weeding

Weeds are generally hardier than cultivated plants since they are genetically closer to the parental plant stock and nearer to the origin of the plant species. They tend to germinate before cultivated plants. Usually you should wait to remove these plants from the beds until the cultured plants catch up with the weeds in height or until the cultured plants become established (about transplanting size)—whichever comes first. Weeding before this time is likely to disturb the germinating cultured plant seeds or to disturb the developing new plant root systems, causing interrupted plant growth and a weakened plant. Be sure to remove any grass plants which develop in the beds even after the first weeding. These plants put out incredibly large root systems which interfere with those of other plants in their competition for nutrients and water.

Planting in Season

Vegetables, flowers, and herbs—all plants for that matter—should be planted in season. This is a good way to love your plants. If they are forced (grown out of season), much of their energy is used up straining to combat unseasonable weather in the form of cold, heat, rain, or drought. Less energy is left for balanced growth, and a plant with limited reserves of energy is more susceptible to disease and insect attack. Plants are not unlike people.

SATISFACTORY (AND OPTIMAL) PLANT GROWING TEMPERATURE RANGES[21]

Determine Planting Range Calendar For Your Own Area

Crop Season	Temp. Range	Optimal Temp. Range	Plant
Cool Season Crops[22]	30° F.		Asparagus • Rhubarb
	45-85° F.	(55-75° F.)	Chicory • Chive • Garlic • Leek • Onion • Salsify • Shallot
	40-75° F.	(60-65° F.)	Beet • Broad Bean • Broccoli • Brussels Sprouts • Cabbage • Chard • Collard • Horseradish • Kale • Kohlrabi • Parsnip • Radish • Rutabaga • Sorrel • Spinach • Turnip
	45-75° F.	(60-65° F.)	Artichoke • Carrot • Cauliflower • Celeriac • Celery • Chicory • Chinese Cabbage • Endive • Florence Fennel • Lettuce • Mustard • Parsley • Pea • Potato
Warm Season Crops	50-80° F.	(60-70° F.)	Bean • Lima Bean
	50-95° F.	(60-75° F.)	Corn • Cowpea • New Zealand Spinach
	50-90° F.	(65-75° F.)	Pumpkin • Squash
	60-90° F.	(65-75° F.)	Cucumber • Muskmelon
Hot Season Crops	65-80° F.	(70-75° F.)	Sweet Pepper • Tomato
	65-95° F.	(70-85° F.)	Eggplant • Hot Pepper • Okra • Sweet Potato • Watermelon

21. From James Edward Knott, *Handbook for Vegetable Growers,* John Wiley & Sons, Inc., New York, 1957, pp. 6-7.

22. Try these crops in shady areas in the summer. Remember, crops need *at least* 4 hours of direct sunlight to grow. Seven hours are preferable, and 11 hours are even better.

SOIL TEMPERATURE CONDITIONS FOR VEGETABLE SEED GERMINATION[23]

CROP	Minimum, °F.	Optimum Range, °F.	Optimum, °F.	Maximum, °F.
Asparagus	50	60-85	75	95
Bean	60	60-85	80	95
Bean, Lima	60	65-85	85	85
Beet	40	50-85	85	95
Cabbage	40	45-95	85	100
Carrot	40	45-85	80	95
Cauliflower	40	45-85	80	100
Celery	40	60-70	70*	85*
Chard, Swiss	40	50-85	85	95
Corn	50	60-95	95	105
Cucumber	60	60-95	95	105
Eggplant	60	75-90	85	95
Lettuce	35	40-80	75	85
Muskmelon	60	75-95	90	100
Okra	60	70-95	95	105
Onion	35	50-95	75	95
Parsley	40	50-85	75	90
Parsnip	35	50-70	65	85
Pea	40	40-75	75	85
Pepper	60	65-95	85	95
Pumpkin	60	70-90	95	100
Radish	40	45-90	85	95
Spinach	35	45-75	70	85
Squash	60	70-95	95	100
Tomato	50	60-85	85	95
Turnip	40	60-105	85	105
Watermelon	60	70-95	95	105

*Daily fluctuation to 60 degrees or lower at night is essential.

23. From James Edward Knott, *Handbook for Vegetable Growers,* John Wiley & Sons, Inc., New York, 1957, p. 8.

Planning Charts

The large planning charts which follow should be helpful. They are in great part based on our experience. They are generally complete and accurate. As testing continues the information will be revised and the chance of error reduced. It should be noted that

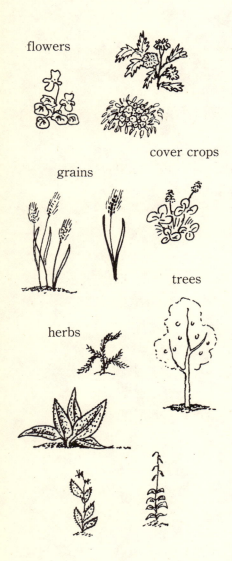

flowers

cover crops

grains

trees

herbs

☐ Maximum yields may not be reached in the first year. Also, one plant, grown alone, will probably not produce as large a yield as one plant grown among several plants under mini-climate conditions.

☐ Seeds grown out of season will take longer to germinate and/or may decompose before they do unless grown under special miniature greenhouse or shade netting house conditions.

☐ Closer spacing may be needed during the winter to make up for the slower plant growth during this period and to create a balanced winter mini-climate. (Try 3/4 or 1/2 the spacing distance with lettuce.) Closer spacing is sometimes also used to promote faster, balanced growth due to a more rapidly reached mini-climate. Extra plants are thinned to make room for larger plants. Baby carrots and beets are a delicacy!

☐ For more cultural detail about each crop, see also the Ten Speed Press edition of *The Vegetable Garden*.

The planning charts on the following tables will let you expand from vegetable crops to the broader and more permanent scope of

☐ Grains, Protein Source, and Vegetable Oil Crops

☐ Cover, Organic Matter, and Fodder Crops

☐ Tree and Cane Food Crops

☐ Energy, Fiber, Paper, and Other Crops

Eventually, we hope to add tree crops for fuel and building materials. If you seek more information than is contained in these detailed charts, you can refer to the books listed in the Bibliography.

One of the exciting things about biointensive growing is its emphasis on the soil. Once you know how to prepare it well for vegetables, a whole world of crops becomes available. The bed preparation, fertilization, and watering approaches remain essentially the same—only the plant spacings are different!

There is a convenient soil improvement succession to know about. Vegetables the first year improve soil for grains the second year, and the vegetables and grains for the even more permanent tree crops the third year. This follows an improvement in your skill as well.

If you want to study the learning process more closely, see Ecology Action's *Backyard Homestead, Mini-Farm and Garden Logbook* crop testing chapter for vegetable, grain, fodder, and tree crops, and our "Soybean Test" booklet.

It is especially important to emphasize that a permanent crop-growing system begins with the soil. Even biological and tree cultivation systems can be environmentally unsound if improperly used. Dr. Hans Jenny, soil scientist emeritus at the University of California, Berkeley, pointed to this in *Science* magazine:

> At the turn of the century, farsighted agricultural experiment stations set up permanent cultivation plots and monitored for decades the nitrogen and carbon balances. Stirring soil and removing crops initiated profound declines in nitrogen, carbon, and humus substances and caused deterioration of soil structure. Under these circumstances water infiltration is reduced and runoff and sheet erosion are encouraged. Crop yields suffer. While applications of nitrogen fertilizers boost yields, they have not restored the soil body. In central Europe, farmers used to remove forest litter and put it on their fields for manuring. Tree production declined markedly, documented by Aaltonen. . . .
>
> I am arguing against indiscriminate conversion of biomass and organic wastes to fuels. The humus capital, which is substantial, deserves being maintained because good soils are a national asset. The question will be raised, How much organic matter should be assigned to the soil? No general formula can be given. Soils vary widely in character and quality.[23a]

The growing of crops must be approached, then, with a sensitivity to how *the way* they are being grown affects the sustainability of the soil's vitality and health. An understanding of this proper relationship will take us all some time to develop and eventually will involve the growing of many different crops, including a large number of trees. Trees beneficially modify our climate, bring up and make available nutrients from deep down in the soil, protect the soil from erosion, help maintain healthy water tables, and provide us with food and building materials.

Some of the charts for grains, cover crops, trees, and other crops are less developed than the ones for vegetables because we have done less work on the crops involved. They do provide a rough picture of what you can begin to accomplish in your own backyard or small farm-holding. (Also see Ecology Action's *Backyard Homestead, Mini-Farm and Garden Log Book*.) More information about additional special seed sources, harvesting, cleaning, grinding, storing, and preserving these crops will be included as time permits.

23a. V. T. Aaltonen, *Boden und Wald,* Parey, Berlin, 1948.

When planning, remember to look closely at *all* the factors involved. For example, sesame seeds are very high in nutrition, but they usually have low yields (compared with other protein crops), are somewhat difficult to harvest, and exhaust the soil. So on a per-square-foot, sustainable nutrition yield basis, sesame seeds are not particularly superior to other protein sources, even though they are great nutritionally and good to eat. A large harvest of sesame seeds would also require a very large growing area. It is important to examine each crop's total *practicality*.

As you begin to plant at an intermediate level, another factor to consider is the quantity of nutrients taken from the soil by each crop. Many "heavy givers" of nitrogen can exhaust the soil of other nutrients over time. Soybeans are "heavy giving" legumes, but continuous cropping of them has been demonstrated to wear out the soil. It is important to develop and work within natural sustainable cycles.

Food value columns have been added to the planning charts for protein, calories, and calcium for each crop. These are key, but many other food values are important—including iron, vitamins, and amino acids. Reference books are listed in the Bibliography so this area can be pursued further. Be sure to explore growing cover crops in between your trees to increase the friability of the soil and its nitrogen and organic matter content. An easy procedure for this is to remove about 1/4 inch of soil from the tree bed after digging it. Shape and fertilize the bed. Then run rake tines lightly over the soil to create small "furrows." Broadcast the seed into the bed and cover the area with the light covering of soil removed earlier. Finish by tamping the bed with the digging board and water gently. Try medium red clover. It can be cut up to three times before it is dug in and has beautiful red flowers.

The spacings and other growing information for grains, fodder crops, fibers, bush and dwarf fruit trees, other tree crops, berries and grapes, and cover crops are under study by Ecology Action. Increasingly more people want to grow them. They are fun to try. One hundred square feet of grain may yield 4, 8, 12, or more pounds of edible seed. If you are in a cooler climate and wish to grow beans for eating, try varieties such as the peanut, yellow-eye, and cranberry beans available from the Vermont Bean Seed Company. Dwarf fruit trees, if nurtured properly, can yield 50 to 100 pounds of fruit annually at maturity. Two trees on 8-foot centers in 100 square feet can yield as high as 200 pounds together, and the average person in the United States eats only about 162 pounds of tree fruit. Fava beans may yield the greatest amount of organic matter for you. Alfalfa and clover are also fun to use.

Our goal with wheat is to eventually get two 26-pound crops in an 8-month period. This would make possible one 1-pound loaf of bread for every week in the year from 100 square feet! Then we could literally raise our own bread in our backyards. Sound impossible? Yields close to this are already occurring in some parts of the world. Wheat can be threshed easily with a mini-thresher[23b] made available by a public organization in your area. Our highest wheat yield to date is at the rate of about 21 pounds per 100-square-foot bed, using about 10 inches of water for the whole season, compost we grew ourselves for fertilizer, and a small amount of purchased organic fertilizers. The Zulus in South Africa use a technique similar to the biointensive method and grow grains with natural rainfall. See what you can do! Let us know if you get to 26 pounds—and how you do it!

23b. One good foot-treadle powered model is available from CeCe Co., P.O. Box 8, Ibaraki City, Osaka, Japan.

Biointensive techniques can be used to grow important protein crops. Research with wheat has been very promising. Tests with soybeans and other seeds, grains, and beans will continue.

VEGETABLES AND GARDEN CROPS

PLANT A	SEED — B Approx. Seeds/Ounces [24]	C Minimum Legal Germination Rate [25]	D Ounces Seed/100 Sq. Ft. (Adj. for Germ. Rate, Offset Spacing, and Curv. Surf.) [26,30]	YIELD — E Possible B/FIM Pounds Yield/100 Sq. Ft. [27,27a]	F Possible B/FIM Pounds Yield/Plant [28]	G Avg. U.S. Pounds Yield/100 Sq. Ft. [29]
1 Artichoke, Jerusalem	Sprouted 2 oz. tuber pieces	—, R	10.5 lbs.	100-206-420+	1.2-5+	D
2 Artichoke, Regular	From divided roots	D	3 roots	D	D	16.5
3 Asparagus	700	.70	.32 or 159 roots	9.5-19-38	.06-.24	5
4 Basil	12,000	.60	.35	26-52-104	.024-.097	D
5 Beans, Broad, Fava	20-70	.70[R]	22.8-6.5 22.8-6.5	5-9-18 Dry 90-180-360 Wet weight above ground biomass	.015-.056 .28-1.1	B
6 Beans, Lima, Bush	20-70	.70[R]	44.3-12.7	11.5-17.2-23 Dry	.018-.037	5.7
7 Beans, Lima, Pole	20-70	.70[R]	22.8-6.5	11.5+-17.2+-23+ Dry	.035+-.071+	5.7+
8 Beans, Snap, Bush	100	.75[R]	7.8	30-72-108	.022-.08	8.2
9 Beans, Snap, Pole[N]	100	.75[R]	8.3	30+-72+-108+	.048+-.171+	8.2+
10 Beets, Cylindra[AA]	1,600	.65[R]	1.35	110-220-540 Roots 55-110-270 Tops	.044-.21 .021-.1	D D
11 Beets, Regular[AA]	1,600	.65[R]	1.35	55-110-270 Roots 55-110-270 Tops	.02-.1 .02-.1	30 D
12 Broccoli	9,000	.75	.01	26-39-53 Heads 52+-78+-106+ Leaves	.3-.63 .6-1.26	17.4 D
13 Brussels Sprouts	8,500	.70	.01	71-106-142	1.3-2.6	23.4
14 Cabbage, Chinese	9,500	.75	.03	96-191-383	.47-1.9	D
15 Cabbage, Regular	8,500	.75	.01	96-191-383	1.1-4.5	45
16 Carrots[BB]	23,000	.55[##]	.2	100-150-1,080	.016-.18	58.9
17 Cauliflower	10,000	.75	.01	44-100-291	.52-3.4	23
18 Celery	70,000	.55	.016	240-480-959+	.38-1.5	110
19 Chard, Swiss	1,200	.65[R]	.76	200-405-810	.62-2.5	D
20 Collards, Annual, Perennial	8,000	.80	.025	96-191-383	.6-2.4	D
21 Corn, Sweet	100-200	.75	1.1-.55 / .7-.35	17-34-68 Shelled, Wet	.2-.8 .3-1.3	15.3
22 Cucumbers	1,000	.80	.2	158-316-581	1.0-3.6	20.6
23 Eggplant	6,000	.60	.015	54-108-163	1.0-3.0	35.6
24 Garlic	12[ZZ]	.5[ZZ]	19.5 lbs.	60-120-240+	.02-.096+	32
25 Horseradish	Live roots used	—	159 roots	D	D	D
26 Kale	10,000	.75	.01	76-114-153	.9-1.8	16.0
27 Kohlrabi	8,000	.75	.22	67-135-270	.05-.2	D
28 Leeks	11,000	.60	.1	240-480-960	.095-.38	D
29 Lettuce, Head	25,000	.80	.007	75-150-300	.47-1.9	48.6
30 Lettuce, Leaf	25,000	.80	.016-.012	135-202-540	.4-1.7	48.6

BEDS/FLATS							MATURITY		RE-MARKS	FOOD NEEDED	SEED YIELD	
H In BED Spacing In Inches	**I** Maximum Number of Plants/100 Sq. Ft.[30]	**J** Short/Long/Extra-Long Germ. Rate	**K** Plant Initially In Flats/Beds	**L** In FLATS Spacing in Inches[31]	**M** Approx. Plants/Flat (Adj. for Germ. Rate)[31,32]	**N** Approx. Time In Flats—In Weeks[31,33]	**O** Approx. Weeks to Maturity	**P** Harvesting Period In Weeks—Up To:	**Q** Remarks and Especially Good Varieties	**R** Pounds Consumed/Year[34] Avg. Person in U.S.	**S** Approx. Max. Pounds Seed Yield/100 Sq. Ft.[40]	Heavy Giver (HG), Light Feeder (LF), Low Nitrogen User (LNU), Heavy Feeder (HF)
15 centers 6 depth	84	L	F	2 / —	60 / —	4 / —	17-26	—	41	D	420+	HF
72	3	L	B	—	—	—	D,P	8		D	D	HF
12	159	L	Seeds in F Roots in B	1 / 2	175 / 60	D	4 Yrs./Seeds 1 Yr./Roots	8	—	1.2	8.7	HF
6	621	L	F	1 / —	150 / —	3-4 / —	6-8	12	—	D	D	HF
8	320	S	B	—	—	—	11-26	8	Fava Beans	D	18.0	HG
6	621	S	F	1 /	175 /	1-2 /	9-11	12	—	} 1.3	17.8	HG
8	320	S	F	1 /	175 /	1-2 /	11-13	12	—		22.3	HG
6	621	S	F	1 /	187 /	1-2 /	8	12	—	} 8.5	17.0	HG
6	621	S	F	1 /	187 /	1-2 /	8-9	12	—		29.7	HG
4	1,343	S	F	1 /	162 /	3-4 /	8-9	—	Twice the Weight	} 1.9	30.6	LF
4	1,343	S	F	1 /	162 /	3-4 /	8-9	—	—		30.6	LF
15	84	S	F	1 / 2	187 / 60	4-6# / 8-10 / 2-3	8-9	4-6	43	1.3	5.5	HF
18	53	S	F	1 / 2	175 / 60	4-6# / 8-10 / 2-3	11-13	12	—	.3	2.8	HF
10	201	S	F	1 / 2	187 / 60	4-6# / 8-10 / 2-3	7-11**	—	—	D	6.1	HF
15	84	S	F	1 / 2	187 / 60	4-6# / 8-10 / 2-3	9-16**	—	—	10.7	3.6	HF
3	2,507	S	B	—	—	—	9-11	—	—	8.4	17.8	LF
15	84	S	F	1 / 2	187 / 60	4-6# / 8-10 / 2-3	8-12**	—	44a	1.3	1.0	HF
6	621	L/EL	F	1 / 2	137 / 60	8-12# / 14-16 / 6-8	15-19	—	—	7.5	9.9	HF
8	320	S	F	1 /	162 /	3-4 /	7-8	44	Burpee Fordhook	D	29.0	HF
12	159	S	F	1 / 2	200 / 60	4-6# / 8-10 / 2-3	12	24	44	D	D	HF
15[z] / 18[z]	84 / 53	S	F	1 /	187 /	2 /	9-13**	—	—	Shelled Wet 14.0	320 / 248	HF
12	159	S	F	2 /	48 /	3-4 /	7-10	26	—	3.1 Reg. 7.6 Pickle	4.1	HF
18	53	L/EL	F	1 / 2	150 / 60	6-8# / 12-14 / 4-6# / 8-12	10-11	13	—	.5	.6	HF
4	1,343	L	F	1 /	122 /	4-6 /	17-26	—	—	.3	240 (Bulbs)	LF
12	159	L	B	—	—	—	26	—	—	D	D	LF
15	84	S	F	1 / 2	187 / 60	4-6# / 8-10 / 2-3	8-9	17	—	D	3.8	HF
4	1,343	S	F	1 / —	187 / —	4-6# / 8-10 / —	7-8	—	—	D	20.1	LF
6	621	S	F	1 /	150 /	8-12 /	19	—	—	D	9.8	LF
12	159	S	F	1 /	200 /	2-3 / 1-2	11-13	—	—	} 22	1.2	HF
8 / 9	320 / 248	S	F	1 / 2	200 / 60	2-3 / 1-2	6-13*	—	—		2.0	HF

VEGETABLES AND GARDEN CROPS (Continued) PLANT A	FOOD NEEDED B _Pounds You Select_	MATERIALS NEEDED C _Approx. Number Plants You Need_[35]	D _Approx. Sq. Ft. You Need_[36]	E _Approx. Flats You Need_[37]	F _Approx. Ounces/Seed You Need_[38]
1 Artichoke, Jerusalem					
2 Artichoke, Regular					
3 Asparagus					
4 Basil					
5 Beans, Broad, Fava					
6 Beans, Lima, Bush					
7 Beans, Lima, Pole					
8 Beans, Snap, Bush					
9 Beans, Snap, Pole[N]					
10 Beets, Cylindra[AA]					
11 Beets, Regular[AA]					
12 Broccoli					
13 Brussels Sprouts					
14 Cabbage, Chinese					
15 Cabbage, Regular					
16 Carrots[BB]					
17 Cauliflower					
18 Celery					
19 Chard, Swiss					
20 Collards, Annual, Perennial					
21 Corn, Sweet					
22 Cucumbers					
23 Eggplant					
24 Garlic					
25 Horseradish					
26 Kale					
27 Kohlrabi					
28 Leeks					
29 Lettuce, Head					
30 Lettuce, Leaf					

G	H	I	J	K	L	M	N	O
Your Actual Yield/100 Sq. Ft.	Your Yield Compared With U.S. Avg. [39]	Time of Year To Plant (SP, SU, FA, WI)	Special Seed Sources	Special Harvesting/ Preparation/ Storage Information	Protein Content/ Pound In Grams (g) (454g/Pound) [44b]	Calorie Content/Pound [44b]	Calcium Content/ Pound In Milligrams (mg) [44b]	
								△ Harvest sequentially as leaves mature. 6-8 times the oxalic acid free calcium yield per unit of area and the same amount of protein in comparison with milk. Also, Mexico and Africa have a perennial "tree" collard variety.
		SP	44e	See Notes	7.2 Raw.	22 Fresh 235 Stored	44 for a long time.	Used in alchol production for gasahol. Good source of organic matter. Harvest when top is dead. 31% Refuse.
		FA	—	—	5.3 Raw.	16 Fresh 85 Stored	93 for a long time.	
		SP	—	—	6.4 Raw.	66	56 44% Refuse.	
		SU	—	—	D	D	D	
		FA, SP	—	—	13.0 / 113.9	162 / 1,533	42 / 463	:In Pods, 66% Refuse. Excellent organic matter crop. :Dry Beans CAUTION: Beans can be toxic to some people.
		SU	—	See Notes	92.5	1,565 Dry Seeds.	327	Pick when beans are bulging through pods so plants will set more beans.
		SU	—	See Notes				
		SP, SU	—	See Notes	7.6	128	224	
		SP, SU	—	See Notes	Raw. 12% Refuse.			
		SP, SU, FA	—	—	5.1 Raw. Roots. 30% Refuse.	137	51	Excellent tops often mean too much nitrogen fertilizer and poor root growth. Cylindra variety can be a good organic matter crop.
		SP, SU, FA	—	—	5.6 Raw. Greens.	6.1	302^M	
		SP, FA	—	—	12.7 / 13.6	113 / 158	364 / 1,189	:Head, Raw, 22% Refuse. :Leaves, Raw. Contain more nutrition than head type.
		SP, FA	—	—	20.4 Raw.	188	150 8% Refuse.	When sprout node begins to bulge, remove leaf below it for best growth.
		SP, FA	—	—	5.3 Raw.	62	189 3% Refuse.	
		SP, FA	—	—	5.3 / 8.2	98 / 127	200 / 171	:Green, Raw 10% Refuse :Red Raw
		SP, SU, FA	—	—	4.1 Raw.	156 Without tops.	134 18% Refuse.	Excellent tops often mean too much nitrogen fertilizer and poor root growth.
		SP, FA	—	—	12.2 Raw.	122	113	Cauliflower head often develops in just a few days.
		SP, FA	—	—	5.3	62	189 25% Refuse.	
		SP, SU, FA	—	See Notes	10.0 Raw.	104	367^M 8% Refuse.	Harvest sequentially as leaves mature. Good organic matter crop.
		SP, FA	—	See Notes	16.3 Raw leaves	181 and stems.	921	See above. △
		SU	—	See Notes	8.7 Raw.	240	7 45% Refuse. (cob)	Harvest when fluid in kernel is half way between clear and milky.
		SU	—	See Notes	3.9 Raw,	65 whole	108 5% Refuse.	Harvest when swollen, but not yellowing for sweetest taste.
		SU	—	—	4.4 Raw.	92	44 19% Refuse.	
		SP, FA	—	—	24.8 / 8.2	547	116 12% Refuse.	Most of bulb growth occurs in last 45 days. Contains antibiotics.
		SP, FA	—	—	10.6 Raw.	288	464 27% Refuse.	
		SP, FA	—	—	14.1 Raw leaves	128 and stems	601 26% Refuse.	Good vitamin and mineral content.
		SP, FA	—	—	6.6 Raw.	96	136 27% Refuse.	
		SP, FA	—	—	5.2 Raw.	123	123 48% Refuse.	
		SP, FA	—	—	3.9 Raw.	56	86 5% Refuse.	Not very nutritious. Harvest in very early morning for best taste.
		SP, FA	—	—	3.8 Raw.	52	197 36% Refuse.	Harvest in very early morning for best taste.

PLANT A	SEED B — Approx. Seeds/Ounces[24]	C — Minimum Legal Germination Rate[25]	D — Ounces Seed/100 Sq. Ft. (Adj. for Germ. Rate, Offset Spacing, and Curv. Surf.)[26,30]	YIELD E — Possible B/FIM Pounds Yield/100 Sq. Ft.[27,27a]	F — Possible B/FIM Pounds Yield/Plant[28]	G — Avg. U.S. Pounds Yield/100 Sq. Ft.[29]
31 Mangels	1,600	.65[R]	.6	200-400-960 Roots 100-200-480 Tops	.46-2.2	D
32 Melons	1,200	.75	.09	50-72-145	.6-1.7	20[C] / 36.5[H]
33 Mustard	15,000	.75	.055	180-225-270	.29-.43	D
34 Okra	500	.50	.64	30-60-120	.19-.75	D
35 Onion, Bunching	9,500	.70[R]	.39	100-200-540	.004-.023	D
36 Onions, Regular	9,500	.70	.21	100-200-540	.04-.2	} 68.6
37 Onions, Torpedo	9,500	.70	.38	200-400-1,080	.08-.43	
38 Parsley	18,000	.60	.07	26-52-136	.02-.08	D
39 Parsnips	12,000	.60[##]	1.9	119-238-479	.047-.19	D
40 Peas, Bush	50-230	.80[R]	3.9 lbs. - 13.7 oz.	25-53-106	.01-.04	} 6.8
41 Peas, Pole[N]	50-230	.80[R]	2.1 lbs. - 7.3 oz.	25+-53+-106+	.02-.08+	
42 Peppers, Cayenne	4,500	.55	.064	10-25-40	.06-.25	D
43 Peppers, Green	4,500	.55	.064	36-83-197	.2-.8	18.8
44 Potatoes, Irish	—[47]	—	23.25 lbs. - 31 lbs.	100-200-780	.4-3.1	52.6
45 Potatoes, Sweet	—[49]	—	12 lbs.	82-164-492	.33-2.0	23.6
46 Pumpkin	110	.75	.44-.16	48-96-191	3.4-13.6	D
47 Radishes	2,000	.75[R]	3.9	100-200-540	.017-.09	D
48 Rhubarb	1,700[Y]	.60[Y]	.025	70-140-280	D	D
49 Rutabagas	12,000	.75	.07	200-400-960	.3-1.5	D
50 Salsify	1,800	.75[R]	4.4	200-400-1,080	.03-.18	D
51 Shallots	8[Y]	.75[Y]	14.8	60-120-240+	.02-.01+	D
52 Spinach, New Zealand, Malabar	350	.40	1.14	180-225-270	1.1-1.7	D
53 Spinach, Regular	2,800	.60	.35	50-100-225	.037-.17	12.1
54 Squash, Crook Neck	300 (Bush)	.75	.37	35-75-150	.4-1.8	D
55 Squash, Patty Pan	300 (Bush)	.75	.37	75-150-307	.9-3.6	D
56 Squash, Winter	100 (Vine)	.75	.53	50-100-350	5.6-13.6	D
57 Squash, Zucchini	300 (Bush)	.75	.24	160-319-478+	3.0-9.0	D
58 Sunflowers[X]	650 (In Shell)[Y]	.50+[Y]	.24-1.68	2.5-5-10 Seeds 20-40-80 Stalks, Dry Weight	.09-.37	2.4
59 Tomatoes	11,000	.75	.006/.004/.003	100-194-418	1.9-16.0	30.7
60 Turnips	13,000	.80[R]	.13	100-200-360	.04-.14	D
61 Watermelon	225-300	.70	1.0-.76/.34-.25/ .22-.17/.17-.12	50-100-320	.31-12.3	24.3

H — In BED Spacing In Inches	I — Maximum Number of Plants/100 Sq. Ft.[30]	J — Short/Long/Extra-Long Germ. Rate	K — Plant Initially In Flats/Beds	L — In FLATS Spacing in Inches[31]	M — Approx. Plants/Flat (Adj. for Germ. Rate)[31,32]	N — Approx. Time In Flats–In Weeks[31,33]	O — Approx. Weeks to Maturity	P — Harvesting Period In Weeks—Up To:	Q — Remarks and Especially Good Varieties	R — Pounds Consumed/Year[34] Avg. Person in U.S.	S — Approx. Max. Pounds Seed Yield/100 Sq. Ft.[40]	Heavy Giver (HG), Light Feeder (LF), Low Nitrogen User (LNU), Heavy Feeder (HF)
7	432	S	F	1 / —	162 / —	3-4+ / —	8-12+	—	Peace Seeds Yellow Intermediate	D	D	LF
15	84	S	F	2 / —	45 / —	3-4 / —	12-17**	13	—[45]	7.8^C	2.9	HF
6	621	S	F	1 / —	187 / —	3-4 / —	5-6	8	—	D	5.7	HF
12	159	L	F	1 / 2	125 / 60	6-8 / 3-4	7-8	13	—	D	9.3	HF
3	2,507	S	F	1 / —	175 / —	6-8 / —	17	—	—	D	39.6	LF
4	1,343	S	F	1 / —	175 / —	10-12* / 12-14	14-17	—	—	} 17.9	10.3	LF
4	1,343	S	F	1 / —	175 / —	10-12# / 12-14	14-17	—	—[46]	} 17.9	10.3	LF
5	833	L/EL	F	1 / 2	150 / 60	8-12 / 6-8	10-13	40	—	D	24.8	HF
4	1,343	L	F	1 / —	200 / —	1-2 / —	15	—	—	D	24.8	LF
3	2,507	S	F	1 / —	200 / —	1-2 / —	8-10	12	—	} 5.9	21.6	HG
4	1,343	S	F	1 / —	137 / 60	6-8 / 3-4	10-11	12	—	} 5.9	12.1	HG
12	159	L/EL	F	1 / 2	137 / 60	6-8# / 12-14 / 4-6	9-11	17	—	D	.1	HF
12	159	L/EL	F	1 / 2	137 / 60	6-8# / 12-14 / 4-6	9-12	17	—	2.5	.3	HF/LNU
9 centers 9 depth	248	L	Sprout in dark place	—	—	—	17	—	—[48]	133.4	200-780	LF
9 centers 6 depth	248	L	F	Q / —	30 / —	4-6 / 4	26-34	—	—	6.2	492	LF/LNU
18/30	53/14	S	F	2 / —	45 / —	3-4 / —	14-16	—	—[50]	.6	5.1	HF
2	5,894	S	B	—	—	—	3-9**	—	—[51]	D	20.6	LF
24	26	L	F	1 / 2	150 / 60	D / D	3 years Roots 1 Yr.	D	—[52]	.03	D	HF
6	621	S	F	1 / —	187 / —	3-4 / —	13	—	—	D	5.4	LF
2	5,894	S	B	—	—	—	17	—	—	D	27.7	LF
4	1,343	L	F	1 / —	122 / —	4-6 / —	17-26	—	—	D	240	HF
12	159	L	F	2 / —	24 / —	3-4 / —	10	42	Drought Resistant	D	17.2	HF
6	621	S	F	1 / —	150 / —	3-4 / —	6-7	—	—	1.8	10.8	HF
15	84	S	F	2 / —	45 / —	3-4 / —	10	17+	—	D	6.1	HF
15	84	S	F	2 / —	45 / —	3-4 / —	7	17+	—	D	6.1	HF
18	53	S	F	2 / —	45 / —	3-4 / —	11-17**	17+	—	D	5.7	HF
18	53	S	F	2 / —	45 / —	3-4 / —	7-9	26	Burpee's Fordhook	D	6.1	HF
24/9	26/298	S	F	1 / —	100+ / —	2-3 / —	12	—	—	D	D	HF
18/21/24T	53/35/26	S	F	1 / 2	187 / 60	6-8# / 12-14 / 3-4	8-13	17+	—	31.1	5.5	HF
4	1,343	S	F	1 / —	200 / —	2-3 / —	5-10**	—	—	D	14.7	LF/LNU
12/18/21/24 W	159/53/35/26	S	F	2 / —	42 / —	3-4 / —	10-13	13	—[53]	13.9	2.6	HF

—Footnotes on Page 98—

VEGETABLES AND GARDEN CROPS (Continued) PLANT A	FOOD NEEDED B	MATERIALS NEEDED C	D	E	F
	Plant	Pounds You Select	Approx. Number Plants You Need[35]	Approx. Sq. Ft. You Need[36]	Approx. Flats You Need[37]	Approx. Ounces/Seed You Need[38]
31 Mangels						
32 Melons						
33 Mustard						
34 Okra						
35 Onion, Bunching						
36 Onions, Regular						
37 Onions, Torpedo						
38 Parsley						
39 Parsnips						
40 Peas, Bush						
41 Peas, Pole[N]						
42 Peppers, Cayenne						
43 Peppers, Green						
44 Potatoes, Irish						
45 Potatoes, Sweet						
46 Pumpkin						
47 Radishes						
48 Rhubarb						
49 Rutabagas						
50 Salsify						
51 Shallots						
52 Spinach, New Zealand, Malabar						
53 Spinach, Regular						
54 Squash, Crook Neck						
55 Squash, Patty Pan						
56 Squash, Winter						
57 Squash, Zucchini						
58 Sunflowers[X]						
59 Tomatoes						
60 Turnips						
61 Watermelon						

G	H	I	J	K	L	M	N	O
Your Actual Yield/100 Sq. Ft.	Your Yield Compared With U.S. Avg.[39]	Time of Year To Plant (SP, SU, FA, WI)	Special Seed Sources	Special Harvesting/Preparation/Storage Information	Protein Content/Pound In Grams (g) (454g/Pound)[44b]	Calorie Content/Pound[44b]	Calcium Content/Pound In Milligrams (mg)[44b]	△ Approximately 12% of the calories, 8% of the protein and 18% of the calcium eaten worldwide is in the form of potatoes grown on 2.4% of the crop land.
		SP, SU, FA	—	—	D	D	D	
		SU	—	—	1.6 / 2.3	68 / 94	32 / 32	:Cantaloup (50% Refuse). / :Honeydew (37% Refuse).
		SP, FA	—	—	9.5 Raw.	98	73 30% Refuse.	
		SU	—	—	9.4 Raw.	140	359 14% Refuse.	
		SP, SU, FA	—	—	6.5 Raw.	157	222 4% Refuse.	
		SP	—	—	6.2 Dry, Raw.	157	111 9% Refuse.	
		SP	—	—	6.2 Dry, Raw.	157	111 9% Refuse.	
		SP	—	—	16.3 Raw.	200	921	
		SP, FA	—	—	6.6 Raw.	293	193 15% Refuse.	
		SP, FA	—	See Notes	10.9 Green.	145	45 (Pods). 62% Refuse	Harvest when seeds are bulging in pods.
		SP, FA	—	—	109.4 Dry.	1,542	290	Try Sugar Snap edible variety.
		SU	—	—	16.1 Raw.	405	126 4% Refuse.	
		SU	—	—	4.5 / 5.1	82 / 112	33 / 47	:Green. 18% Refuse. / :Red. 20% Refuse.
		SP, FA	44c	Harvest when tops dead.	7.7 Raw.	279	26 19% Refuse.	Green parts poisonous. }See above △
		SU	44d		6.6 / 6.2	375 / 430	118 / 118 19% Refuse.	:Jersey (firm). :Puerto Rican (soft).
		SU	—	—	131.5 Raw	2,508 seeds.	231 Hulled.	Hulls 30% of unhuled weight. 3.2 Raw Fruit. 83 30% 67 Refuse.
		SP, FA	—	—	4.1 Raw	69 without	122 tops.	10% Refuse.
		SP	—	—	2.3 Raw	62 without	374 leaves.	14% Refuse Green parts poisonous.
		SP, FA	—	—	4.2 Raw.	177	254 15% Refuse.	Very flavorful when biointensively grown.
		SP, FA	—	—	11.4	51 Fresh	185	Caloric content rises to 324 after being stored for some time.
		SP, FA	44e	—	10.0 Raw.	287	148 12% Refuse.	
		SP, SU, FA	—	—	10.0 Raw.	86	263	
		SP, FA	—	—	10.5 Raw.	85	304[M] 28% Refuse.	
		SU	—	—	5.3 Raw.	89	124 2% Refuse.	
		SU	—	See Notes	4.0 Raw.	93	124 2% Refuse.	Harvest when bone white with only a little tinge of green left.
		SU	—	See Notes	5.2 / 4.4 / 4.2	152 / 171 / 117	107 / 102 / 57	:Acorn: :Butternut: :Hubbard: Harvest when neck stem is dry. Raw. 24, 30 and 34% refuse respectively.
		SU	—	See Notes	5.2 Raw.	73	121 5% Refuse.	Harvest when 10 inches long. One pound contains a lot of protein and calcium.
		SU	—	—	108.9 Dry seeds	2,540 without	544 hulls.	Hulls 46% of unhulled weight.
		SU	—	—	5.0	100	59	
		SP, FA	—	—	3.9 Raw.	117	152	
		SU	—	—	1.0 Raw.	54	15 54% Refuse.	

GRAIN, PROTEIN SOURCE, VEGETABLE OIL CROPS

For protein also see: Beans, Lima—Beans, Broad, Fava—Buckwheat—Collards—Corn, Sweet—Garlic—Peas—Potatoes, Irish and Sweet—Squash, Zucchini—Sunflowers.

PLANT	SEED			YIELD		
A — Plant	B — Approx. Seeds/Ounces [24]	C — Minimum Legal Germination Rate [25]	D — Ounces Seed/100 Sq. Ft. (Adj. for Germ. Rate, Offset Spacing, and Curv. Surf.) [26,30]	E — Possible B/FIM Pounds Yield/100 Sq. Ft. [27,27a]	F — Possible B/FIM Pounds Yield/Plant [28]	G — Avg. U.S. Pounds Yield/100 Sq. Ft. [29]
1 Amaranth	53,400 Grain-type	.70[A]	.0014	Greens: 68-136-272+ Seed: 4-8-16+	1.3-5.1+ .075-.3+	D D
2 Barley, Beardless	900	.70[A]	3.5-4.4	Seed: 5-10-24[K,U]	D	4.9
3 Beans, Kidney	50	.70[A]	17.7	Seed: 4-10-24	.003-.012	2.7
4 Beans, Lentil	600	.70[A]	6.0	Seed: 4-6-8+	.003-.019+	1.4
5 Beans, Mung	500	.70[A]	3.8	Seed: 4-10-24	.006-.038	2.7
6 Beans, Pinto	70	.70[A]	12.7	Seed: 4-10-24	.006-.038	2.7
7 Beans, Red	50-100	.70[A]	17.7-8.3	Seed: 4-10-24	.006-.038	2.7
8 Beans, White	90-180	.70[A]	4.9-2.5	Seed: 4-10-24	.006-.038	2.7
9 Chickpea (Garbanzo)	50	.70[A]	38.4	Seed: 4-10-24	.003-.012	D
10 Corn, Fodder	100-200	.70[A]	.7-.35	Seed: 11-17-32+	.2-.4+	11.3
11 Cowpea	150	.70[A]	.5/1/2+	Seed: 4-10-24	.025-.3.0	D
12 Grains, Perennial	The major work in this field is being performed by Wes Jackson at: The Land Institute,					
13 Millet, Proso	2,200 Unhulled	.70[A]	.28	Seed: 3-6-12+[K]	.009-.07+	3.4
14 Oats	950	.70[A]	2.3-3.5	Seed: 3-7-13+[K,U]	D	3.3
15 Peanuts	20-70 Unshelled 30-90 Shelled	.70[A]	11.8-3.9 Shelled	Seed: 4-10-24	.016-.096	5.6
16 Pigeon Pea	D	.70[A]	D	Seed: 4-10-24	.003-.018	D
17 Quinoa	D	.70[A]	.0014	Seed: 4-8-16+	.025-.1	D
18 Rape	8,000	.70[A]	D	Seed: D	D	D
19 Rice	1,100 Unhulled	.70[A]	1.7	Seed: 4-10-24	.003-.018	10.7
20 Rye, Cereal	1,300-1,700	.70[A]	.9-.7	Seed: 4-10-24[K,U]	.005-.029	2.6
21 Safflower	640 Unhulled	.70[A]	1.2	Seed: 4-9-17+	.08-.33+	4.3
22 Sesame	11,000	.70[A]	.08	Seed: 1.5-3-6+	.007-.028+	D
23 Soybeans	100-180+	.70[A]	8.3-4.6	Seed: 4-8-14.4+	.006-.023+	3.6
24 Wheat, Durum	500 Hulled	.70[A]	2.4	Seed: 4-10-26[K,U]	.005-.03	4.0
25 Wheat, Early Stone Age	800 Unhulled	.70[A]	1.5	Seed: 4-10-17+[K,U]	.005-.02+	D
26 Wheat, Hard Red Spring	500 Hulled	.70[A]	2.4	Seed: 4-10-26[K,U]	.005-.03	3.7
27 Wheat, Red Winter	500 Hulled	.70[A]	2.4	Seed: 4-10-26[K,U]	.005-.03	4.3
28 Wheat, White	500 Hulled	.70[A]	2.4	Seed: 4-10-26[K,U]	.005-.03	3.7

BEDS/FLATS							MATURITY		RE-MARKS	FOOD NEEDED	SEED YIELD	
H	**I**	**J**	**K**	**L**	**M**	**N**	**O**	**P**	**Q**	**R**	**S**	
In BED Spacing In Inches	Maximum Number of Plants/100 Sq. Ft.[30]	Short/Long/ Extra-Long Germ. Rate[30]	Plant Initially In Flats/Beds	In FLATS Spacing in Inches[31]	Approx. Plants/Flat (Adj. for Germ. Rate)[31,32]	Approx. Time In Flats-In Weeks[31,33]	Approx. Weeks to Maturity	Harvesting Period In Weeks—Up To:	Remarks and Especially Good Varieties	Pounds Consumed/Year[34] Avg. Person in U.S.	Approx. Max. Pounds Seed Yield/100 Sq. Ft.[40]	Heavy Giver (HG), Light Feeder (LF), Low Nitrogen User (LNU), Heavy Feeder (HF)
6 Greens 18 Grains	53	S	F	1 / 2	175 / 42	.3 / 2	8 (Greens) 17 (Seed)	4	—	D	16.0	HF
5	D	S	F	1 / —	175 / —	2 / —	9-10	—	—	1.2	24.0	HF
6	621	S	F	1 / —	175 / —	1-2 / —	12	8	—	} 6.3 All Dry Edible Beans	24.0	HG
4	1,343	S	F	1 / —	175 / —	1-2 / —	12	8	—		8.0+	HF
4	1,343	S	F	1 / —	175 / —	1-2 / —	12	8	—		24.0	HG
6	621	S	F	1 / —	175 / —	1-2 / —	12	8	—		24.0	HG
6	621	S	F	1 / —	175 / —	1-2 / —	12	8	—		24.0	HG
6	621	S	F	1 / —	175 / —	1-2 / —	12	8	—		24.0	HG
4	1,343	S	F	1 / —	175 / —	1-2 / —	9	8	—	D	24.0	HG
18	53	S	F	1 / —	187 / —	1-2 / —	11-16	—	—	51.4 for Foodstuffs	22.6+	HF
12/24/ 36E	159/26 18	S	F	1 / —	175 / —	2 / —	9-12	8	—	D	24.0	HG
Route 3, Salina, Kansas 67401. Send stamped, self-addressed envelope for publications information.												
7	432	S	F	1 / —	175 / —	2-4 / —	10-13	—	—	D	30.0	HF
D	D	S	F	1 / —	175 / —	1-2 / —	13-17	—	—	3.2 for Food Products	13.4+	HF
9	248	S	F	2 / —	42 / —	2-4 / —	17	—	—	6.4	24.0	HG
8 ft.	2	S	F	1 / —	175 / —	2-3 / —	8-10	8	—	D	24.0	HG
12	159	S	F	1 / —	175 / —	3 / —	16	—	—	D	16.0	HF
D	D	S	B	—	—	—	D	D	—	D	D	HF
4	1,343	S	F	1 / —	175 / —	2 / —	17	—	Calrose	7.7	24.0	HF
5	833	S	F	1 / —	175 / —	2 / —	17	—	—	.8	24.0	HF
18	53	S	F	1 / —	175 / —	2-3 / —	17	—	—	D	17.4+	HF
6	621	L	F	1 / —	175 / —	3 / —	13-17	8	—	D	5.6+	HF
6	621	S	F	1 / —	187 / —	2 / —	8-9 Green 16-17 Dry	2-4	Altona	225.0	14.4+	HG
5	833	S	F	1 / —	175 / —	1-2 / —	16-18	—	—	111.9 All Wheat	26.0	HF
5	833	L	F	1 / —	175 / —	2-3 / —	16-20	—	—	D	17.0+	HF
5	833	S	F	1 / —	175 / —	1-2 / —	16-18	—	—	} 111.9 All Wheat	26.0	HF
5	833	S	F	1 / —	175 / —	1-2 / —	16-18	—	—		26.0	HF
5	833	S	F	1 / —	175 / —	1-2 / —	16-18	—	—		26.0	HF

GRAIN, PROTEIN SOURCE, VEGETABLE OIL CROPS (Continued) PLANT A	FOOD NEEDED B Pounds You Select	MATERIALS NEEDED C Approx. Number Plants You Need[35]	D Approx. Sq. Ft. You Need[36]	E Approx. Flats You Need[37]	F Approx. Ounces/Seed You Need[38]
1 Amaranth					
2 Barley, Beardless					
3 Beans, Kidney					
4 Beans, Lentil					
5 Beans, Mung					
6 Beans, Pinto					
7 Beans, Red					
8 Beans, White					
9 Chickpea (Garbanzo)					
10 Corn, Fodder					
11 Cowpea					
12 Grains, Perennial					
13 Millet, Proso					
14 Oats					
15 Peanuts					
16 Pigeon Pea					
17 Quinoa					
18 Rape					
19 Rice					
20 Rye, Cereal					
21 Safflower					
22 Sesame					
23 Soybeans					
24 Wheat, Durum					
25 Wheat, Early Stone Age					
26 Wheat, Hard Red Spring					
27 Wheat, Red Winter					
28 Wheat, White					

G	H	I	J	K	L	M	N	O
Your Actual Yield/100 Sq. Ft.	Your Yield Compared With U.S. Avg. [39]	Time of Year To Plant (SP, SU, FA, WI)	Special Seed Sources	Special Harvesting/ Preparation/ Storage Information	Protein Content/ Pound In Grams (g) (454g/Pound) [44b]	Calorie Content/Pound [44b]	Calcium Content/ Pound In Milligrams (mg) [44b]	
		SU	44e	—	15.9 / 69.5	200 / 1,775	1,212 / 2,224	:Greens: Good calcium source. For latest information contact: Rodale :Seed. Amaranth Project, 33 East Minor St., Emmaus, PA 18049
		SP, FA	44g	—	37.2 / 43.5	1,583 / 1,579	73 / 154	:Light. :Pearled or Scotch. } Hulling Difficult
		SU	44e	See Notes	102.1 Dry.	1,556	449	
		SP	44i	See Notes	112.0 Dry.	1,542	538	
		SU	44e	See Notes	109.8 Dry.	1,542	535	
		SU	44e	See Notes	103.9 Dry.	1,583	612	Harvest sequentially when seeds bulge through pods.
		SU	—	See Notes	103.9 Dry.	1,583	612	
		SU	44h	See Notes	101.2 Dry.	1,542	653	
		SU	44g	See Notes	93.0 Dry.	1,633	680	
		SU	44f	—	40.4 Dry.	1,579	100	Also produces a lot of organic matter.
		SU	44f,44h	See Notes	103.4 Dry.	1,556	336	Harvest sequentially when seeds bulge through pods.
		—	—	—	—	—	—	
		SU	44f	—	44.9 Dry.	1,483	91	High in iron.
		SP, FA	44e	—	64.4 Dry.	1,769	240	Hulling difficult.
		SU	44i	—	117.9 Shelled.	2,558 Raw.	313	Shells 27% of unshelled weight. Can be carcinogenic if not stored properly.
		SP	44h	See Notes	92.5 Dry.	1,551	485	Hulls 61% of unhulled weight.
		SU	44q	—	73.5	1,600	640	
		SU	44f	—	D Dry.	D	D	Helps eradicate weeds.
		SU	—	—	34.0 / 30.4	1,633 / 1,647	145 / 109	:Brown. :White.
		SP, FA	44e	—	54.9 Dry.	1,515 Whole.	172 Grain.	15% in wheat bread buffers phytates which otherwise tie-up iron.
		SU	44o	See Notes	86.6 Hulled.	2,790 Dry.	—	Source of organic matter and vegetable oil. Harvest when 98-100% of heads dry. Hulls 49% unhulled weight.
		SU	—	—	84.4 Dry.	2,554	5,262	Exhausts soil. Very high in calcium.
		SU	44e	—	49.9 / 154.7	608 / 1,828	304 / 1,025	:Green. :Hulled, dry.
		SP,(FA)	—	—	57.6 Dry.	1,506	168	
		SP, SU	44i	—	83.0 Dry.	D	D	*Triticum monococcum var. Hornemanii.* Variety up to 12,000 years old.
		SP,(FA)	44e	—	63.5 Dry.	1,497	163	
		FA	44e	—	55.8 / 46.3	1,497 / 1,497	209 / 191	:Hard Variety. :Soft Variety.
		SP	—	—	42.6 Dry.	1,520	163	

COVER, ORGANIC MATTER, FODDER CROPS

For Organic Matter also see: Artichoke, Jerusalem—Beans, Broad, Fava—Beets, Cylindra—Beets, Tops.

PLANT A	SEED B — Approx. Seeds/Ounces [24]	C — Minimum Legal Germination Rate [25]	D — Ounces Seed/100 Sq. Ft. (Adj. for Germ. Rate, Offset Spacing, and Curv. Surf.) [26,30]	YIELD E — Possible B/FIM Pounds Yield/100 Sq. Ft. [27,27a]	F — Possible B/FIM Pounds Yield/Plant [28]	G — Avg. U.S. Pounds Yield/100 Sq. Ft. [29]
1 Alfalfa	14,000	.70[A]	.085	43-80-120 Air Dry Weight/3 Cuttings	D	13.6
2 Beans, Bell, Cold Weather Favas	40	.70[A]	11.4	90-180-360 Wet Weight: Above Ground Biomass	.28-1.1	D
3 Buckwheat	1,000	.70[A]	2.6	4-8-16+ Grain	D	D
4 Clover, Alsike	44,875	.70[A]	.3-.55+	12-25-38 Air Dry Weight	D	4.1
5 Clover, Crimson	7,000	.70[A]	.6+	12-25-38 Air Dry Weight	D	4.1
6 Clover, Sweet, Hubam	11,400	.70[A]	1.1+	12-25-38 Air Dry Weight	D	4.1
7 Clover, Medium Red	14,500	.70[A]	.36 For Hay / .72 For Green Manure	25-50-75 Air Dry Weight	D	8.3
8 Clover, Sweet, White	45,750	.70[A]	1.1+	12-25-38 Air Dry Weight	D	4.1
9 Clover, Timothy	82,500	.96[A]	2.2-3.7	12-25-38 Air Dry Weight	D	4.1
10 Comfrey, Russian	—	—	53 Roots	92-220-339 Wet Weight 10-24-37 Dry Weight 3 Cuttings	1.7-6.4	62.6 World High (12 mo. season) Dry Wt.
11 Grass, Rye, Italian	16,875	.70[A]	4.4-6.6	D	D	D
12 Holy Hay (*Sainfoin*)	1,560 In Pods 2,040 Cleaned	.70[A]	1.1 Hulled	25-50-75 Air Dry Weight/Multiple Cuttings	D	D
13 Kudzu	2,000	.70[A]	Propagated by seeds, cuttings, and roots. More research needs to			
14 Millet, Pearl	2,200 Unhulled	.70[A]	.3	230-560-1,120 Wet Weight: Above Ground Biomass	.65-2.6	280
15 Roots, General	An important hidden cover crop beneath the ground. This information needs to					
16 Sorghum	1,000	.65[A]	.68	6.2-12.4-25 Seed 42-84-168 Wet Weight: Above Ground Biomass	.004-.018 .03-.12	6.2 42.6
17 Sow Thistle (*Sonchus oleraceus*)	D	.70[A]	D	D	D	D
18 Straw and Chaff, Barley	See Protein Source Crops for General Information			12-30-72 Dry	D	7.3 Approx.
19 Straw and Chaff, Oats				12-30-72 Dry	D	5.0 Approx.
20 Straw and Chaff, Rice				12-30-72 Dry	.014-.086	16.0 Approx.
21 Straw and Chaff, Rye				12-30-72 Dry	.014-.086	3.9 Approx.
22 Straw and Chaff, Wheat, Early Stone Age				12-30-51 Dry	.014-.06	D
23 Straw and Chaff, Wheat, General				12-30-72 Dry	.014-.086	6.0 Approx.
24 Teosinte	440	.70[A]	.08	17-30-60 Wet Weight 2-4-6 Grain	2.4-8.0	83.0 Approx.
25 Trefoil, Narrow Leaf	35,000	.70[A]	D	D	D	D
26 Vetch, Hairy[BB]	800	.70[A]	5.5	D	D	D
27 Weeds, Amaranth, Green	D	.70[A]	D	D	D	D
28 Weeds, Dandelion, Greens	42,000	.70[A]	D	D	D	D
29 Weeds, Lamb's Quarters	52,000	.70[A]	D	D	D	D
30 Weeds, Purslane	104,000	.70[A]	D	D	D	D

BEDS/FLATS							MATURITY		RE-MARKS	FOOD NEEDED	SEED YIELD	
H In BED Spacing In Inches	**I** Maximum Number of Plants/100 Sq. Ft.[30]	**J** Short/Long/Extra-Long Germ. Rate	**K** Plant Initially In Flats/Beds	**L** In FLATS Spacing in Inches[31]	**M** Approx. Plants/Flat (Adj. for Germ. Rate)[31,32]	**N** Approx. Time In Flats-In Weeks[31,33]	**O** Approx. Weeks to Maturity	**P** Harvesting Period In Weeks—Up To:	**Q** Remarks and Especially Good Varieties	**R** Pounds Consumed/Year[34] Avg. Person in U.S.	**S** Approx. Max. Pounds Seed Yield/100 Sq. Ft.[40]	Heavy Giver (HG), Light Feeder (LF), Low Nitrogen User (LNU), Heavy Feeder (HF)
5	833	S	F	1 / —	175 / —	12 / —	17 to First Cutting	3-50+ Years	—	730.7	1.1	HG
8	320	S	F	1 / —	175 / —	2 / —	17-26	—	—	D	4.5	HG
Broadcast	D	S	B	—	—	—	9-13	—	—	D	16+	HF
Broadcast	D	S	F	1 / —	175 / —	8 / —	17-26	1 Cutting	—	228.0		HG
Broadcast	D	S	F	1 / —	175 / —	8 / —	17-26	1 Cutting	—	Including Timothy		HG
Broadcast	D	S	F	1 / —	175 / —	8 / —	17-26	1 Cutting	—		2.2+	HG
Broadcast	D	S	F	1 / —	175 / —	8 / —	17 to First Cutting. 9 Thereafter.	2+ Cuttings	—			HG
Broadcast	D	S	F	1 / —	240 / —	8 / —	17-26	1 Cutting	—			HG
Broadcast	D	S	B	—	—	—	17	D	—	228.0 Incl. All Clovers	.46+	HG
12	159	S	B	—	—	—	17 to First Cutting	Years	—	D	D	HF
Broadcast	D	S	B	—	—	—	D	D	—	D	6.9+	HF
D	D	S	F	1 / —	175 / —	—	17 to First Cutting. 9 Thereafter.	D	—	D	.46+	HG

be performed. For some information see Kudzu book in Bibliography.

7	432	L	F	1 / —	175 / —	2-4 / —	17-21	—	—	D	18.3	HF

be developed.

7	432	S	F	1 / —	162 / —	2-3 / —	13	—	—	D	25.0	HF
D	D	S	B	—	—	—	D	—	—	D	D	HF
21	35	S	F	1 / —	175 / —	2-3 / —	D	D	—	D	D	HF
Broadcast	D	S	B	—	—	—	D	D	—	D	D	HG
Broadcast	D	S	B	—	—	—	D	D	—	D	1.1+	HG
D	D	S	B	—	—	—	D	D	—	D	D	HF
D	D	L	B	—	—	—	D	D	—	D	D	HF
D	D	L	B	—	—	—	D	D	—	D	D	HF
D	D	L	B	—	—	—	D	D	—	D	D	HF

COVER, ORGANIC MATTER, FODDER CROPS
(Continued)

PLANT	FOOD NEEDED	MATERIALS NEEDED			
A *Plant*	B *Pounds You Select*	C *Approx. Number Plants You Need*[35]	D *Approx. Sq. Ft. You Need*[36]	E *Approx. Flats You Need*[37]	F *Approx. Ounces/Seed You Need*[38]
1 Alfalfa					
2 Beans, Bell, Cold Weather Favas					
3 Buckwheat					
4 Clover, Alsike					
5 Clover, Crimson					
6 Clover, Sweet, Hubam					
7 Clover, Medium Red					
8 Clover, Sweet, White					
9 Clover, Timothy					
10 Comfrey, Russian					
11 Grass, Rye, Italian					
12 Holy Hay (*Sainfoin*)					
13 Kudzu					
14 Millet, Pearl					
15 Roots, General					
16 Sorghum					
17 Sow Thistle (*Sonchus oleraceus*)					
18 Straw and Chaff, Barley					
19 Straw and Chaff, Oats					
20 Straw and Chaff, Rice					
21 Straw and Chaff, Rye					
22 Straw and Chaff, Wheat, Early Stone Age					
23 Straw and Chaff, Wheat, General					
24 Teosinte					
25 Trefoil, Narrow Leaf					
26 Vetch, Hairy					
27 Weeds, Amaranth, Green					
28 Weeds, Dandelion, Greens					
29 Weeds, Lamb's Quarters					
30 Weeds, Purslane					

G	H	I	J	K	L	M	N	O
Your Actual Yield/100 Sq. Ft.	Your Yield Compared With U.S. Avg.[39]	Time of Year To Plant (SP, SU, FA, WI)	Special Seed Sources	Special Harvesting/ Preparation/ Storage Information	Protein Content/ Pound In Grams (g) (454g/Pound)[44b]	Calorie Content/Pound[44b]	Calcium Content/ Pound In Milligrams (mg)[44b]	△ Excellent organic matter crop. Biomass yield similar to Fava Beans, but seeds smaller and much less expensive. Harvest biomass when plants as a whole begin to lose their maximum green. **CAUTION:** Plants and seeds are reportedly toxic.
		SP	44f	See Notes	53.1* Air Dry:	411 10% Bloom	667 point	Harvest when in 10-90% flowering range.
		FA, SP	—	See Notes	D	D	D	See above. △
		SP, Mid-SU	44e	—	53.1 Dry	1,520 grain.	517	Good honeybee plant. ½ lb. honey/100 sq. ft. Fairly good organic matter crop. Hulling difficult.
		SP	44f	—	36.7* Dry	436	522	See Voisin books in Bibliography for way to increase grazing yields significantly. Try 3-5 times the seeding rate for hay if growing crop seed. Roots can equal biomass weight above ground.
		SP	44f	—	44.5*	391 Dry	558	
		SP	44f	—	42.6*	355 Dry	567	
		SP	44f	—	51.3*	450 Before	767 bloom	
		SP	44f	—	42.6*	355 Dry	567	
		SP	44f	—	18.6* Dry	D Early	186 bloom	
		SP	44i	—	3.4	D	D	
		SP	44f	—	15.4*	D	—	Not good for soil.
		SP	44o	—	34.0* Dry	D	—	Does best in slightly dry climates.
		D	44i	—	13.3 / 11.3	D / D	D / D	:Dried Root. :Cured Hay. } Plus cloth can be made from the root.
		SP	—	—	19.0*	D Dry	—	Can easily exhaust soil if not returned to it. Seeds form when days become shorter in about 45 days.
		—	—	—	—	—	—	—
		SU	44f	—	49.9 / 15.0*	1,506 / 351	127 / 154	:Grain. :Fodder. Dry.
		SP, SU, FA	44i	—	D	D	D	Medium deep rooting system.
					3.2* Dry	224 Dry	145	Roger Revelle, "The Resources Available for Agriculture," *Scientific American*, September 1976, p. 168: ". . . most—perhaps all—of the energy needed in high yielding agriculture could be provided by the farmers themselves" from the crop residues of cereal grains!
					3.2*	233 Dry	86	
					2.7*	D Dry	86	
					—*	90 Dry	118	
					D	D	D	
					1.3*	100 Dry	95	
		D	44i	—	22.2*	D		
		SP	—	—	D	D	D	
		SP	44f	—	69.0*	D Dry	513	
		SU	—	—	3.5	36	267	
		SP, SU, FA	44o	—	2.7	45	187	Good biomass crops. Vitamins and minerals.
		SP, SU, FA	44o	—	4.2	43	309	
		SP, SU, FA	44o	—	1.7	21	103	

ENERGY, FIBER PAPER AND OTHER CROPS

PLANT A		SEED			YIELD			
	Plant	B _Approx. Seeds/Ounces [24]_	C _Minimum Legal Germination Rate [25]_	D _Ounces Seed/100 Sq. Ft. (Adj. for Germ. Rate, Offset Spacing, and Curv. Surf.) [26,30]_	E _Possible B/FIM Pounds Yield/100 Sq. Ft. [27,27a]_		F _Possible B/FIM Pounds Yield/Plant [28]_	G _Avg. U.S. Pounds Yield/100 Sq. Ft. [29]_
1 Bamboo, Paper		Under research.						27.5 General
2 Bamboo, Regular								
3 Beets, Sugar [AA]		1,600	.65 [P]	2.2-2.9	91-182-364		.21-.84	91.3
4 Cheese		Approx. 1 pound/gallon of milk. Heat milk to 180° F. Add ⅓ cup vinegar/gallon of milk.						
5 Cotton, Regular		300	.70 [A]	.76	1.2-2.4-4.8+		.007-.03+	1.2
6 Cotton, Tree		An African perennial variety. Under research.						
7 Eggs, Chicken		See Ecology Action's _Backyard Homestead, Mini-Farm and Garden Log Book._						
8 Flax		6,000	.70 [A]	.6 for Seed .32 for Fiber	D		D	D
9 Gopher Plant		For automotive oil. Under research. Also, a <u>toxic</u> plant for gopher control. Not to be used						
10 Guayule		For rubber. Under research.						
11 Jojoba		50	D	For oil. Under research.				
12 Kenaf		For newsprint, toilet paper, fiber, twine, rope. (Also see Intermediate Technology in						
13 Milk, Cow		See Ecology Action's _Backyard Homestead, Mini-Farm and Garden Log Book._						
14 Milk, Goat		A cow requires about twice the fodder as a goat and produces about twice the milk.						
15 Sprouts, Alfalfa		To be developed. Nutritious, but a large area is required for the production of the seed.						
16 Sprouts, Wheat								

	BEDS/FLATS							MATURITY		RE-MARKS	FOOD NEEDED	SEED YIELD	
H	**I**	**J**	**K**	**L**	**M**	**N**		**O**	**P**	**Q**	**R**	**S**	
In BED Spacing In Inches	*Maximum Number of Plants/100 Sq. Ft.* [30]	*Short/Long/ Extra-Long Germ. Rate*	*Plant Initially In Flats/Beds*	*In FLATS Spacing in Inches* [31]	*Approx. Plants/Flat (Adj. for Germ. Rate)* [31,32]	*Approx. Time In Flats-In Weeks* [31,33]		*Approx. Weeks to Maturity*	*Harvesting Period In Weeks—Up To:*	*Remarks and Especially Good Varieties*	*Pounds Consumed/Year* [34] *Avg. Person in U.S.*	*Approx. Max. Pounds Seed Yield/100 Sq. Ft.* [40]	*Heavy Giver (HG), Light Feeder (LF), Low Nitrogen User (LNU), Heavy Feeder (HF)*
											(596 All paper and paper-board.)		
7	432	L	F	1 / —	162 / —	3-4 / —		12	—	—	(94.7 All sugar.)	30.6	LF

Stir. Let sit for 5 minutes. Pour through cheese cloth lining a colander. Let drain until excess moisture is gone. Result: soft cheese.

12	159	L	F	1 / —	175 / —	3-4 / —		17-26	—	—	D	15.2	HF
											258 Eggs (Approx. 24.2 lbs.)		
3: Seed 4: Fiber	2,507 1,343	S	F	1 / —	175 / —	3 / —		12-14	—	—	D	D	HF

around young children.

Bibliography under Tools Section.)

											238 Lbs. (29¾ Gal.)		
											D		

ENERGY, FIBER PAPER AND OTHER CROPS (Continued)	FOOD NEEDED	MATERIALS NEEDED			
PLANT **A** / Plant	**B** Pounds You Select	**C** Approx. Number Plants You Need[35]	**D** Approx. Sq. Ft. You Need[36]	**E** Approx. Flats You Need[37]	**F** Approx. Ounces/Seed You Need[38]
1 Bamboo, Paper					
2 Bamboo, Regular					
3 Beets, Sugar[AA]					
4 Cheese					
5 Cotton, Regular					
6 Cotton, Tree					
7 Eggs, Chicken					
8 Flax					
9 Gopher Plant					
10 Guayule					
11 Jojoba					
12 Kenaf					
13 Milk, Cow					
14 Milk, Goat					
15 Sprouts, Alfalfa					
16 Sprouts, Wheat					

G — *Your Actual Yield/100 Sq. Ft.*	H — *Your Yield Compared With U.S. Avg.* [39]	I — *Time of Year To Plant (SP, SU, FA, WI)*	J — *Special Seed Sources*	K — *Special Harvesting/Preparation/Storage Information*	L — *Protein Content/Pound In Grams (g) (454g/Pound)* [44b]	M — *Calorie Content/Pound* [44b]	N — *Calcium Content/Pound In Milligrams (mg)* [44b]	O
								Bambusea Gramince. 40% paper yield. For wrapping, news, and book quality paper. Paper can also be made from many fibrous plants, including cabbage! △
								See above △
								Building materials, piping.
		SP, SU, FA	44f	—	D	D	D	
		—	—	—	36.3 Cream	1,696 cheese.	281	Add parsley, dill seeds, chives for flavor!
		SU	44i	—	—	—	—	Minimum clothes replacement rate per year: 2.5 lbs. Thousands of years ago in India people placed a mineral in the soil with the cotton plants and colored fibers resulted!
		SU		—	—	—	—	
		—	—	—	52.1 11%	658 Refuse.	218	
		SP	44i	—	—	—	—	
		—	—	—	—	—	—	
		—	—	—	—	—	—	
			44i	—	—	—	—	For more information on Kenaf, write for information packet: The Newspaper Paper Mill Center, Box 17047, Dulles International Airport, Washington, DC 20041.
		—	—	—	15.9 3.7%	299 Fat.	531	
		—	—	—	14.5	304	585	Has only $\frac{1}{3}$ the vitamin B_{12} that cow milk has.
		All Year	—	—	} Nutritive amounts given for sprouts differ.			
		All Year	—	—				

PLANT A		SEED			YIELD		
Plant	B Approx. Seeds/Ounces [24]	C Minimum Legal Germination Rate [25]	D Approx. Number of Plants/Acre	E Possible B/FIM Pounds Yield/100 Sq. Ft. [27, 27a]	F Possible B/FIM Pounds Yield/Plant [28]	G Good U.S. Pounds Yield/100 Sq. Ft. [29]
1 Almond	12-15	D	160	2.8-5.6-8.4+ In Shell	7.6-22.8+	2.8
2 Apple, Dwarf	600-1,000	D	681	50-75-100	50-100	54.1
3 Apple, Regular	600-1,000	.65[A]	27	50-75-100	800-1,600	54.1
4 Apple, Semi-Dwarf	600-1,000	D	194	50-75-100	112-225	54.1
5 Apricot, Dwarf	18-20	D	681	25-50-100	25-100	24.3
6 Apricot, Regular	18-20	.90[A]	70	25-50-100	156-625	24.3
7 Apricot, Semi-Dwarf	18-20	D	303	25-50-100	36-144	24.3
8 Avocado Tall / Dwarf	D	D	302-193 / 681	9-18-36	13-81 / 6-23	D
9 Banana Tall / Dwarf	—	D	302-193 / 681	27-60-92+	39-208 / 12-59	D
10 Blackberries	10,000	—	2,723 Propagated by "cuttings"	24-36-48+	3.8-7.6+	23.8
11 Boysenberries	—	—	681 Propagated by "cuttings"	26-39-52+	16.6-33+	25.7
12 Cherry, Sour, Bush	D	D	4,840	8-17-34	.8-3.0	D
13 Cherry, Sour, Dwarf	200-250	.80[A]	681	17-34-51	11-32.6	16.5
14 Cherry, Sour, Regular	200-250	D	1,089	17-34-51	68-204	16.5
15 Cherry, Sweet, Bush	D	D	4,840	8-17-34	.8-3.0	D
16 Cherry, Sweet, Dwarf	150-160	D	681	17-34-51	11-32.6	16.5
17 Cherry, Sweet, Regular	150-160	.75[A]	481	17-34-51	153-459	16.5
18 Chestnut	1	.72[A]	27	3.5-7-15 In Shell	56-240	D
19 Coconut	—	D	48	3-6-13	27-118	D
20 Currants, Black	—	—	2,723 Propagated by "cuttings"	D	D	D
21 Dates	40	—	48 Propagated by "cuttings"	23-46-70	207-630	22.9
22 Filbert	10-20	—	194 Propagated by "cuttings"	13-27-55 In Shell	17-123	D
23 Fig	—	—	194 Propagated by "cuttings"	12-24-36++	27-81++	11.9
24 Grapefruit	150-200	D	76	63-95-126	362-724	63.3
25 Grapes, Raisin	—	—	681 Propagated by "cuttings"	38-57-76	24-48	45.4
26 Grapes, Table	—	—	681 Propagated by "cuttings"	45-67-90	28.8-57.6	37.6
27 Grapes, Wine	—	—	681 Propagated by "cuttings"	32-48-64	20.5-41	31.6
28 Guava	D	D	303	D	D	D
29 Hickory	1-5 Depends on variety	.55-.80 J Depends on variety	27	D	D	D

	BEDS/FLATS						MATURITY		RE-MARKS	FOOD NEEDED	SEED YIELD	
H In BED Spacing In Feet	**I** Sq. Ft. Required/Plant[30]	**J** Short/Long/Extra-Long Germ. Rate	**K** Plant Initially In Flats/Beds	**L** In FLATS Spacing in Inches[31]	**M** Approx. Plants/Flat (Adj. for Germ. Rate)[31,32]	**N** Approx. Time In Flats-In Weeks[31,33]	**O** Approx. Years to Bearing / Approx. Years to Max. Bearing	**P** Harvesting Period In Weeks—Up To: / Maximum Bearing Years	**Q** Remarks and Especially Good Varieties	**R** Pounds Consumed/Year[34] Avg. Person in U.S.	**S** Approx. Max. Pounds Seed Yield/100 Sq. Ft.[40]	Heavy Giver (HG), Light Feeder (LF), Low Nitrogen User (LNU), Heavy Feeder (HF)
16.5	272	L	F	4 / I	D / —	D / D	3-4 / D	D / D	—	.4	8.4 In Shell	HF
8	64	EL	F	2 / I	D / —	D / D	3 / D	D / D	—	} 18.5	D	HF
40	1,600	EL	F	2 / I	D / —	162 / D	5 / 10	D / 35-50	—	18.5	D	HF
15	225	EL	F	2 / I	D / —	D / D	4 / 10	D / D	—		D	HF
8	64	L	F	4 / I	D / —	D / D	2 / D	D / D	—		D	HF
25	625	L	F	4 / I	D / —	225 / D	3 / D	D / D	Manchurian	} D	D	HF
12	144	L	F	4 / I	D / —	D / D	3 / D	D / D			D	HF
12-15 / 8	144-225 / 64	D	F	4 / I	D / —	D / D	D / D	D / D	—	D	D	HF
12-15 / 8	144-225 / 64	D	F	4 / I	D / —	D / D	D / D	D / D	—	D	D	HF
4	16	D	Deep Flat	6 / I	D / —	D / D	2 / D	D / 6-10	—	D	D	HF
8	64	D	Deep Flat	6 / I	D / —	D / D	2 / D	D / 6-10	—	D	D	HF
3	9	L	F	3 / I	D / —	D / D	3 / D	D / D	2 Varieties for Pollination	D	D	HF
8	64	L	F	3 / I	200 / —	D / D	3 / D	D / D		D	D	HF
20	400	L	F	3 / I	D / —	D / D	4 / 10-20	D / D		D	D	HF
3	9	L	F	3 / I	D / —	D / D	3 / D	D / D		D	D	HF
8	64	L	F	3 / I	D / —	D / D	3 / D	D / D		D	D	HF
30	900	L	F	3 / I	187 / —	D / D	4 / 10-20	D / D		D	D	HF
40	1,600	D	Deep Flat	6 / I	180 / —	D / D	D / D	D / D	—	D	15.0 In Shell	HF
30	900	D	F	4 / I	D / —	D / D	D / D	D / D	—	D	D	HF
4	16	D	Deep Flat	6 / I	D / —	D / D	3 / D	D / 20	—	D	D	HF
30	900	D	Deep Flat	9 / I	D / —	D / D	5-6 / 10-15	D / D	—	D	D	HF
15 (18-25)	225	D	Deep Flat	9 / I	D / —	D / D	D / D	D / D	—	.07	55.0 In Shell	HF
15	225	D	Deep Flat	9 / I	D / —	D / D	D / D	D / 17	—	D	D	HF
24	576	L	F	3 / I	D / —	D / D	3 / D	D / D	—	29.4 All Citrus	D	HF
8	64	D	F	6 / I	D / —	D / D	3 / D	D / D	—	2.0 Dry Wt.	D	HF
8	64	D	F	6 / I	D / —	D / D	3 / D	D / D	—	6.3	D	HF
8	64	D	F	6 / I	D / —	D / D	3 / D	D / D	—	20.4	D	HF
12	144	D	F	1 / I	D / —	D / D	D / D	D / D	—	D	D	HF
40	1,600	D	F	4 / I	137-200 / —	D / D	D / D	D / 25-350	—	D	D	HF

TREE, CANE CROPS (Continued)		FOOD NEEDED	MATERIALS NEEDED			
PLANT A	Plant	B Pounds You Select	C Approx. Number Plants You Need[35]	D Approx. Sq. Ft. You Need[36]	E Approx. Flats You Need[37]	F Approx. Ounces/Seed You Need[38]
1 Almond						
2 Apple, Dwarf						
3 Apple, Regular						
4 Apple, Semi-Dwarf						
5 Apricot, Dwarf						
6 Apricot, Regular						
7 Apricot, Semi-Dwarf						
8 Avocado Tall Dwarf						
9 Banana Tall Dwarf						
10 Blackberries						
11 Boysenberries						
12 Cherry, Sour, Bush						
13 Cherry, Sour, Dwarf						
14 Cherry, Sour, Regular						
15 Cherry, Sweet, Bush						
16 Cherry, Sweet, Dwarf						
17 Cherry, Sweet, Regular						
18 Chestnut						
19 Coconut						
20 Currants, Black						
21 Dates						
22 Filbert						
23 Fig						
24 Grapefruit						
25 Grapes, Raisin						
26 Grapes, Table						
27 Grapes, Wine						
28 Guava						
29 Hickory						

YIELDS		MISC.						NOTES
G	H	I	J	K	L	M	N	O
Your Actual Yield/100 Sq. Ft.	Your Yield Compared With U.S. Avg.[39]	Time of Year To Plant (SP, SU, FA, WI)	Special Seed Sources	Special Harvesting/ Preparation/ Storage Information	Protein Content/ Pound In Grams (g) (454g/Pound)[44b]	Calorie Content/Pound[44b]	Calcium Content/ Pound In Milligrams (mg)[44b]	
		Early SP	—	—	84.4 Shelled.	2,713	1,061	Shells 49% of unshelled weight.
		Early SP	44j, 44h	—	.8 Raw.	242	29 8% Refuse.	Spur-type yields higher.
		Early SP	—	—	.8 Raw.	242	29 8% Refuse.	
		Early SP	—	—	.8 Raw.	242	29 8% Refuse.	
		Early SP	—	—	4.3 Raw.	217	72 6% Refuse.	A fall yielding variety also exists.
		Early SP	44k	—	4.3 Raw.	217	72 6% Refuse.	30 feet high.
		Early SP	—	—	4.3 Raw.	217	72 6% Refuse.	
		Early SP	—	—	7.1	568	34 25% Refuse.	
		Early SP	—	—	3.4 3.7	262 278	25 31	:Yellow. :Red. 32% Refuse.
		Early SP	44i	—	5.3 Raw.	264	145	2-foot-wide beds.
		Early SP	—	—	3.2 Canned.	163	86 8% Refuse.	2-foot-wide beds.
		Early SP	44k, 44l	—	5.0 Raw.	242	92 8% Refuse.	
		Early SP	—	—	5.0 Raw.	242	92 8% Refuse.	
		Early SP	—	—	5.0 Raw	242	92 8% Refuse.	Bear in 3-5 years.
		Early SP	44k, 44l	—	3.6 Canned.	195 Without	68 pits.	
		Early SP	—	—	3.6 Canned.	195 Without	68 pits.	One self-pollinating variety exists.
		Early SP	—	—	3.6 Canned.	195 Without	68 pits.	
		Early SP	—	—	30.4 Dried	1,710 and	236 shelled.	Shells (dried): 18% of unshelled weight. Problems with blight.
		Early SP	—	—	8.3 15.9	816 1,569	31 59	:Fresh. 48% Refuse. :Meat.
		Early SP	—	—	7.6 Raw.	240	267 2% Refuse.	2-foot-wide beds.
		Early SP	44i	—	10.0 Dry	1,243 and	268 pitted.	1 male to 100 female plants for pollination. Pits: 13% of dried weight.
		Early SP	44i	—	57.2 Shelled.	2,876	948	Shells: 54% of unshelled weight.
		Early SP	—	—	5.4 Raw.	363	159	Drying ratio 3:1.
		Early SP	—	—	1.0 Raw.	84	33 55% Refuse.	
		Early SP	—	—	11.3 Dry.	1,311 18%	281 moisture.	
		Early SP	—	—	2.4 Raw.	270	48 11% Refuse.	
		Early SP	—	—	3.7 Raw.	197	46 37% Refuse.	
		Early SP	44i	—	3.5 Raw.	273	101 3% Refuse.	15 feet high.
		Early SP	44i	—	59.9 Shelled.	3,053	Trace	Shells: 65% of unshelled weight.

PLANT A		SEED			YIELD			
	Plant	**B** *Approx. Seeds/Ounces* [24]	**C** *Minimum Legal Germination Rate* [25]	**D** *Approx. Number of Plants/Acre*	**E**	*Possible B/FIM Pounds Yield/100 Sq. Ft.* [27, 27a]	**F** *Possible B/FIM Pounds Yield/Plant* [28]	**G** *Good U.S. Pounds Yield/100 Sq. Ft.* [29]
30 Honey Locust		180	.50[J]	27	Pods and Beans 6-13-26+		128-320	D
31 Lemon		200-300	D	76	75-112-150		432-864	74.6
32 Lime		300-400	D	194	D		D	D
33 Mango		D	D	48 Propagated by seed or grafting.	D		D	D
34 Mesquite		D	D	109	D Seed D Pods		D D	D
35 Nectarine, Dwarf		D	D	681	40-60-80		25.6-51+	39.9
36 Nectarine, Regular		D	D	194	40-60-80		90-180+	39.9
37 Olive		D	D	27	8-17-35		129-564	D
38 Orange, Sweet		200-300	D	97 76	Navel: 32-48-64 Valencia: 42-63-84		155-310 242-484	31.8 42.0
39 Peach, Dwarf		610	D	681	60-90-120 Clingstone		38-76	60.1
40 Peach, Regular		610	D	194	Clingstone: 60-90-120 Freestone: 39-59-78		135-270 88-176	60.1 38.5
41 Pear, Dwarf		750	D	681	36-72-108		23-70	35.8
42 Pear, Regular		750	D	170	36-72-108		92-276	35.8
43 Pecan		6	.50[J]	27	6-12-25+ In Shell		96-400+	D
44 Persimmon		74	D	134	8-16-32+		26-103	D
45 Pistachio		28 In Shell	D	109	D		D	D
46 Plum, Bush		D	D	4,840	9.5-19-38		.85-3.4	D
47 Plum, Regular		50-55	D	134	Regular: 19-38-57 Prune: 11-22-33		61-184 36-107	19.2 11.4
48 Pomegranate		D	D	435	50-75-100		50-100	D
49 Raspberries		—	—	2,723 Propagated by "cuttings."	6-12-24+		.95-.38+	12.3
50 Strawberries		40,000	D	43,560 Propagated by seed or runners.	40-80-320		.4-1.6	16.7 U.S. Avg.
51 Tangello		200-300	D	109	D		D	D
52 Tangerine		300-400	D	109	D		D	D
53 Walnut, No. Calif. Black		3	.40[A]	27	5-7.5-10+ In Shell		80-160+	4.7
54 Walnut, English (Persian)		2	.80[A]	27	5-7.5-10+ In Shell		80-160+	4.7
55 Walnut, Eastern, Black		3	.50[A]	27	5-7.5-10+ In Shell		80-160+	4.7

H	I	J	K	L	M	N	O	P	Q	R	S	HG/LF/LNU/HF
In BED Spacing In Feet	Sq. Ft. Required/Plant[30]	Short/Long/Extra-Long Germ. Rate	Plant Initially In Flats/Beds	In FLATS Spacing in Inches[31]	Approx. Plants/Flat (Adj. for Germ. Rate)[31,32]	Approx. Time In Flats-In Weeks[31,33]	Approx. Years to Bearing / Approx. Years to Max. Bearing	Harvesting Period In Weeks—Up To: / Maximum Bearing Years	Remarks and Especially Good Varieties	Pounds Consumed/Year[34] Avg. Person in U.S.	Approx. Max. Pounds Seed Yield/100 Sq. Ft.[40]	Heavy Giver (HG), Light Feeder (LF), Low Nitrogen User (LNU), Heavy Feeder (HF)
40	1,600	D	F	4 / I	125 / —	D / D	D / D	D / 10-100	—	D	13.0 In Shell	HF
24	576	D	F	2 / I	D / —	D / D	3 / D	D / 50+	—	} 29.4 All Citrus-Fresh	D	HF
15	225	D	F	2 / I	D / —	D / D	3 / D	D / D	—		D	HF
30	900	D	F	2 / I	D / —	D / D	D / D	D / D	—	D	D	HF
20	400	D	F	2 / I	D / —	D / D	D / D	D / D	—	D	D	HF
8	64	D	B Sapling	—	—	—	3-4 / 8-12	D / D	—	D	D	HF
15	225	D	F	4 / I	D / —	D / D	D / D	D / D	—	D	D	HF
40	1,600	D	F	2 / I	D / —	D / D	D / D	D / D	—	D	D	HF
22 24	448 576	D	F	2 / I	D / —	D / D	3 / D	D / 50+	—	D	D	HF
8	64	D	B Sapling	—	—	—	3 / D	D / D	—	D	D	HF
15	225	D	F	4 / I	D / —	D / D	3-4 / 8-12	D / 8-12	—	D	D	HF
8	64	D	B Sapling	—	—	—	3 / D	D / D	—	D	D	HF
16(-20)	256	EL	F	1 / I	D / —	D / D	4 / D	D / 50-75	—	D	D	HF
40(-70)	1,600	L	F	4 / I	125 / —	D / D	D / D	D / Up to 150	—	.4	25.0+ In Shell	HF
18	324	D	F	1 / I	D / —	D / D	2-3 / D	D / 20-300	—	D	D	HF
20	400	D	F	2 / I	D / —	D / D	D / D	D / 35-50	—	D	D	HF
3	9	D	B Sapling	—	—	—	3 / D	D / D	—	D	D	HF
18(-24)	324	D	F	4 / I	D / —	D / D	4 / D	D / 20-25	—	D	D	HF
10	100	D	F	2 / I	D / —	D / D	D / D	D / D	—	D	D	HF
4	16	D	Deep Flat	6 / I	D / —	D / D	2 / D	D / 6-10	—	D	D	HF
1	1	D	F	1 / 2	D / —	D / D	2 / D	D / 4	Tioga-Everbearing	D	D	HF
20	400	D	F	1 / I	3 / —	D / D	3 / D	D / D	—	} 29.4 All Citrus-Fresh	D	HF
20	400	D	F	1 / I	D / —	D / D	3 / D	D / D	—		D	HF
40	1,600	EL	F	4 / I	100 / —	D / D	D / D	D / D	—	} .46	10.0+ In Shell	HF
40	1,600	L	F	4 / I	200 / —	D / D	D / D	D / D	—		10.0+ In Shell	HF
40	1,600	EL	F	4 / I	125 / —	D / D	D / D	D / D	—		10.0+ In Shell	HF

TREE, CANE CROPS (Continued)	FOOD NEEDED	MATERIALS NEEDED				
	B	**C**	**D**	**E**	**F**	
PLANT **A**	*Plant*	*Pounds You Select*	*Approx. Number Plants You Need*[35]	*Approx. Sq. Ft. You Need*[36]	*Approx. Flats You Need*[37]	*Approx. Ounces/Seed You Need*[38]
30 Honey Locust						
31 Lemon						
32 Lime						
33 Mango						
34 Mesquite						
35 Nectarine, Dwarf						
36 Nectarine, Regular						
37 Olive						
38 Orange, Sweet						
39 Peach, Dwarf						
40 Peach, Regular						
41 Pear, Dwarf						
42 Pear, Regular						
43 Pecan						
44 Persimmon						
45 Pistachio						
46 Plum, Bush						
47 Plum, Regular						
48 Pomegranate						
49 Raspberries						
50 Strawberries						
51 Tangello						
52 Tangerine						
53 Walnut, No. Calif. Black						
54 Walnut, English (Persian)						
55 Walnut, Eastern, Black						

| YIELDS | | MISC. | | | | | | | NOTES |
| G | H | I | J | K | L | M | N | O | |
Your Actual Yield/100 Sq. Ft.	Your Yield Compared With U.S. Avg. [39]	Time of Year To Plant (SP, SU, FA, WI)	Special Seed Sources	Special Harvesting/ Preparation/ Storage Information	Protein Content/ Pound In Grams (g) (454g/Pound) [44b]	Calorie Content/Pound [44b]	Calcium Content/ Pound In Milligrams (mg) [44b]		
		Early SP	44i	—	72	D	D	Can make a flour from the beans. Pods and beans a good fodder. A very important tree. *Gleditsia triancanti.*	
		Early SP	—	—	3.3	82	79 33% Refuse.		
		Early SP	—	—	2.7	107	126 16% Refuse.		
		D	44i	—	2.1	201	30 33% Refuse.	90 feet high at maturity.	
		Early SP	—	—	17.0 76.2	D D	260 D	:Seed. :Pod.	
		Early SP	44j	—	2.5	267	263 8% Refuse.	8 feet high.	
		Early SP	44j	—	2.5	267	263 8% Refuse.	25 feet high.	
		Early SP	—	—	5.3 8.0	442 1,227	232 —	:Green. 16% Refuse. Pasquale, up to 40%. :Ripe. 20% Refuse. All other, 16.5-21.8%.	
		Early SP	—	—	4.0 4.1	157 174	123 136	:Navels (winter bearing). 32% Refuse. :Valencias (summer bearing). 25% Refuse.	
		Early SP	—	—	2.4	150	36 13% Refuse.	8 feet high.	
		Early SP	—	—	2.4	150	36 13% Refuse.	25 feet high.	
		Early SP	44j	—	2.9	252	33 9% Refuse.	8 feet high.	
		Early SP	44j	—	2.9	252	33 9% Refuse.	30-40 feet high.	
		Early SP	—	—	41.7 Shelled.	3,116	331	Shell: 47% of unshelled weight.	
		Early SP	44i	—	2.6	286	22 18% Refuse.	30 feet high.	
		Early SP	44i	—	87.5 Shelled.	2,694	594	30 feet high. Shell: 50% of unshelled weight.	
		Early SP	44k, 44l	—	2.1	272	74 9% Refuse.	3 feet high.	
		Early SP	44j	—	2.1 3.4	272 320	74 51	:Damson. 9% Refuse. :Prune. 6% Refuse.	
		Early SP	—	—	1.3	160	8 44% Refuse.		
		Early SP	—	—	6.6 5.3	321 251	132 97	:Black. Refuse 3%. :Red. 2-foot-wide beds.	
		Early SP	44m	—	3.0	161	91 4% Refuse.	Bear well second through fourth year. Use new plants on end of runners to renew bed.	
		Early SP	—	—	1.3	104	— 44% Refuse.	30 feet high.	
		Early SP	—	—	2.7	154	134 26% Refuse.	30 feet high.	
		Early SP	44i	—	D	D	D	30-60 feet high.	
		Early SP	—	—	93.0 Shelled.	2,849	449 55% Refuse.	Up to 60 feet high.	
		Early SP	—	—	67.1 Shelled.	2,953	Trace 78% Refuse.	Up to 150 feet high. A good tree to plant for your great-great grandchildren!	

CODES

A — Approximate germination rate as sold by seed companies. No known minimum germination rate. Can be higher or lower.

B — In beds.

C — Cantaloup.

D — Do not know yet.

E — Spacing increases with warmth of climate.

F — In flats.

G — Best "seed" is a seed packet of 2–6 seeds, of which approximately 1.62 germinate.

H — Honeydew.

I — Transplant into 1- to 5-gallon container as appropriate. Raise sapling until 1 year old. Then transplant into soil.

J — Germination average in laboratory.

K — Straw weight is generally 1 to 3+ times harvested and cleaned seed weight.

L — Long-germinating seed (8–21 days).

M — Cook to minimize oxalic acid, calcium tie-up.

N — Use narrow bed: 2 feet wide.

P — Perennial.

Q — Whole sweet potatoes side by side in flat. Approximately 4 flats per 100 square feet.

R — Replant at points where germination fails. We call this "spotting."

S — Short germinating seed (1–7 days).

T — 18 inches for cherry tomatoes; 21 inches for regular tomatoes; 24 inches for large tomatoes. Sequential information in columns D, H, and I should be used according to spacing chosen.

U — A loaf of bread requires 2/3 lb. flour (2-1/2 cups).

V — Approximate minimum.

W — 12 or 15 inches for midget varieties; 18 inches for 5- to 7-lb. varieties; 21 inches for 10- to 15-lb. varieties; 24 inches for largest varieties.

X — Sow 3 seeds per center and thin to 1 plant if sowing directly in growing bed.

Y — Estimate.

Z — 15-inch spacing for non-hybrids; 18-inch spacing for hybrids. Sequential information in columns D, F, H, and I should be used according to spacing chosen.

AA — Each "seed" contains about 3 seeds, of which half germinate.

BB — Soak seeds overnight for best germination.

EL — Extra-long-germinating seed (22-28 days).

FA — Fall.

SP — Spring.

SU — Summer.

WI — Winter.

ZZ — Based on Ecology Action experience.

* — Digestible protein for animals.

** — Depending on variety selected.

— — Not applicable.

\# — First set of figures: summer growing in lathhouse for fall set-out.
Second set of figures: winter growing in greenhouse for spring set-out.
Harden off for 2 days outside in flat before transplanting into bed.

\#\# — Plant 2 seeds per center to compensate for low germination rate.

\+ — Yield may be significantly higher.

FOOTNOTES

24. From James Edward Knott, *Handbook for Vegetable Growers,* John Wiley & Sons, Inc., New York, 1975, p. 17; and other reference sources.

25. Ibid., pp. 192 and 193; and other reference sources.

26. To determine amount divide Column I by Column B by Column C.

27. Estimates based on our experience and research. Use lower figure if you are a beginning gardener; middle, if a good one; third, if an excellent one. (The testing and development process is requiring a long time and has involved many failures. Its direction, however, has been encouraging over the years, as the soil, our skills, and yields have improved, and as resource consumption levels have decreased. There is still much left to be done.)

27a. The approximate plant yield averages are in some instances much lower than one would expect. For example, a beginning gardener will get carrots much larger than the 1/4 ounce noted, but all of his or her carrots will probably not germinate as well as a good or excellent gardener's and will probably not be as large. Therefore it is estimated that the average weight of the carrots would be 1/4 ounce (based as if all 5,894 seeds germinated).

28. E ÷ I.

29. From U.S. Department of Agriculture, *Agricultural Statistics—1972,* U.S. Government Printing Office, Washington, DC, pp. 151–188; and other reference sources.

30. Curved surface adds about 20% to planting surface, so 159 plants fit in 120 square feet of curved surface on 12-inch (1-foot) centers, rather than fewer plants. It is 159 plants rather than 120 because the hexagonal "offset" spacing uses up less space than equidistant spacing.

31. Upper part of box is for initial seeding in flat. Lower part is for later transplanted spacing in another flat, when that is recommended.

32. Assumes flat with *internal* dimensions of 13 inches by 21 inches (or 273 square inches) in which at least 250 plants fit on 1-inch centers and 60 plants on 2-inch centers.

33. From James Edward Knott, *Handbook for Vegetable Growers,* John Wiley & Sons, Inc., New York, 1957, p. 14; and from our experience and research.

34. U.S. Department of Agriculture, *Agricultural Statistics—1972,* U.S. Government Printing Office, Washington, DC, pp. 238, 239, 241, 242, 244, 245; and other sources.

35. B (pp. 72, 76, 80, 84, 88, 92, 96) ÷ F (pp. 70, 74, 78, 82, 86, 90, 94).

36. B (pp. 72, 76, 80, 84, 88, 92, 96) ÷ E (pp. 70, 74, 78, 82, 86, 90, 94). Use lower figure in E if you are a beginning gardener; middle, if a good one working with good soil; third, if an excellent one working with excellent soil.

37. C (pp. 72, 76, 80, 84, 88, 92, 96) ÷ M (pp. 71, 75, 79, 83, 87, 91, 95).

38. D (pp. 72, 76, 80, 84, 88, 92, 96) × D (pp. 70, 74, 78, 82, 86, 90, 94).

39. G (pp. 73, 77, 81, 85, 89, 93, 97) ÷ G (pp. 70, 74, 78, 82, 86, 90, 94).

40. Based in part on standard yield figures from James Edward Knott, *Handbook for Vegetable Growers,* John Wiley & Sons, Inc., New York, 1975, pp. 198–199, in combination with a multiplier factor based on our research and experience, and other reference sources. The result, however, is preliminary, for your guidance, and very experimental. Remember, if growing seed, to adjust for germination rate when determining amount to grow for your use.

41. Harvest after die-back of plants.

42. From James Edward Knott, *Handbook for Vegetable Growers,* John Wiley & Sons, Inc., New York, 1975, p. 14.

43. Can cut smaller heading secondary and tertiary side shoots also. In addition, leaves generally have twice the nutritive value of the "heads"!

44. Contains the same amount of general protein (not amino acids) as milk and 50–100% more calcium per cup, yet may produce up to 6 times the cups per unit of area!

44a. The Redwood City Seed Company carries an interesting tropical variety, Snow Peak, which heads only in the summer. A good variety with small heads for out-of-season growing.

44b. United States Department of Agriculture, *Composition of Foods,* U.S. Government Printing Office, Washington, DC, 1963, 190 pp.; and other reference sources.

44c. Irish Potatoes: White Rose and Red. LaSoda varieties. 100-lb. orders or more. Order in September *untreated* for next Spring in 100-lb. bags from Cal-Ore Seed Company, 1212 Country Club Blvd., Stockton, CA 95204, if your nursery does not carry seed potatoes. Ask for prices with a stamped, self-addressed return envelope.

44d. Sweet Potatoes: Jewel, Centennial, Garnett, Jersey varieties. Order in September *untreated,* number two size, for following summer in 40-lb. boxes from Joe Alvernaz, P.O. Box 474, Livingston, CA 95334. Ask for prices with a stamped, self-addressed return envelope.

44e. Johnny's Selected Seeds. (See Bibliography.)

44f. R. H. Shumway Seed Company.

44g. Burpee Seed Company.

44h. Vermont Bean Seed Company.

44i. Redwood City Seed Company.

44j. Tree Crops Nursery.

44k. Hansen New Plants Company.

44l. Gurney's Seed Company.

44m. Nourse Farms.

44n. Stark Brothers Company.

44o. J. L. Hudson Seed Company.

44p. Stokes Seeds.

44q. Bountiful Gardens.

45. Use French variety (Vilmorin's Cantalun—orange-fleshed) or Israeli variety (Haogen—green-fleshed). Both have smooth exterior without netting. This minimizes rotting.

46. Try the Torpedo onion. Its long shape is particularly suited to intensive raised bed gardening and farming, and it can produce twice the yield per unit of area.

47. 1.5- to 2.0-ounce pieces of slightly sprouted tubers use only 1 or 2 sprouted eyes left on potato piece.

48. Red "Lasoda" variety recommended. Note that stems and leaves are poisonous, as is any part of the tuber which has turned green. Get "seed" potatoes. Many in stores have been treated to retard sprouting.

49. Stem and root sections nicked in one piece from one end of sprouted tuber. About 3 to 4 of these "starts" will be obtained from each 8-ounce potato started in a flat. Get "seed" potatoes. Many in stores have been treated to retard sprouting.

50. Burpee's Triple Treat variety with hull-less seeds. No shelling of nutritious and tasty seeds!

51. Burpee's Sparkler variety: red top with white bottom half. Good looking.

52. Green parts poisonous.

53. Burpee's New Hampshire Midget variety.

NOTES ON THE PLANNING CHARTS

FLOWER SPACING CHART

Spacings vary for flowers depending on the variety and how the flowers are used. The following may help you start out with the most common flowers.

Annuals—replant each year from seed

	height	inches apart*		height	inches apart*
African Daisy	4–16″	12	Phlox	6–18″	9
Aster	1–3′	10–12	(*P. Drummondii*)**		
Calif. Poppy***	9–12″	12	Portulaca	6″	6–9
Columbine	2–3′	12	Pansy	6–9″	8–10
Calendula***	1½–2′	12	Scabiosa	2½–3′	12–18
Cosmos***	2–3′	12–18	Scarlet Sage	12–18″	12
Flowering Tobacco	3″	18–24	(*Salvia splendens*)		
Hollyhock***	4–6′	12	Schizanthus	1½–2′	12–18
Marigold, African	2–4′	12–24	Shirley Poppy	1½–2′	18
Marigold, French	6–18″	8–12	Snapdragons	1½–3′	12
Nasturtium, Dwarf***	12″	8	Stocks	12–30″	12
Nasturtium, Climbing***	Trails	10	Strawflower	2–3′	12–18
Petunia	12–16″	12	Sweet Peas	Climbing	12
			Zinnia	1–3′	12–18

Perennials—need a permanent space in the garden

	height	inches apart		height	inches apart
Alyssum	4–6″	10–12	Gazania	6–12″	10
(*Lobularia maritima*)			Iceland Poppy	1′	12
Aubrieta	Trailing	12–15	Jacob's Ladder	6″–3′	12–15
Baby's Breath	3–4′	14–16	(*Polemonium caeruleum*)		
Bachelor Buttons	2′	12	Marguerite	2½–3′	18–24
Carnation	1′	12	Oriental Poppy	2½–3′	12–14
Chrysanthemum	2–3′	18–24	Pinks (*Dianthus*)	1′	12
Coral Bells	2′	12	Peony	2′	14–16
(*Heuchera sanguinea*)			Painted Daisy	3′	12
Coreopsis	2′	9–18	Scabiosa	2′	12
Delphinium	1–5′	24	Sea Pink (*Armeria*)	4–6″	10–12
Foxglove	3′	12	Shasta Daisy	2½–3′	12
Gaillardia	2–3′	12	Sweet William	1–2′	12

* These are spacings for standard-sized plants. For smaller varieties, the spacings should be reduced in proportion to the reduced plant size.

**Botanical Latin names also given when confusion might occur without it.

***Reseed themselves easily by dropping many seeds on ground.

NOTE: Most flowers have long-terminating seeds (8–21 days).

HERB SPACING CHART

Annuals—plant seed in spring for late summer harvest

	height	inches apart		height	inches apart
Anise	2′	8	Cilantro	1–1½′	5
Sweet Basil	1–2′	6	Coriander	1–1½′	6
Borage	1½′	15	Cumin	1′	18
Caraway	2½′	6	Dill	2½′	8
Chamomile	2½′	6–10	Fennel	3–5′	12
(Matricaria chamomilla)			Parsley	2½′	5
Chervil	1½′	4	Summer Savory	1½′	6

Perennials[54a]—need a permanent place in the garden

	height	inches apart		height	inches apart
Angelica	4–6′	36	Santolina	2′	30
*Bee Balm	3′	30	Winter Savory	1′	12
Burnet	15″	15	Southernwood	3–5′	30
Catnip	2–3′	15 (spreads)**	*Spearmint	2–3′	15 (spreads)**
*Chamomile, Roman	3–12″	12	Stinging Nettle	4–6′	24 (spreads)**
(Anthemis nobilis)			Tansy	4′	30
Chives	10–24″	5	Tarragon	2′	12–18
Costmary	2–6′	12	Thyme	1′	6
Comfrey	15–36″	15–36	Valerian	4′	18
*Feverfew	1–3′	10–15	*Woodruff	6–10″	8–12 (spreads)**
Horehound	2′	9 (spreads)**	Wormwood	3–5′	12–24
Hyssop	2′	12	Yarrow—Common	3–5′	12–18
Lavender	3′	24	*(Achillea millefolium)*		
Lemon Balm	3′	12 (spreads)**			
Lemon Verbena	10′	24	*Yarrow—White, red		
Lovage	6′	36	or pink flowered	2½–3′	12
Marjoram	1′	12	*Scented Geraniums		
*Oregano	2′	18–24	Rose	3′	30
Peppermint	2½″	12 (spreads)**	Lemon	2–3′	***
*Pineapple Sage	4′	24–36	Apple	10″	18
Rosemary	3–4′	18–24	Peppermint	2′	48
Rue	3′	18	Coconut	8–12″	18
Sage	2′	18	Lime	2′	18

* Based on our experience. Others are from the *Herb Chart* by Evelyn Gregg, Biodynamic Farming and Gardening Assn., Wyoming, Rhode Island.

** Spreads underground—keep it contained or plant where it can keep going.

*** Do not yet know height and/or spacing information.

NOTE: Many herbs are long germinating seeds (22–28 days).

54a. Normally started from cuttings or root divisions; often takes 1–4 years to reach full size from seed.

Use this space to record your favorite flowers and herbs which are not included in the preceding spacing charts. *Use within-the row spacings given on the back of the seed packets.*

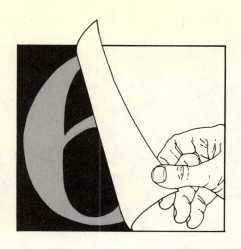

Making The Garden Plan

Now we come to the art of putting the theory into a garden plan. No book is detailed enough to make gardening foolproof. If growing plants did not involve real learning and *experimentation* it would not be nearly so satisfying. The plans that follow are meant to illustrate some of the considerations that make a successful garden. They are based on what the average American consumes each year, but do not take the precise amounts too seriously. Everyone has different tastes and your use of the "Average American Diet" changes rapidly when you have abundant fresh vegetables to use. You will probably want to eat many more fresh fruits and vegetables.

Before you start, there is some local information you will need. Talk to neighbors who garden, check with the county agricultural agent, or ask at the local nursery. You want to know:

Which vegetables grow well in your area?

When does the main planting season start?

What are the special requirements of your specific soil?

Are there any special climatic conditions to be aware of, such as heavy winds, hot dry spells, or excessive rain?

How do people usually plan for this?

The first plan is for a one-person garden. The first year includes the easiest crops to grow in 100 square feet based on yields expected of a good gardener. The second year, *the square footage doubles* and more difficult crops are added. The third and fourth years, trees, herbs, strawberries, and asparagus are included—these permanent plantings being placed in soil that has now been worked and improved for 2 years—and a third bed is added. After 3 or 4 years, the skills gained may enable one to condense vegetable growing from 200 square feet to 100 square feet, leaving 100 square feet of improved soil for protein crops (wheat, rye, peanuts, lentils, soybeans, and rice), fibers (cotton or flax), or special interest crops (chicken, goat, or bee forage, grapes, blueberries, bamboo, herbs, nut trees, and so on).

Lastly, a garden plan for a family of four is shown. We recommend using a similar 3- to 4-year progression, starting with approximately 300 square feet the first year, and adding 300 more square feet each year until the entire garden is developed.

Buying seeds for a backyard garden easily runs up a $10–20+ bill. At our garden supply store in Palo Alto we purchase seeds in bulk and sell them out of jars like penny candy using teaspoons and tablespoons to measure. One can easily spend less than $2 in our store for 6 months of vegetables. You can take advantage of the same low prices by having bulk seeds ordered and carried at your favorite local co-op grocery store.

The plans specify twice as many seedlings as are needed in the garden beds. Plant the best ones and give any extras to a friend or save them in case of damage to first transplants. Leaf lettuce matures sooner than head lettuce. Planting both insures a continuous harvest. Similarly, half of the tomatoes planted should be an early variety (maturing in 65 days) for continuous harvesting. Save space by tying tomatoes up to stakes. Pumpkins take a lot of space. Plant them at the edge of the garden where they can sprawl over uncultivated areas. Corn is pollinated by the wind. A square block of 4 plants in each direction (not in a row) is the minimum for adequate pollination. In small plantings you may want to hand-pollinate it so all ears can fill out optimally.

When choosing a site for your garden the amount of available direct sunlight should be taken into consideration. *Optimally,* your garden area should have 11 hours of sunlight or more—7 hours may allow plants to grow acceptably and in some instances 4 hours may work for Cool Season Crops (see page 64). Experimentation will probably be needed if you plan to garden in soil which receives less than 11 hours of sun.

THE GARDEN YEAR

Winter
□ Plan garden.
□ Order *untreated* seeds (allow 2 months for delivery if ordering by mail).
□ Make flats, trellises, mini-greenhouses, and shade-netting units.[54b]

Spring
□ Plant flats so they can mature while soil is being prepared.
□ Start new compost piles with plentiful weeds and grass clippings.
□ Spread fall compost and dig garden beds.
□ Plant cool weather crops in early spring and warm and hot weather crops in late spring and early summer.

Summer
□ Plant summer crops.
□ Keep garden watered and weeded.
□ Harvest and enjoy the fruits of your work.
□ In mild winter areas, plant fall gardens of cool weather crops at the end of summer.

Fall
□ Start additional compost piles with plentiful leaves and garden waste.
□ Harvest summer crops.

54b. See Ecology Action's *Backyard Homestead, Mini-Farm and Garden Log Book* for miniature greenhouse and shade-netting house plans.

SIMPLE MINI-GARDEN, 6-MONTH GROWING SEASON
100–140 + SQUARE FEET

As early as possible in spring plant (optional):
1 bare root fruit tree — 1 tree   40+   sq. ft.

6 weeks before last frost of spring _____
                                        (date)

Start seedlings in flats:
leaf lettuce   — 12 seeds⑤
head lettuce   — 6 seeds⑤
parsley   — 4 seeds

2 weeks before last frost _____
                                    (date)

Start seedlings in flat:
cherry tomatoes   — 16 seeds
Set out:
leaf lettuce   — 6 plants⑤Ⓜ   2   sq. ft.
head lettuce   — 3 plants⑤   2   sq. ft.
Plant:
bush peas   — 252 seeds*   10   sq. ft.
carrots   — 206 seeds   1.75 sq. ft.
          (2 seeds/center: thin to 1 plant/center)
bunching onions   — 234 seeds   1 sq. ft.
radishes   — 15 seeds   .25 sq. ft.

On last frost date _____
                              (date)

Plant:
red potatoes   —75 starts   30 sq. ft.
                         (9.4 lbs.)

Start seedlings in flats:
cucumbers   — 4 seeds
cantaloup   — 16 seeds
New Hampshire
  midget water-
  melons   —32 seeds
dwarf marigolds   — 4 seeds

2 weeks after last frost date _____
                                        (date)

Set out:
cherry tomatoes
  (18″ centers)   —8 plants   15 sq. ft.
parsley   —1 plant   1 sq. ft.
Plant:
early corn
  (15″ centers)   —34 seeds   20 sq. ft.
          (2 seeds/center: thin to 1 plant/center)

4 weeks after last frost _____
                                   (date)

Set out:
cucumbers   —2 plants   —   sq. ft.
cantaloup   —8 plants   10   sq. ft.
New Hampshire
  midget water-
  melon   —16 plants   10   sq. ft.
dwarf marigold   — 2 plants   —   sq. ft.
Plant:
pumpkins   —4 seeds   —   sq. ft.
          (thin to 2 plants)
sunflowers   —4 seeds   —   sq. ft.
      (2 seeds/center: thin to 1 plant/center)
zucchini   —2 seeds   —   sq. ft.
          (thin to 1 plant)
acorn winter
  squash   —2 seeds   —   sq. ft.
          (thin to 1 plant)

8 weeks after last frost _____
                                   (date)

As first planting comes out, plant:
red potatoes   —75 starts   30   sq. ft.
                         (9.4 lbs.)

10 weeks after last frost _____
                                    (date)

Plant:
bush beans   —134 seeds*   10   sq. ft.

12 weeks after last frost _____
                                     (date)

Start seedlings in flats:
leaf lettuce   —12 seeds⑤
head lettuce   — 6 seeds⑤
Plant:
early corn
  (15″ centers)   —34 seeds   20   sq. ft.
       (2 seeds/center: thin to 1 plant/center)

16 weeks after frost _____
                                (date)

Set out:
leaf lettuce   —6 plants⑤   2   sq. ft.
head lettuce   —3 plants⑤   2   sq. ft.
Plant:
chard   — 2 seeds   —   sq.ft.
          (thin to 1 plant)
carrots   —206 seeds   1.75 sq. ft.
       (2 seeds/center: thin to 1 plant/center)
radishes   — 15 seeds   .25 sq. ft.

⑤ = Stagger planting for a more continuous
      harvest.

* = Spot additional seeds later where seeds
      do not germinate.

Ⓜ = Numbers given are the maximum which
      should be required for each crop for area
      involved. Less may be needed.

NORTH

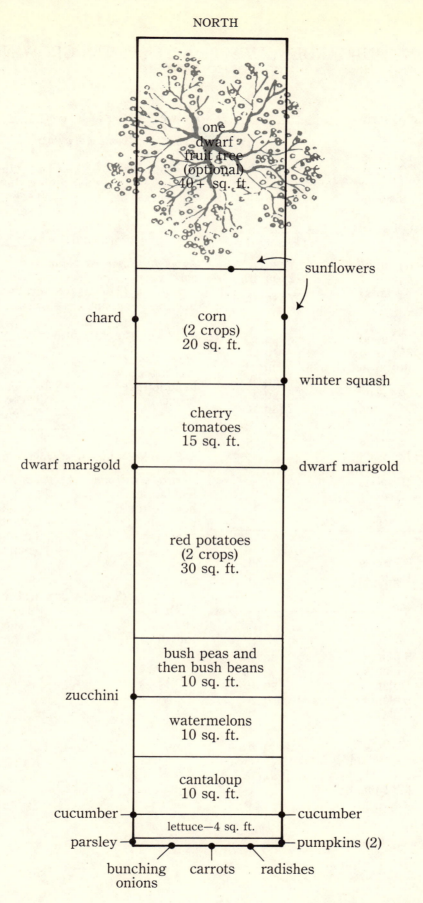

sunflowers

chard
corn
(2 crops)
20 sq. ft.

winter squash

cherry
tomatoes
15 sq. ft.

dwarf marigold
dwarf marigold

red potatoes
(2 crops)
30 sq. ft.

bush peas and
then bush beans
10 sq. ft.

zucchini

watermelons
10 sq. ft.

cantaloup
10 sq. ft.

cucumber
cucumber

lettuce—4 sq. ft.

parsley
pumpkins (2)

bunching
onions
carrots
radishes

Scale: 5/16 inch to 1 foot

ONE PERSON MINI-GARDEN, *FIRST* YEAR, 6-MONTH GROWING SEASON
100 SQUARE FEET

6 weeks before last frost of spring _____
(date)

Start seedlings in flats:
cabbage	— 12 seeds	
broccoli	— 6 seeds	
leaf lettuce	— 14 seeds Ⓢ	
head lettuce	— 10 seeds Ⓢ	

2 weeks before last frost of spring _____
(date)

Set out:
cabbage	— 6 plants Ⓜ	6.7 sq. ft.
broccoli	— 3 plants	3.2 sq. ft.
leaf lettuce	— 7 plants Ⓢ	5.25 sq. ft.
head lettuce	— 5 plants Ⓢ	

Plant:
bush peas	— 172 seeds*	6.8 sq. ft.
carrots	— 354 seeds	3 sq. ft.

(2 seeds/center: thin to 1 plant/center)
cylindra beets	— 25 seeds	1 sq. ft.
onions	— 95 sets	3.8 sq. ft.
radishes	— 15 seeds	.25 sq. ft.

Start seedlings in flats:
tomatoes	— 10 seeds	
peppers	— 12 seeds	
sweet basil	— 2 seeds	
zinnias	— 6 seeds	
cucumbers	— 12 seeds	

On last frost date _____
(date)

Plant:
potatoes	— 87 starts	35 sq. ft.
	(10.9 lbs.)	

2 weeks after last frost date _____
(date)

Set out:
tomatoes (21″ centers)	— 5 plants	15 sq. ft.
bell peppers	— 6 plants	4 sq. ft.
sweet basil	— 1 plant	1 sq. ft.
cucumbers	— 6 plants	4 sq. ft.
zinnias	— 3 plants	3 sq. ft.

Plant:
pumpkins	— 2 seeds for 1 plant	6.3 sq. ft.
zucchini	— 1 seed for 1 plant	2.3 sq. ft.

6-8 weeks after last frost _____
(date)

As first crops come out, plant:
early corn (15″ centers)	— 34 seeds	20 sq. ft.

(2 seeds/center: thin to 1 plant/center)
bush limas	— 56 seeds	9 sq. ft.
cosmos	— 1 seed	1 sq. ft.

14 weeks after last frost _____
(date)

As potatoes come out, plant:
early corn	— 42 seeds	25 sq. ft.

(2 seeds/center: thin to 1 plant/center)
bush green beans	— 135 seeds*	10 sq. ft.

8–12 weeks before first frost _____
(date)

Start seedlings in flats:
leaf lettuce	— 24 seeds Ⓢ	
head lettuce	— 14 seeds Ⓢ	
broccoli	— 2 seeds	
stocks	— 10 seeds	
calendulas	— 10 seeds	

4–8 weeks before first frost of fall _____
(date)

As early corn comes out, set out:
leaf lettuce	— 12 plants Ⓢ	
head lettuce	— 7 plants Ⓢ	7.8 sq. ft.
broccoli	— 1 plants	1.6 sq. ft.
stocks	— 5 plants	5 sq. ft.
calendulas	— 5 plants	5 sq. ft.

Plant:
carrots	— 318 seeds	2.7 sq. ft.

(2 seeds/center: thin to 1 plant/center)
bush peas	— 172 seeds*	6.8 sq. ft.
chard	— 3 seeds	1 sq. ft.
radishes	— 15 seeds	.25 sq. ft.

Ⓢ = Stagger planting for a more continuous harvest.

★ = Spot additional seeds later where seeds do not germinate.

Ⓜ = Numbers given are the maximum which should be required for each crop for area involved. Less may be needed.

Spring
BED 1

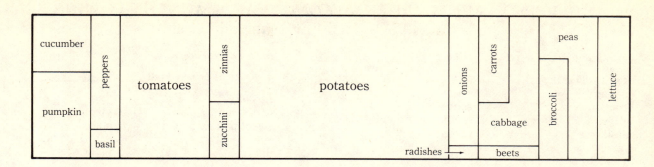

cucumber

peppers

pumpkin

basil

tomatoes

zinnias

zucchini

potatoes

onions

carrots

cabbage

radishes →

beets

peas

broccoli

lettuce

Summer
(BED 1)

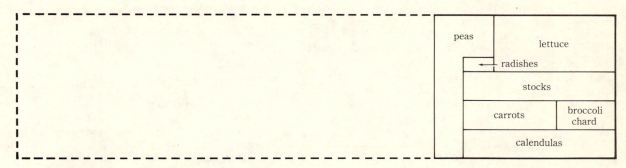

bush beans

corn

early corn

bush limas

Fall
(BED 1)

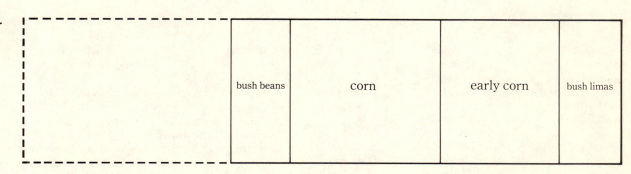

peas

lettuce

← radishes

stocks

carrots

broccoli chard

calendulas

Scale: 5/16 inch to 1 foot

ONE PERSON MINI-GARDEN, *SECOND* YEAR, 6-MONTH GROWING SEASON
240 SQUARE FEET (including path)

6 weeks before last frost of spring _____
(date)

Start seedlings in flat:

cabbage	— 8 seeds		
broccoli	— 4 seeds		
brussels sprouts	— 2 seeds		
cauliflower	— 2 seeds		
leaf lettuce	— 24 seeds Ⓢ		
head lettuce	— 14 seeds Ⓢ		
celery	— 24 seeds		
parsley	— 4 seeds		

2 weeks before last frost _____
(date)

Set out:

cabbage	— 4 plants Ⓜ	5.2	sq. ft.
broccoli	— 2 plants	2.6	sq. ft.
cauliflower	— 1 plant	1.3	sq. ft.
brussels sprouts	— 1 plant	2.3	sq. ft.
leaf lettuce	— 12 plants Ⓢ	7.8	sq. ft.
head lettuce	— 7 plants Ⓢ		

Plant:

spinach	— 60 seeds	2.2	sq. ft.
(2 seeds/center: thin to 1 plant/center)			
bush peas	— 172 seeds*	6.8	sq. ft.
carrots	— 318 seeds	2.7	sq. ft.
(2 seeds/center: thin to 1 plant/center)			
cylindra beets	— 25 seeds	1	sq. ft.
onion sets	— 95 sets	3.8	sq. ft.
radishes	— 15 seeds	.25	sq. ft.
garlic	— 8 cloves	.3	sq. ft.

Start seedlings in flats:

tomatoes	— 14 seeds		
bell peppers	— 12 seeds		
eggplant	— 2 seeds		
dill	— 2 seeds		

On last frost date _____
(date)

Plant:

potatoes	— 100 starts	40.2	sq. ft.
(12.5 lbs.)			

Start seedlings in flats:

cucumbers	— 12 seeds		
sweet basil	— 2 seeds		
cantaloup	— 10 seeds		
honeydew melons	— 10 seeds		
New Hampshire midget watermelons	— 50 seeds		
zinnias	— 6 seeds		
cosmos	— 6 seeds		

2 weeks after last frost _____
(date)

Set out:

tomatoes (21″ centers)	— 7 plants	20	sq. ft.
eggplant	— 1 plant	2.3	sq. ft.
bell peppers	— 6 plants	4	sq. ft.
parsley	— 1 plant	.7	sq. ft.

Plant:

early corn (15″ centers)	— 42 seeds	25	sq. ft.
(2 seeds/center: thin to 1 plant/center)			

Move celery to deeper flat.

4 weeks after last frost _____
(date)

Set out:

cucumbers	— 6 plants	4	sq. ft.
sweet potatoes	— 11 starts	4.5	sq. ft.
	(1.8 lbs.)		
dill	— 1 plant	.4	sq. ft.
sweet basil	— 1 plant	1	sq. ft.
cantaloup	— 5 plants	12.5	sq. ft.
honeydew melons	— 5 plants		
New Hampshire midget watermelons (12″ centers)	— 25 plants	16	sq. ft.
zinnias	— 3 plants	3	sq. ft.
cosmos	— 3 plants	3	sq. ft.

Set out:

celery	— 12 plants	2.5	sq. ft.

Plant:

bush green beans	— 188 seeds*	14	sq. ft.
bush lima beans	— 56 seeds*	9	sq. ft.
pumpkins	— 2 seeds for 1 plant	6.3	sq. ft.
zucchini	— 2 seeds for 1 plant	2.3	sq. ft.

8 weeks after last frost _____
(date)

As first planting comes out, plant:

potatoes	— 100 starts	40.2	sq. ft.
	(12.5 lbs.)		

12 weeks after frost _____
(date)

Start seedlings in flats:

broccoli	— 2 seeds		
cabbage	— 8 seeds Ⓢ		
stocks	— 8 seeds Ⓢ		
leaf lettuce	— 24 seeds		
head lettuce	— 14 seeds		
calendulas	— 8 seeds		

14 weeks after frost _____
(date)

As first potatoes come out, plant:

early corn	— 42 seeds	25	sq. ft.
(2 seeds/center: thin to 1 plant/center)			

16 weeks after frost _____
(date)

Set out:

broccoli	— 1 plant Ⓢ	1.3	sq. ft.
leaf lettuce	— 12 plants Ⓢ	7.8	sq. ft.
head lettuce	— 7 plants	2.7	sq. ft.
calendulas	— 4 plants	4	sq. ft.
stocks	— 4 plants	4	sq. ft.
cabbage	— 4 plants	5.2	sq. ft.

Plant:

chard	— 3 seeds	1	sq. ft.
radishes	— 15 seeds	.25	sq. ft.
peas	— 172 seeds*	6.8	sq. ft.
carrots	— 318 seeds	2.7	sq. ft.
(2 seeds/center: thin to 1 plant/center)			
spinach	— 60 seeds	2.2	sq. ft.
(2 seeds/center: thin to 1 plant/center)			

NOTE: By the second year, the curved bed surface gives you 120 square feet of planting area in each 100 square feet of bed.

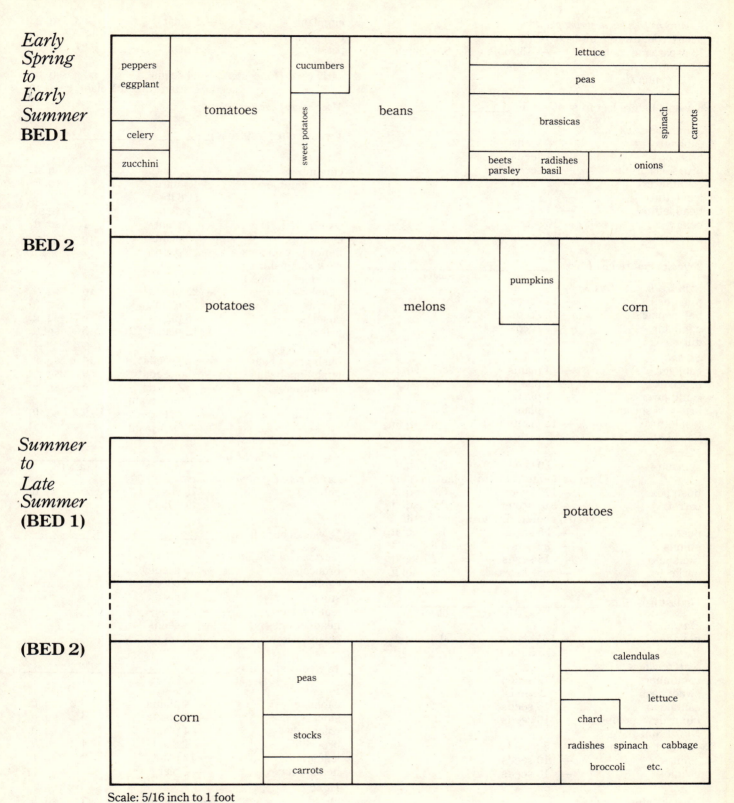

Early Spring to Early Summer **BED 1**

peppers
eggplant

celery

zucchini

tomatoes

cucumbers

sweet potatoes

beans

lettuce

peas

brassicas

spinach

carrots

beets parsley | radishes basil | onions

BED 2

potatoes

melons

pumpkins

corn

Summer to Late Summer **(BED 1)**

potatoes

(BED 2)

corn

peas

stocks

carrots

calendulas

lettuce

chard

radishes spinach cabbage

broccoli   etc.

Scale: 5/16 inch to 1 foot

Ⓢ = Stagger planting for a more continuous harvest.

✳ = Spot additional seeds later where seeds do not germinate.

Ⓜ = Numbers given are the maximum which should be required for each crop for area involved. Less may be needed.

ONE PERSON MINI-GARDEN, *THIRD* YEAR, 6-MONTH GROWING SEASON
380 SQUARE FEET (including paths)

As early as possible in spring plant:

1 bare root dwarf fruit tree	— 1 tree	64	sq. ft.
13 asparagus roots	— 13 roots	8	sq. ft.
32 strawberries (12″ centers)	— 32 plants	20	sq. ft.

6 weeks before last frost of spring _____ (date)

Start seedlings in flats:

cabbage	— 8 seeds
broccoli	— 4 seeds
brussels sprouts	— 2 seeds
cauliflower	— 2 seeds
leaf lettuce	— 24 seeds Ⓢ
head lettuce	— 14 seeds Ⓢ
celery	— 16 seeds
parsley	— 4 seeds

2 weeks before last frost _____ (date)

Start seedlings in flats:

tomatoes	— 14 seeds
bell peppers	— 12 seeds
eggplant	— 2 seeds
dill	— 2 seeds

Set out:

cabbage	— 4 plants	5.2	sq. ft.
broccoli	— 2 plants	2.6	sq. ft.
cauliflower	— 1 plant	1.3	sq. ft.
brussels sprouts	— 1 plant	2.3	sq. ft.
leaf lettuce	— 12 plants Ⓢ	7.8	sq. ft.
head lettuce	— 7 plants Ⓢ		

Plant:

spinach	— 60 seeds	2.2	sq. ft.
(2 seeds/center: thin to 1 plant/center)			
bush peas	— 172 seeds*	6.8	sq. ft.
carrots	— 318 seeds	2.7	sq. ft.
(2 seeds/center: thin to 1 plant/center)			
beets	— 25 seeds	1	sq. ft.
onions	— 95 sets	3.8	sq. ft.
radishes	— 15 seeds	.25	sq. ft.
garlic	— 8 cloves	.3	sq. ft.

On last frost date _____ (date)

Plant:

potatoes	— 124 starts (15.5 lbs.)	50	sq. ft.

Start seedlings in flats:

cucumbers	— 12 seeds
sweet basil	— 2 seeds
cantaloup	— 10 seeds
honeydew melons	— 10 seeds
New Hampshire midget watermelons	— 50 seeds
zinnias	— 10 seeds
cosmos	— 10 seeds

2 weeks after last frost _____ (date)

Set out:

tomatoes (21″ centers)	— 7 plants	20	sq. ft.

eggplant	— 1 plant	2.3	sq. ft.
bell peppers	— 6 plants	4	sq. ft.
parsley	— 1 plant	.7	sq. ft.

Plant:

early corn (15″ centers)	— 84 seeds	50	sq. ft.
(2 seeds/center: thin to 1 plant/center)			

Move celery to deeper flat

4 weeks after last frost _____ (date)

Set out:

cucumbers	— 6 plants	4	sq. ft.
sweet potatoes	— 11 starts (1.8 lbs.)	4.5	sq. ft.
dill	— 1 plant	.4	sq. ft.
sweet basil	— 1 plant	1	sq. ft.
cantaloup	— 5 plants	12.5	sq. ft.
honeydew melons	— 5 plants		
New Hampshire midget watermelons	— 25 plants	16	sq. ft.
zinnias	— 5 plants	5	sq. ft.
cosmos	— 5 plants	5	sq. ft.
celery	— 12 plants	2	sq. ft.

Plant:

bush green beans	— 188 seeds*	14	sq. ft.
bush lima beans	— 56 seeds*	9	sq. ft.
pumpkins	— 2 seeds for 1 plant	6.3	sq. ft.
zucchini	— 2 seeds for 1 plant	2.3	sq. ft.

8 weeks after last frost _____ (date)

As first planting comes out plant:

potatoes	— 75 starts (9.4 lbs.)	30	sq. ft.

12 weeks after frost _____ (date)

Start seedlings in flats:

broccoli	— 2 seeds
cabbage	— 8 seeds
stocks	— 8 seeds
leaf lettuce	— 24 seeds Ⓢ
head lettuce	— 14 seeds Ⓢ
calendulas	— 8 seeds

16 weeks after frost _____ (date)

Set out:

cabbage	— 4 plants	5.2	sq. ft.
stocks	— 4 plants	4	sq. ft.
calendulas	— 4 plants	4	sq. ft.
broccoli	— 1 plant	1.3	sq. ft.
leaf lettuce	— 12 plants Ⓢ	7.8	sq. ft.
head lettuce	— 7 plants Ⓢ		

Plant:

chard	— 3 seeds	1	sq. ft.
carrots	— 318 seeds	2.7	sq. ft.
(2 seeds/center: thin to 1 plant/center)			
radishes	— 15 seeds	.25	sq. ft.
bush peas	— 172 seeds*	6.8	sq. ft.

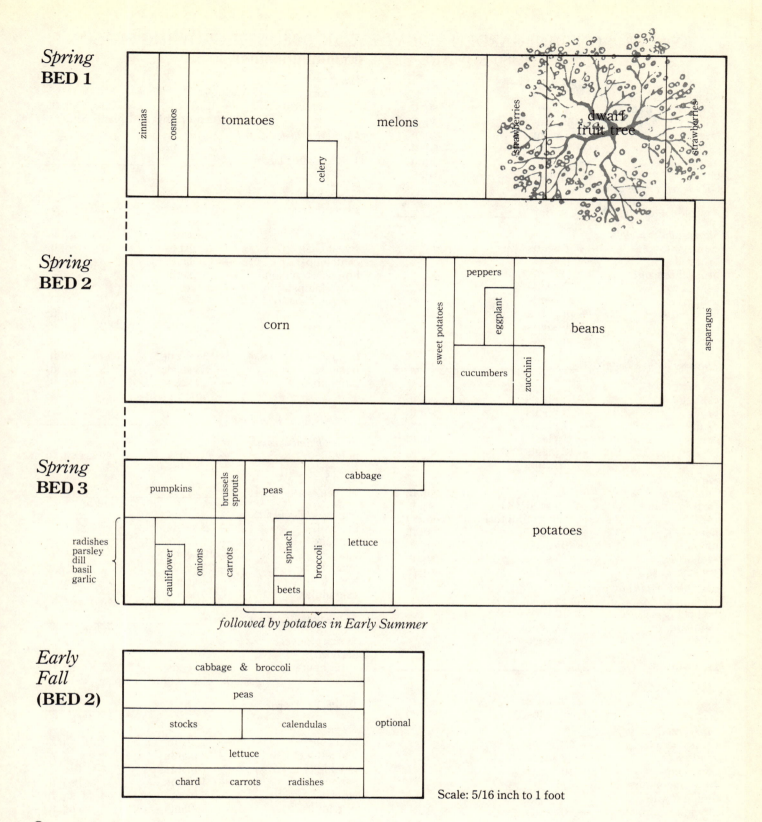

Spring
BED 1

zinnias | cosmos | tomatoes | melons | celery | strawberries | dwarf fruit tree | strawberries

Spring
BED 2

corn | sweet potatoes | peppers | eggplant | cucumbers | zucchini | beans | asparagus

Spring
BED 3

pumpkins | brussels sprouts | peas | cabbage | potatoes

radishes
parsley
dill
basil
garlic

cauliflower | onions | carrots | spinach | beets | broccoli | lettuce

followed by potatoes in Early Summer

Early Fall
(BED 2)

cabbage & broccoli
peas
stocks | calendulas | optional
lettuce
chard   carrots   radishes

Scale: 5/16 inch to 1 foot

Ⓢ = Stagger planting for a more continuous
      harvest.

✱ = Spot additional seeds later where seeds do
      not germinate.

Ⓜ = Numbers given are the maximum which
      should be required for each crop for area
      involved. Less may be needed.

ONE PERSON MINI-GARDEN, *FOURTH* YEAR, 6-MONTH GROWING SEASON
380 SQUARE FEET (including paths)

As soon as possible in spring, plant:
An additional bare root

dwarf fruit tree	— 1 tree	64	sq. ft.
relocate strawberries	— 32 plants Ⓜ	20	sq. ft.
lavender	— 1 plant	4	sq. ft.
sage	— 1 plant	2.3	sq. ft.
marjoram	— 1 plant	1	sq. ft.
chives	— 3 plants	.5	sq. ft.

OR whatever herbs desired

6 weeks before last frost of spring _____
(date)

Start seedlings in flats:

cabbage	— 8 seeds
broccoli	— 4 seeds
brussels sprouts	— 2 seeds
cauliflower	— 2 seeds
leaf lettuce	— 24 seeds Ⓢ
head lettuce	— 14 seeds Ⓢ
celery	— 16 seeds
parsley	— 4 seeds

2 weeks before last frost _____
(date)

Set out:

cabbage	— 4 plants	5.2	sq. ft.
broccoli	— 2 plants	2.6	sq. ft.
cauliflower	— 1 plant	1.3	sq. ft.
brussels sprouts	— 1 plant	2.3	sq. ft.
leaf lettuce	— 12 plants Ⓢ	7.8	sq. ft.
head lettuce	— 7 plants Ⓢ		

Plant:

bush peas	— 172 seeds*	6.8	sq. ft.
carrots	— 318 seeds	2.7	sq. ft.

(2 seeds/center: thin to 1 plant/center)

beets	— 25 seeds	1	sq. ft.
onions	— 95 sets	3.8	sq. ft.
radishes	— 15 seeds	.25	sq. ft.
garlic	— 8 sets	.3	sq. ft.

Start seedlings in flats:

tomatoes	— 14 seeds
bell peppers	— 12 seeds
eggplant	— 2 seeds
dill	— 2 seeds

On last frost date _____
(date)

Plant:

potatoes	— 99 starts	40	sq. ft.
	(12.4 lbs.)		

Start seedlings in flats:

cucumbers	— 12 seeds
sweet basil	— 2 seeds
cantaloup	— 10 seeds
New Hampshire midget water- melons	— 10 seeds

2 weeks after last frost _____
(date)

Set out:

tomatoes (21″ centers)	— 7 plants	20	sq. ft.
eggplant	— 1 plant	2.3	sq. ft.
bell peppers	— 6 plants	4	sq. ft.
parsley	— 1 plant	.7	sq. ft.

Plant:

early corn (15″ centers)	— 42 seeds	25	sq. ft.

(2 seeds/center: thin to 1 plant/center)

Move celery to deeper flat

4 weeks after last frost _____
(date)

Set out:

cucumbers	— 6 plants	4	sq. ft.
sweet potatoes	— 11 starts	4.5	sq. ft.
	(1.8 lbs.)		
dill	— 1 plant	.4	sq. ft.
sweet basil	— 1 plant	1	sq. ft.
cantaloup	— 5 plants	12.5	sq. ft.
honeydew melons	— 5 plants		
New Hampshire midget water- melons	— 25 plants	16	sq. ft.
celery	— 12 plants	2	sq. ft.

Plant:

bush green beans	— 188 seeds*	14	sq. ft.
bush lima beans	— 56 seeds*	9	sq. ft.
pumpkins	— 2 seeds	6.3	sq. ft.
	for 1 plant		

8 weeks after last frost _____
(date)

As first planting comes out plant:

potatoes	— 99 starts	40	sq. ft.
	(12.4 lbs.)		

12 weeks after frost _____
(date)

Start seedlings in flats:

broccoli	— 2 seeds
cabbage	— 8 seeds
stocks	— 10 seeds
leaf lettuce	— 24 seeds Ⓢ
head lettuce	— 14 seeds Ⓢ
calendulas	— 10 seeds

14 weeks after frost _____
(date)

As first potatoes come out plant:

early corn (15″ centers)	— 42 seeds	25	sq. ft.

(2 seeds/center: thin to 1 plant/center)

16 weeks after frost _____
(date)

Set out:

broccoli	— 1 plant	1.3	sq. ft.
leaf lettuce	— 12 plants Ⓢ	7.8	sq. ft.
head lettuce	— 7 plants Ⓢ		
cabbage	— 4 plants	5.2	sq. ft.
stocks	— 5 plants	5	sq. ft.
calendulas	— 5 plants	5	sq. ft.

Plant:

carrots	— 318 seeds	2.7	sq. ft.

(2 seeds/center: thin to t plant/center)

chard	— 3 seeds	1	sq. ft.
radishes	— 15 seeds	.25	sq. ft.
bush peas	— 172 seeds	6.8	sq. ft.
spinach	— 60 seeds	2.2	sq. ft.

(2 seeds/center: thin to 1 plant/center)

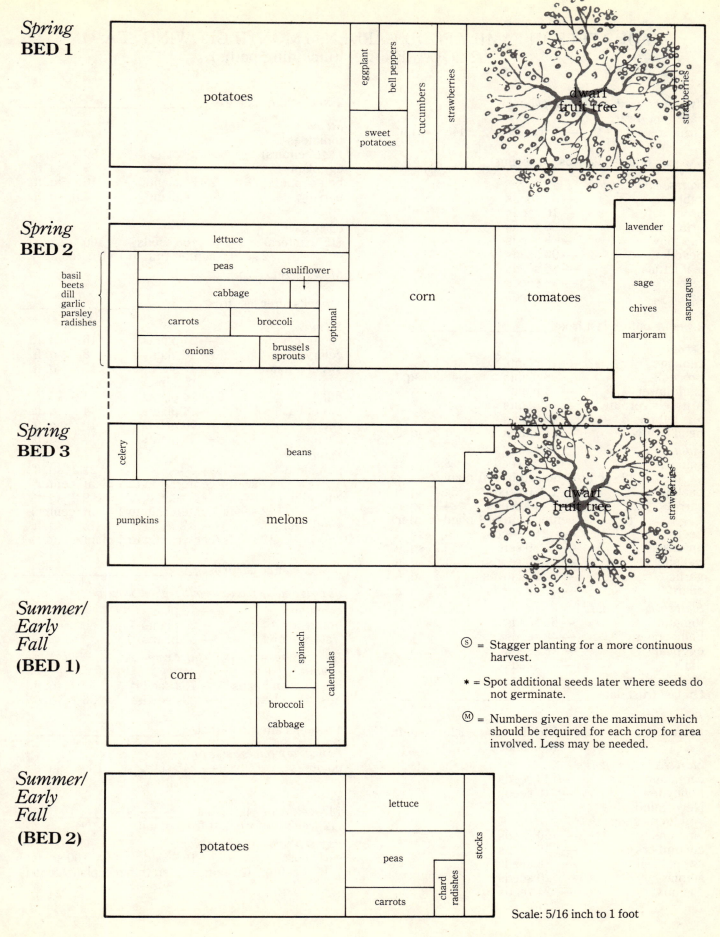

Spring **BED 1**

potatoes

eggplant

bell peppers

sweet potatoes

cucumbers

strawberries

dwarf fruit tree

strawberries

Spring **BED 2**

basil
beets
dill
garlic
parsley
radishes

lettuce

peas

cauliflower

cabbage

carrots

broccoli

onions

brussels sprouts

optional

corn

tomatoes

lavender

sage

chives

marjoram

asparagus

Spring **BED 3**

celery

beans

pumpkins

melons

dwarf fruit tree

strawberries

Summer/ Early Fall **(BED 1)**

corn

spinach

broccoli

cabbage

calendulas

S = Stagger planting for a more continuous harvest.

* = Spot additional seeds later where seeds do not germinate.

M = Numbers given are the maximum which should be required for each crop for area involved. Less may be needed.

Summer/ Early Fall **(BED 2)**

potatoes

lettuce

peas

carrots

chard

radishes

stocks

Scale: 5/16 inch to 1 foot

FOUR PERSON FAMILY FOOD GARDEN, 6-MONTH GROWING SEASON
1,302 SQUARE FEET (including paths)

As soon as possible in spring, plant:

bare root dwarf fruit trees	— 7 trees	448	sq. ft.

6 weeks before last frost of spring _____
(date)

Start seedlings in flats:

cabbage	— 32 seeds
broccoli	— 16 seeds
brussels sprouts	— 8 seeds
cauliflower	— 8 seeds
head lettuce	— 96 seeds Ⓢ
leaf lettuce	— 56 seeds Ⓢ
celery	— 96 seeds
parsley	— 16 seeds

2 weeks before last frost _____
(date)

Set out:

cabbage	— 16 plants Ⓜ		
broccoli	— 8 plants	45.6	sq. ft
cauliflower	— 4 plants		
brussels sprouts	— 4 plants		
leaf lettuce	— 48 plants Ⓢ		
head lettuce	— 28 plants Ⓢ	31.2	sq. ft.

Plant:

spinach	— 234 seeds	8.8	sq. ft.
(2 seeds/center: thin to 1 plant/center)			
bush peas	— 1,370 seeds*	54.4	sq. ft.
carrots	— 1,414 seeds	24	sq. ft.
(2 seeds/center: thin to 1 plant/center)			
beets	— 100 seeds	4	sq. ft.
onions	— 380 sets	15.2	sq. ft.
radishes	— 60 seeds	1	sq. ft.
garlic	— 32 cloves	1.2	sq. ft.
chard	— 12 seeds	4	sq. ft.

Start seedlings in flats:

tomatoes	— 56 seeds
bell peppers	— 48 seeds
eggplant	— 8 seeds
dill	— 8 seeds

On last frost date _____
(date)

Plant:

potatoes	— 546 starts	220	sq. ft.
	(68.25 lbs.)		

Start seedlings in flats:

cantaloup	— 40 seeds
honeydew	— 40 seeds
New Hampshire midget watermelons	— 160 seeds
cucumbers	— 48 seeds
sweet basil	— 8 seeds
zinnias	— 20 seeds
cosmos	— 24 seeds

2 weeks after last frost _____
(date)

Set out

tomatoes (21″ centers)	— 28 plants	80	sq. ft.
eggplant	— 4 plants	9.2	sq. ft.
bell peppers	— 24 plants	16	sq. ft.
parsley	— 4 plants	2.8	sq. ft.

Plant:

early corn (15″ centers)	— 168 seeds	100	sq. ft.
(2 seeds/center: thin to 1 plant/center)			

Move celery to deeper flat

4 weeks after last frost _____
(date)

Set out:

cucumbers	— 24 plants	16	sq. ft.
celery	— 48 plants	8	sq. ft.
sweet potatoes	— 44 starts	18	sq. ft.
	(7.2 lbs.)		
dill	— 4 plants	1.6	sq. ft.
sweet basil	— 4 plants	4	sq. ft.
zinnias	— 10 plants	10	sq. ft.
cosmos	— 12 plants	12	sq. ft.

Plant:

pumpkins	— 8 seeds	25.2	sq. ft.
(2 seeds/center: thin to 1 plant/center)			
zucchini	— 8 seeds	9.2	sq. ft.
(2 seeds/center: thin to 1 plant/center)			
sunflowers	— 8 seeds	15	sq. ft.
(2 seeds/center: thin to 1 plant/center)			

6 weeks after last frost _____
(date)

As peas and carrots come out, replant bed with:

cantaloup	— 20 plants		
honeydew	— 20 plants	50	sq. ft.
watermelons	— 80 plants		

As early brassicas and lettuce come out, replant bed with:

bush green beans	— 752 seeds*	56	sq. ft.
bush lima beans	— 224 seeds*	36	sq. ft.

12 weeks after last frost _____
(date)

As first corn comes out, plant:

potatoes	— 248 starts	100	sq. ft.
	(31 lbs.)		

14 weeks after last frost _____
(12 weeks before first frost of fall)
(date)

As first potatoes come out plant:

early corn	— 168 seeds	100	sq. ft.
(15″ centers) (2 seeds/center: thin to 1 plant/center)			

Start seedlings in flats:
broccoli   — 16 seeds
cabbage   — 32 seeds
stocks   — 20 seeds
leaf lettuce   — 96 seeds Ⓢ
head lettuce   — 56 seeds Ⓢ
calendulas   — 20 seeds

18 weeks after last frost _____
(8 weeks before first fall frost)   (date)

As last potatoes come out:

Set out:

broccoli	— 4 plants	5.2	sq. ft.
leaf lettuce	— 48 plants Ⓢ		
head lettuce	— 28 plants Ⓢ	31.2	sq. ft.
calendulas	— 10 plants	10	sq. ft.
stocks	— 10 plants	10	sq. ft.
cabbage	— 16 plants	20.8	sq. ft.

Plant:

chard	— 12 seeds	4	sq. ft.
radishes	— 60 seeds	1	sq. ft.
spinach	— 240 seeds	8	sq. ft.

(2 seeds/center: thin to 1 plant/center)

Ⓢ = Stagger planting for a more continuous harvest.

⋆ = Spot additional seeds later where seeds do not germinate.

Ⓜ = Numbers given are the maximum which should be required for each crop for area involved. Less may be needed.

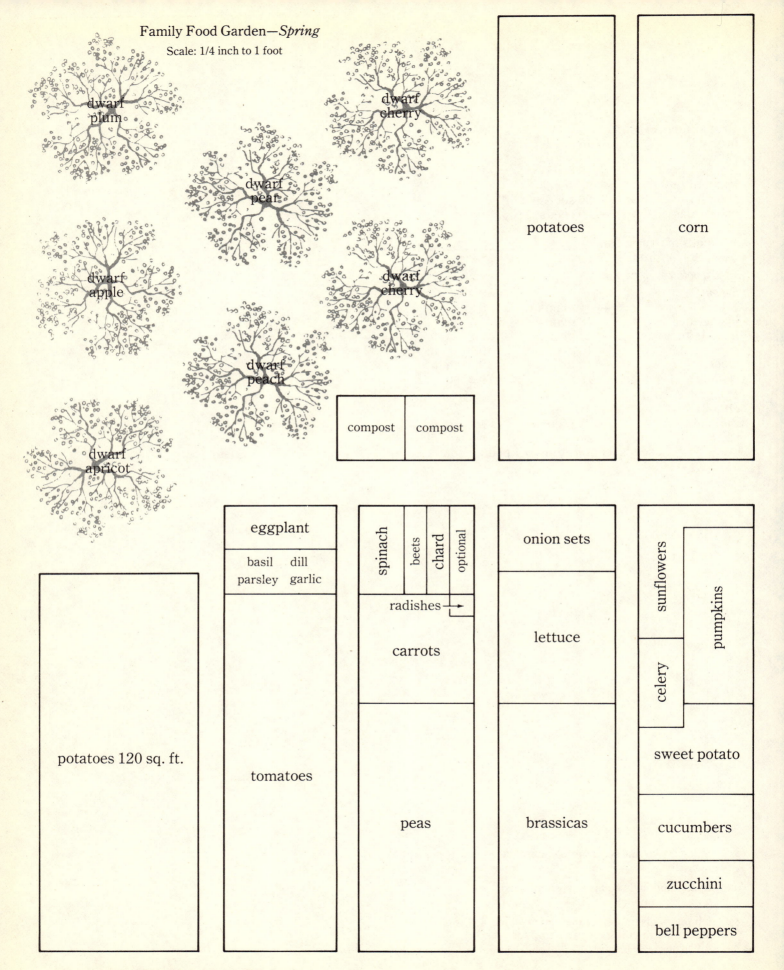

Family Food Garden—*Spring*
Scale: 1/4 inch to 1 foot

dwarf
plum

dwarf
cherry

dwarf
pear

dwarf
apple

dwarf
cherry

dwarf
peach

dwarf
apricot

potatoes

corn

compost | compost

eggplant

basil   dill
parsley   garlic

potatoes 120 sq. ft.

tomatoes

spinach | beets | chard | optional

radishes →

carrots

peas

onion sets

lettuce

brassicas

sunflowers

pumpkins

celery

sweet potato

cucumbers

zucchini

bell peppers

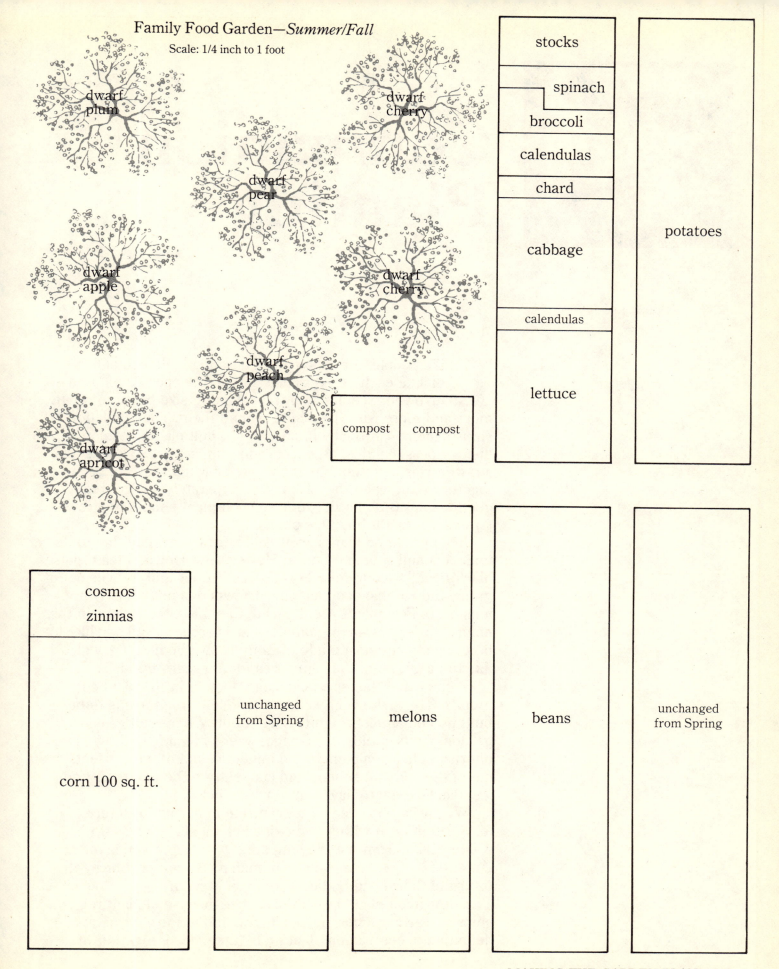

Family Food Garden—*Summer/Fall*

Scale: 1/4 inch to 1 foot

dwarf
plum

dwarf
cherry

dwarf
pear

dwarf
apple

dwarf
cherry

dwarf
peach

dwarf
apricot

stocks

spinach

broccoli

calendulas

chard

cabbage

calendulas

lettuce

potatoes

compost   compost

cosmos

zinnias

corn 100 sq. ft.

unchanged
from Spring

melons

beans

unchanged
from Spring

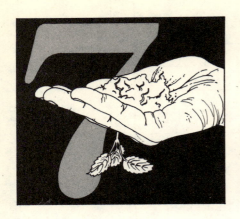

Companion Planting

L ike people in relationships, certain plants like and dislike each other, depending on the specific natures involved. Seedlings of transplanting size begin to relate more and more with the plants around them. These relationships become especially important as adult plants develop distinct personalities, essences, and aromas. Green beans and strawberries, for example, thrive better when they are grown together than when they are grown separately. To get really good tasting Bibb lettuce, one spinach plant should be grown for every four Bibb lettuce plants.

In contrast, no plants grow well near wormwood due to its toxic leaf and root excretions. However, wormwood tea repels black fleas, discourages slugs, keeps beetles and weevils out of grain, and combats aphids. So wormwood is not a totally noxious herb. Few plants are. Instead, they have their place in the natural order of things. Tomatoes are narcissistic. They like to be grown in compost made from their own bodies. They also like to be grown in the same area for a 5-year period.

Weeds are often specialists and doctors in the plant community. They take very well to a sick soil which needs to be built up and almost seem to seek it out. Where cultivated garden plants could not manage, weeds are able to draw phosphorus, potash, calcium, trace minerals, and other nutrients out of the soil and subsoil and concentrate them in their bodies. Plants seem to have uncanny instincts.

Weeds can be used to concentrate nutrients for future fertilization or to withdraw noxious elements, such as unwanted salts, from the growing area. A deficient soil is often enriched by the use of weeds in man-made compost or by the return of their dead bodies to the soil in nature.

Companion planting is the constructive use of plant relationships by the gardener, horticulturist, and farmer. A scientific definition of companion planting is "the placing together of plants having complementary physical demands." A more accurate, living, and spiritual description is "the growing together of all those elements and beings which encourage *life* and *growth:* the creation of a microcosm that includes vegetables, fruits, trees, bushes, wheat, flowers, weeds, birds, soil, microorganisms, water, nutrients, insects, toads, spiders, and chickens."

Companion planting is still an experimental field in which much more research needs to be performed. The age of the plants involved and the percentage of each of the types of plants grown together can be critical, as can be their relative proximity to one another. Companion planting should, therefore, be used with some caution and much observation. You may want to study the causes of some of these beneficial relationships. Are they due to root excretions, plant aroma, or the pollen of composite flowers that attracts certain beneficial predatory insects? Companion planting is a fascinating field.

Some of the companion planting techniques you can eventually try and experience are ones for Health, Nutrition, Physical Complementarity, and Weed, Insect, and Animal Relationships.

Health

Better Growth—The growing together of green beans and strawberries, and Bibb lettuce and spinach, has already been mentioned. On the other side of the spectrum, onions, garlic, chives, and shallots seriously inhibit the growth of peas and beans. In between the extremes, *bush* beans and beets may be grown together with no particular advantage or disadvantage to either plant. *Pole* beans and beets, on the other hand, do not get along well. The nuances are amazing. What is the difference between bush and pole beans? No one appears to know the scientific reason yet, but the difference can be observed. Ehrenreid Pfeiffer developed a method known as crystallization, from which one can predict in advance whether or not plants are good companions. In this technique, part of a plant is ground up and mixed with a chemical solution. After the solution dries, a crystalline pattern remains. Different plants have distinct, representative patterns. When two plant solutions are mixed, the patterns increase, decrease, or stay the same in strength and regularity. Sometimes both patterns improve, indicating a reciprocal, beneficial influence. Or both may deteriorate in a reciprocal negative reaction. One pattern may improve while another deteriorates, indicating a one-sided advantage. Both patterns may remain the same, indicating no particular companion advantage or disadvantage. And one plant pattern may increase or decrease in quality while the other undergoes no change. Two plants which suffer a decrease in quality on a one-to-one basis may show an increase in strength in a one-to-ten ratio.

Spacing for Better Companions—Using biointensive spacing with the plant leaves barely touching allows good companions to be better friends.

All Round Beneficial Influence—Certain herbs and one tree have a beneficial influence on the plant community. These plants and their characteristics are:[55]

- ☐ Lemon Balm
  Creates a beneficial atmosphere around itself and attracts bees. Part of the mint family.

- ☐ Marjoram
  Has a "beneficial effect on surrounding plants."

- ☐ Oregano
  Has a "beneficial effect on surrounding plants."

- ☐ Stinging Nettle *(Urtica dioica)*
  "Helps neighboring plants to grow more resistant to spoiling." Increases essential oil content in many herbs. "Stimulates humus formation." Helps stimulate fermentation in compost piles. As a tea, promotes plant growth and helps strengthen plants. Concentrates sulfur, potassium, calcium, and iron in its body.

- ☐ Valerian *(Valeriana officinalis)*
  "Helps most vegetables." Stimulates phosphorus activity in its vicinity. Encourages health and disease resistance in plants.

- ☐ Chamomile *(Chamomile officinalis)*
  A lime specialist. "Contains a growth hormone which . . . stimulates the growth of yeast." In a 1:100 ratio helps growth of wheat. As a tea, combats diseases in young plants such as damping off. Concentrates calcium, sulfur, and potash in its body.

- ☐ Dandelion *(Taraxacum officinale)*
  Increases "aromatic quality of all herbs." "In small amounts" helps most vegetables. Concentrates potash in its body.

- ☐ Oak Tree
  Concentrates calcium in its bark (bark ash is 77% calcium). In a special tea, it helps plants resist harmful diseases. The oak tree provides a beneficial influence around it which allows excellent soil to be produced underneath its branches. An excellent place to build a compost pile for the same reason, but keep the pile at least 6 feet from the tree trunk so an environment will not be created near the tree which is conducive to disease or attractive to harmful insects.

Stinging nettle and tomatoes. Good garden companions.

55. Helen Philbrick and Richard B. Gregg, *Companion Plants and How to Use Them*, Devin-Adair Company, Old Greenwich, CT, 1966, pp. 16, 57, 58, 60, 65, 84, 85, 86, 92. Rudolf Steiner, *Agriculture—A Course of Eight Lectures*, Biodynamic Agricultural Association, London, 1958, pp. 93–95, 97, 99, 100.

NOTE: Lemon balm, marjoram, oregano, dandelion, chamomile, stinging nettle, and valerian are perennials. They are traditionally planted in a section along one end of the bed so they need not be disturbed when the bed is replanted.

Soil Life Stimulation—Stinging nettle helps stimulate the microbial life and this helps plant growth.

Soil Improvement—Sow thistle *(Sonchus oleraceus)* brings up nutrients from the subsoil to enrich a depleted topsoil. After years of dead sow thistle bodies have enriched the topsoil, heavier-feeding grasses return. This is part of nature's recycling program, in which leached-out nutrients are returned to the topsoil, as well as a natural method for raising new nutrients to the upper layers of the soil. It has been estimated that *one* rye plant grown in good soil produces an average of 3 miles of roots per day, 387 miles of root and 6,603 miles of root hairs during a season. Plants are continuously providing their own composting program underground. In one year 800–1,500 pounds of roots per acre are put into the soil by plants in a small garden, and red clover puts 1,200–3,850 pounds of roots into the soil in the same period of time.[56]

Plant root systems improve the topsoil by bringing up nutrients from the subsoil.

Nutrition

Over Time—Companion planting "over time" has been known for years as "crop rotation." After proper preparation of the soil, heavy feeders are planted. These are followed by heavy givers and then light feeders. This is a kind of *agricultural recycling* in which man and plants participate to return as much to the soil as has been taken out.

Heavy feeders, most of the vegetables we like and eat (including corn, tomatoes, squash, lettuce, and cabbage), take large amounts of nutrients, especially nitrogen, from the soil. In the biointensive method, after heavy feeders have been harvested, phosphorus and potash are returned to the soil in the form of compost. This is supplemented with some bone meal (calcium, phosphorus, and a little nitrogen) and a small amount of wood ash (potash and some trace minerals). To return nitrogen to the soil, heavy givers are grown. Heavy givers are nitrogen-fixing plants or legumes, such as peas, beans, alfalfa, clover, and vetch. Fava beans are good for this purpose. Not only do they bring large amounts of nitrogen into the soil, they also excrete substances which help eradicate tomato wilt–causing organisms. (*Caution:* some people of Mediterranean descent *are fatally allergic* to fava beans, even though the beans are very popular and widely eaten by these people. People on certain medications experience the same

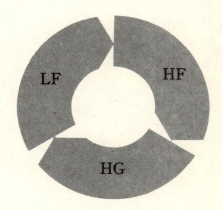

AGRICULTURAL
RECYCLING

56. Helen Philbrick and Richard B. Gregg, *Companion Plants and How to Use Them,* Devin-Adair Company, Old Greenwich, CT, 1966, pp. 75–76.

reaction. Check with your physician first.) After heavy givers, light feeders (all root crops) should be planted to give the soil a rest before the next heavy feeder onslaught. Three vegetables are low nitrogen lovers: turnips (a light feeder), sweet potatoes (a light feeder), and green peppers (a heavy feeder of nutrients other than nitrogen). The two light feeders would normally be planted after heavy givers, which put a lot of nitrogen into the soil. You may find it useful to have them follow a heavy feeder instead. It would also be good to have the green pepper follow a heavy feeder. (It normally comes after a heavy giver and a light feeder.) You should experiment with these out-of-sequence plantings.

In Space—Companion planting of heavy feeders, heavy givers, and light feeders can be done in the same growing area at the same time. For example, corn, beans, and beets can be intermingled in the same bed. Just as with companion planting "over time," the gardener should proceed with care. In the above combination, the beans must be bush beans, since pole beans and beets do not grow well together. Also, pole beans have been reported to pull the ears off corn stalks. Pole beans have been grown successfully with corn, however; and a vegetable such as carrots may be substituted for the beets to allow you to use the tall beans. When different plants are grown together, you sacrifice some of the *living mulch* advantage to companion planting "in space" because of the different plant heights. One way to determine the spacing for different plants

TWO-CROP COMPANION PLANTING
Circles show average root growth diameters.

C = Corn
B = Beets

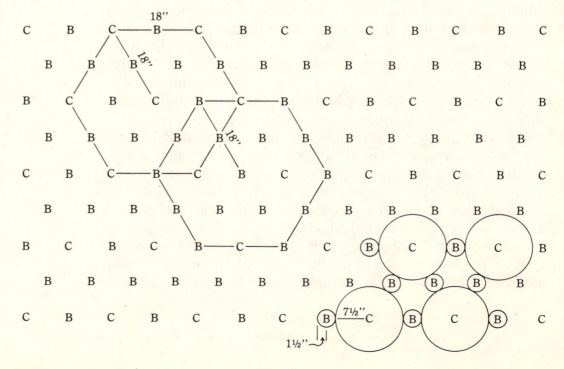

grown together is to add their spacing together and divide by 2. If you grow corn and beets together, add 15 inches to 3 inches for a total of 18 inches. Divide by 2 and you get a per-plant spacing of 9 inches. The beets, then, would be 9 inches from each corn plant and vice versa. Each corn plant will be 18 inches from each corn plant and most beet plants will be 9 inches from the other beet plants nearest to them. In the drawing on page 124, note that each corn plant gets the 7-1/2 inches in each direction that it requires for a total growing area with a "diameter" of 15 inches. Each beet plant, at the same time, gets the 1-1/2 inches it requires in each direction for a growing space with a 3-inch "diameter."

An easier, and probably just as effective, method of companion planting "in space" is to divide your planting bed into separate sections (or beds within a bed) for each vegetable. In this method, a grouping of corn plants would be next to a group of bush beans and a group of beets. In reality, this is a kind of companion planting "over time," since there are heavy feeder, heavy giver, and light feeder sections within a bed. Roots extend 1 to 4 feet around each plant, so it is also companion planting "in space." *We recommend you use this approach.* Additional spacing patterns no doubt exist and will be developed for companion planting "in space."

MULTI-CROP COMPANION PLANTING "IN SPACE"

corn	bush beans	beets	corn	bush beans	beets

A spacing example for 3 crops grown together—corn (a heavy feeder), bush beans (a heavy giver), and beets (a light feeder)—is given on page 126. You should note that this approach to companion planting "in space" uses more bush bean and beet plants than corn.

Compromise and Planning—You can see by now that companion planting involves selecting the combination of factors which works best in your soil and climate. Fortunately, the myriad of details fall into a pattern of simple guidelines. Within the guidelines, however, there are so many possible combinations that the planning process can become quite complex. Be easy on yourself. Do only as much companion planting as is easy for you and comes naturally. What you learn this year and

THREE-CROP COMPANION PLANTING
Circles show average root growth diameters.

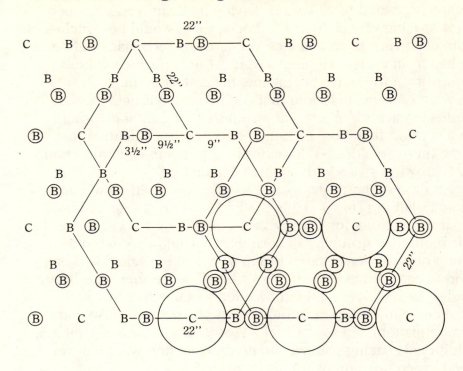

C = Corn
B = Beets
Ⓑ = Beans

Using the sun/shade technique is one way to make the most of your plants' physically complementary characteristics.

Lettuce plants can be nestled among other larger plants for partial shade.

Corn can provide the shade which cucumbers enjoy.

become comfortable with can be applied next year, and so on. An easy place to start is with salad vegetables, since these are generally companions. Also, it is easier to companion-plant over time rather than in space. Since you probably will not have enough area to use an entire bed for each crop, you might create several heavy feeder, heavy giver, and light feeder sections within each bed. You may want to grow a preponderance of crops from one group such as the heavy feeders. (It is unlikely that you will want to grow 1/3 of each crop type.) Therefore, you will need to make adjustments, such as adding extra fertilizer and compost, when you follow one heavy feeder with another. Because of lack of space, you may have to grow some plants together that are not companions. If so, you may need to be satisfied with lower yields, lower-quality vegetables, and less healthy plants. Or, you might try to alter your diet to one which is still balanced but more in line with the balances of nature. At any rate, you can see it is useful to plan your garden in advance. You will need to know how many pounds of each vegetable you want during the year, how many plants are needed to grow the weight of vegetables you require, when to plant seeds both in flats and in the ground, when and how to rotate your crops, and when to raise and transplant herbs so they will be at the peak of their own special influence. Use the charts at the end of the Seed Propagation chapter to assist in this work. To have their optimum effect as companions, herb plants should be reasonably mature when transplanted into a bed for insect control or general beneficial influence. It is easiest to plan your garden 12 months at a time and always at least 3 months in advance.

Physical Complementarity

Sun/Shade—Many plants have a special need for sunlight or a lack of it. Cucumbers, for example, are very hard to please. They like heat, moisture, a well-drained soil, and some shade. One way to provide these conditions is to grow cucumbers with corn. The corn plants, which like heat and sun, can provide partial shade for the cucumber plants. Lettuce or carrot plants nestled among other plants for partial shade is another example. Sunflowers, which are tall and like lots of sun, should be planted at the north side of the garden. There they will not shade other plants and will receive enough sun for themselves.

Shallow/Deep Rooting—There *is* no good, detailed example available. A dynamic process does occur over time, however, as plants with root systems of differing depths and breadths work different areas of the soil in the planting bed.[57]

Fast/Slow Maturing—The French intensive gardeners were able to grow as many as four crops in a growing bed at one time due to the staggered growth and maturation rates of different vegetables. The fact that the edible portions of the plants appear in different vertical locations also helped. Radishes, carrots, lettuce, and cauliflower were grown together in one combination used by the French to take advantage of these differences.

Vertical Location of the Plant's Edible Portion—See Fast/Slow Maturing example.

Weed, Insect, and Animal Relationships

"Weed" Control—The growth of beets, members of the cabbage family, and alfalfa is slowed down significantly by the presence of "weeds." To minimize the "weed" problem for sensitive plants, you can grow other plants during the previous season that discourage "weed" growth in the soil. Two such plants are kale and rape. Another example is the *Tagetes minuta,* a Mexican marigold.[58] "In many instances it has killed even couch grass, convolvulus (wild morning glory), ground ivy, ground elder, horsetail and other persistent weeds that defy most poisons. Its lethal action works only on starch roots and had no effect on woody ones like roses, fruit bushes and shrubs. Where it had grown, the soil was enriched as well as cleansed, its texture was refined and lumps of clay were broken up."[59]

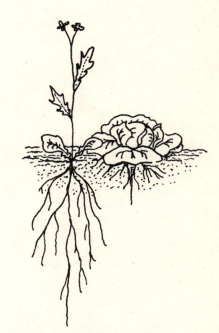

Sow thistle grown with lettuce is one example of shallow/deep rooting symbiosis. Their roots do not compete with each other.

An example of using fast/slow maturing to advantage is to interplant carrots with radishes.

57. Also see Emanuel Epstein, "Roots," *Scientific American,* May 1973, pp. 48–58.

58. Illegal in California, where it is considered a noxious weed which aggressively takes over cattle lands and prevents fodder from growing. It is probably also toxic to the cattle.

Some care should be taken when using this marigold, however, since vegetable crops might also be killed by it and the plant does give off toxic excretions. Tests should be performed to determine how long the influence of these excretions stays with the soil. But to cleanse a soil of pernicious weeds and thereby get it ready for vegetables, *Tagetes minuta* appears to be a useful plant.

Insect/Pest Control—At least two elements are important in companion planting for insect control. Older plants with well-developed aroma and essential oil accumulations should be used. You want the insects to know the plant is there. Second, it is important to use a large variety of herbs. Five different herbs help discourage the cabbage worm butterfly, although one herb may work better than another in your area. Testing several herbs will help you determine the ones that work best. The more "unpleasant" plants there are in the garden, the sooner harmful insects will get the idea that your garden is not a pleasant place to eat and propagate. The use of a large number of herbs also fits in with the diversity of plant life favored by nature. Much more research needs to be performed to determine the optimum ages for control plants and number of control plants per bed which provides optimum control. Too few plants will not control an insect problem and too many may reduce your yields. Some insect controls are:

☐ *Whiteflies:* Marigolds—but not pot marigolds (calendula)—and flowering tobacco. The first are supposed to excrete substances from their roots which are absorbed by the other plants. When the whiteflies suck on the other plants, they think they are on a strong-tasting marigold and leave. The flowering tobacco plant has a sticky substance on the underside of its leaves where whiteflies stick and die when they come there for a meal.

☐ *Ants:* Spearmint, tansy and pennyroyal. (Mint often attracts whiteflies so you may want to grow a few marigolds around for control, but not so many as to possibly impair the taste of the mint and certainly not one of the more poisonous marigolds. This is another area for compromise. A few insects are probably less of a problem than mint with a strange taste.)

☐ *Nematodes and Root Pests:* Mexican marigold *(Tagetes minuta)* "eliminates all kinds of destructive eelworms . . . wireworms, millipedes and various root eating pests from its vicinity." The French marigold, *Tagetes patula,* eliminates some "plant-destroying nematodes . . . at up to a range of three feet . . . The beneficial . . . eelworms which do not feed on healthy roots were not affected."[60]

59. Audrey Wynne Hatfield, *How to Enjoy Your Weeds,* Sterling Publishing Co., Inc., New York, 1971. ©1969 by Audrey Wynne Hatfield.

- *Aphids: Yellow* Nasturtiums are a *decoy* for black aphids. They may be planted at the base of tomatoes for this purpose. Remove the plants and aphids before the insects begin to produce young with wings. Spearmint, stinging nettle, southernwood and garlic help repel aphids.

- *Tomato Worms:* Borage reportedly helps repel tomato worms and/or serves as a decoy. Its blue flowers also attract bees.

- *Gophers:* Elderberry cuttings placed in gopher holes and runs reportedly repel these animals. Daffodils, castor beans, and gopher plant *(Euphorbia lathyrus)* are all poisonous to gophers. Be careful with the latter two, however, as they are also *very* toxic to children, especially infants.

Birds, Bees, and Animals—Sow thistle attracts birds. Some birds are vegetarian and some are omnivorous. The omnivorous birds may stay for a main course of insects after a seed snack. If you are having trouble with birds eating the berries in your berry patch you could erect a wren house in the middle of it. Wrens are insectivores and they will not bother the berries. But they will attack any bird, however large, that comes near the nest.

Hummingbirds are attracted to red flowers. They especially like the tiny, red, torchlike flowers of the pineapple sage in our garden. Bees may be attracted by hyssop, thyme, catnip, lemon balm, pot marjoram, sweet basil, summer savory, borage, mint, and *blue* flowers. Once in the garden they help pollinate.

Animals are good for the garden. Their manures can be used as fertilizers. Chickens are one of the few reliable controllers of earwigs, sowbugs, pill bugs, snails, grasshoppers, and maggots, though you may have to protect young seedlings from chickens pecking tasty plant morsels.

Companion planting in all its aspects can be a complex and often mind-boggling exercise—if you worry too much about the details. Nature is complex and we can only assist and approximate her in our creations. If we are gentle in relation to her forces and balances, she can correct our errors and fill in for our lack of understanding. As you gain more experience, sensitivity and feeling, more companion planting details will come naturally. Don't let too much planning spoil the fun and excitement of working with nature!

Birds and plants can work together too. The *sonchus* plant seeds attract the finch, which afterwards eats aphids from the cabbage.

60. Ibid., p. 17.

A LIST OF COMMON GARDEN VEGETABLES, THEIR COMPANIONS AND THEIR ANTAGONISTS[61]

	COMPANIONS	ANTAGONISTS
Asparagus	Tomatoes, parsley, basil	
Beans	Potatoes, carrots, cucumbers, cauliflower, cabbage, summer savory, most other vegetables and herbs	Onions, garlic, gladiolus
Bush Beans	Potatoes, cucumbers, corn, strawberries, celery, summer savory	Onions
Pole Beans	Corn, summer savory	Onions, beets, kohlrabi, sunflowers
Beets	Onions, kohlrabi	Pole beans
Cabbage Family (cabbage, cauliflower, kale, kohlrabi, broccoli)	Aromatic plants, potatoes, celery, dill, chamomile, sage, peppermint, rosemary, beets, onions	Strawberries, tomatoes, pole beans
Carrots	Peas, leaf lettuce, chives, onions, leeks, rosemary, sage, tomatoes	Dill
Celery	Leeks, tomatoes, bush beans, cauliflower, cabbage	
Chives	Carrots	Peas, beans
Corn	Potatoes, peas, beans, cucumbers, pumpkins, squash	
Cucumbers	Beans, corn, peas, radishes, sunflowers	Potatoes, aromatic herbs
Eggplant	Beans	
Leeks	Onions, celery, carrots	
Lettuce	Carrots and radishes (lettuce, carrots, and radishes make a strong team grown together), strawberries, cucumbers	
Onions (and garlic)	Beets, strawberries, tomatoes, lettuce, summer savory, chamomile (sparsely)	Peas, beans

61. From *Organic Gardening and Farming*, February 1972, p. 54.

	COMPANIONS	ANTAGONISTS
Parsley	Tomatoes, asparagus	
Peas	Carrots, turnips, radishes, cucumbers, corn, beans, most vegetables and herbs	Onions, garlic, gladiolus, potatoes
Potatoes	Beans, corn, cabbage, horse-radish (should be planted at corners of patch), marigolds, eggplant (as a lure for Colorado potato beetle)	Pumpkins, squash, cucumbers, sunflowers, tomatoes, raspberries
Pumpkins	Corn	Potatoes
Radishes	Peas, nasturtiums, lettuce, cucumbers	
Soybeans	Grows with anything, helps everything	
Spinach	Strawberries	
Squash	Nasturtiums, corn	
Strawberries	Bush beans, spinach, borage, lettuce (as a border)	Cabbage
Sunflowers	Cucumbers	Potatoes
Tomatoes	Chives, onions, parsley, asparagus, marigolds, nasturtiums, carrots	Kohlrabi, potatoes, fennel, cabbage
Turnips	Peas	

A COMPANIONATE HERBAL FOR THE ORGANIC GARDEN[62]

A list of herbs, their companions, their uses, including some beneficial weeds and flowers.

Basil	Companion to tomatoes, dislikes rue intensely. Improves growth and flavor. Repels flies and mosquitoes.
Bee Balm	Companion to tomatoes; improves growth and flavor.
Borage	Companion to tomatoes, squash, and strawberries; deters tomato worm; improves growth and flavor.
Caraway	Plant here and there; loosens soil.

62. From *Organic Gardening and Farming,* February 1972, pp. 52 and 53.

Catnip	Plant in borders; deters flea beetle.
Chamomile	Companion to cabbage and onions; improves growth and flavor.
Chervil	Companion to radishes; improves growth and flavor.
Chives	Companion to carrots; improves growth and flavor.
"Dead" Nettle	Companion to potatoes; deters potato bug; improves growth and flavor.
Dill	Companion to cabbage; dislikes carrots; improves growth and health of cabbage.
Fennel	Plant away from gardens. Most plants dislike it.
Flax	Companion to carrots, potatoes; deters potato bug; improves growth and flavor.
Garlic	Plant near roses and raspberries; deters Japanese beetles; improves growth and health.
Horseradish	Plant at corners of potato patch to deter potato bug.
Henbit	General insect repellent.
Hyssop	Deters cabbage moth; companion to cabbage and grapes. Keep away from radishes.
Lamb's Quarters	This edible weed should be allowed to grow in moderate amounts in the garden, especially in corn.
Lemon Balm	Sprinkle throughout garden.
Lovage	Improves flavor and health of plants if planted here and there.
Marigolds	The workhorse of the pest deterrents. Plant throughout garden; they discourage Mexican bean beetles, nematodes, and other insects.
Mint	Companion to cabbage, and tomatoes; improves health and flavor; deters white cabbage moth.
Marjoram	Here and there in garden; improves flavors.
Mole Plant	Deters moles and mice if planted here and there.
Nasturtium	Companion to radishes, cabbage, and cucurbits*; plant under fruit trees. Deters aphids, squash bugs, striped pumpkin beetles. Improves growth and flavor.
Petunia	Protects beans.

Pot Marigold (Calendula)	Companion to tomatoes, but plant elsewhere in garden too. Deters asparagus beetle, tomato worm, and general garden pests.
Purslane	This edible weed makes good ground cover in the corn.
Pigweed	One of the best weeds for pumping nutrients from the subsoil, it is good for potatoes, onions, and corn. Keep weeds thinned.
Peppermint	Planted among cabbages, it repels the white cabbage butterfly.
Rosemary	Companion to cabbage, beans, carrots, and sage; deters cabbage moth, bean beetles, and carrot fly.
Rue	Keep it far away from sweet basil; plant near roses and raspberries; deters Japanese beetle.
Sage	Plant with rosemary, cabbage, and carrots; keep away from cucumbers. Deters cabbage moth, carrot fly.
Southernwood	Plant here and there in garden; companion to cabbage, improves growth and flavor; deters cabbage moth.
Sow Thistle	This weed in moderate amounts can help tomatoes, onions, and corn.
Summer Savory	Plant with beans and onions; improves growth and flavor. Deters bean beetles.
Tansy	Plant under fruit trees; companion to roses and raspberries. Deters flying insects, Japanese beetles, striped cucumber beetles, squash bugs, ants.
Tarragon	Good throughout garden.
Thyme	Here and there in garden. It deters cabbage worm.
Valerian	Good anywhere in garden.
Wild Morning Glory**	Allow it to grow in corn.
Wormwood	As a border, it keeps animals from the garden.
Yarrow	Plant along borders, paths, near aromatic herbs; enhances essential oil production.

*Plants in the gourd family.

**We discourage the growing of wild morning glory anywhere in your garden, since it is a pernicious weed. Cultured morning glory is fine, however.

This information was collected from many sources, most notably the Bio-Dynamic Association and the Herb Society of America.

A Balanced Natural Backyard Ecosystem and Insect Life

Insects and people are only one part of the complex, interrelated world of life. Both are important, integral parts of its living dynamism. Insects are an important part of the diet for many birds, toads, frogs, and other insects in nature's complex food chain. With the biointensive method comes a realization that every time you relate to an insect you are relating with the whole system of life, and that, if you choose to dominate the insect world system of life, rather than work in harmony with it, part of the system dies. For example, we depend on insects for pollination of many of our vegetables, fruits, flowers, herbs, fibers, and cover crops. When we choose dominating, death-oriented control, then the scope and depth of our life become narrower and smaller. So, in reality, we are detracting from our own lives rather than adding to them. In trying to isolate an insect and deal with it separately out of relation to the ecosystem in which it lives, we work against the whole life support system, which in turn works against us in counterproductive results.

When an excess of insects appears in a garden, nature is indicating that a problem exists in the life of that garden. In each case, we need to become sensitive to the source of the imbalance. Observation and gentle action will produce the best results. In contrast, when poisons are used, beneficial predators are killed as well as the targeted harmful insects. Spraying trees to eliminate worms or beetles often results in a secondary outbreak of spider mites or aphids because ladybugs and other predators cannot reestablish themselves as quickly as the destructive species.

Paying attention to the soil and plant health, planning a varied environment, and leaving a few wild spaces for unexpected benefactors minimizes pest losses more effectively than the use of poisons. Also, in order to have beneficial insects in your food producing area, there must be their food—some of the harmful ones! If there are no harmful insects, then there will be few, if any, beneficial insects ready to act as a seed population of friendly guardians. This seeming paradox—the presence of both kinds of insects for the most healthy garden—is symbolic of nature's balances. Not too much moisture, but enough. Not too much aeration, but enough. Not too many harmful insects, but enough. You find the need for these balances everywhere—in the compost pile, in the soil, in the mini-climate, and in the backyard microcosm as a whole.

In a small backyard garden ecosystem or mini-farm it is especially important to welcome all life forms as much as possible. Ants destroy fruitfly and housefly larvae and keep the garden cleaned of rotting debris. Have you ever squashed a snail and watched how the ants come to whisk the remains away almost within a day? Earwigs are carnivorous and prey on other insects. Tachinid flies parasitize caterpillars, earwigs, tomato worms, and grasshoppers by laying their eggs in them. We've found cabbage worms immobilized and bristling with cottony white torpedoes the size of a pinhead—larvae of the braconid wasp, which will hatch and go in search of more cabbage worms. Toads eat earwigs, slugs, and other pests. Chickens control earwigs, sowbugs, and flies. Even the ancient and fascinating snails have a natural predator: humans!

The first step in insect control is to cultivate strong, vigorous plants by cultivating a healthy place in which they can grow. Normally (about 90% of the time), insects only attack unhealthy plants. Just as a healthy person who eats good food is less susceptible to disease, so are healthy plants that are on a good diet less susceptible to plant diseases and insect attack. It is *not* the insect which is the source of the problem, but rather an unhealthy soil. The soil needs your energy, not the insect. The uninterrupted growth stressed by the biointensive method is also important to the maintenance of plant health. In short, we are shepherds providing the conditions our plants need for healthy, vigorous growth.

Some elements to consider:

☐ Is the soil being dug properly?

☐ Are the proper plant nutrients available in the soil?

☐ Is enough compost being used?

☐ Is the soil pH within reasonable limits for the plant being grown?

☐ Are the seedlings being transplanted properly?

☐ Are the plants being watered properly?

☐ Is weeding being done effectively?

- [ ] Is the soil being maintained in a way which will enable it to retain moisture and nutrients?

- [ ] Are the plants receiving enough sun?

- [ ] Are the plants being grown in season?

Another method of providing for plant health and for minimizing insect and disease problems is to keep a correct balance of phosphorus and potash in the soil in relation to the amount of nitrogen present. (See page 32.) The optimal ratio among these elements is still to be determined. Research also needs to be completed to determine the *minimum* amounts of these elements (in pounds per 100 square feet) which should be in the soil. (Smaller amounts of organic fertilizer elements are required in comparison with soluble synthetic chemical fertilizers, since they break down more slowly and remain available to the plants for a longer period of time.)

Proper planning of the garden can eliminate many insect and disease problems!

- [ ] Use seeds which grow well in your climate and soil.

- [ ] Use plant varieties which are weather hardy, insect resistant, and disease resistant. New strains, especially hybrids (whether developed for higher yields, disease resistance, or other reasons), should usually be avoided. Some hybrids produce food of lower nutritive value in comparison with older strains, and often use up nutrients from the soil at a more rapid rate than a living soil can sustain over time. Hybrids are also often very susceptible to a few diseases even when they are greatly resistant to many prevalent ones.

- [ ] Companion plant: grow vegetables and flowers together that grow well with each other.

- [ ] Normally, do not put the same vegetable in the same growing bed each year. This practice invites disease.

- [ ] Rotate your crops: follow heavy feeders with heavy givers and then light feeders.

Encourage natural insect control by enlisting the aid of nature:

Birds—Some are vegetarians. Others are omnivorous. A bird which stops for a seed snack may remain for an insect dinner. A house wren feeds 500 spiders and caterpillars to her young in one afternoon, a brown thrasher consumes 6,000 insects a day, a chickadee eats 138,000 canker worm eggs in 25 days, and a pair of flickers eat 5,000 ants as a snack. A Baltimore oriole can consume 17 hairy caterpillars a minute. The presence of birds may be encouraged by the use of moving water, the planting of bushes for their protection, the planting of sour berry bushes for food, and the growing of plants that have seeds the birds like to eat.

Toads, Snakes, and Spiders—also eat insects and other garden pests. Toads eat as many as 10,000 insects in 3 months, including cutworms, slugs, crickets, ants, caterpillars, and squash bugs.

Ladybugs—are good predators since they eat one particular pest, aphids, and do not eat beneficial insects. Ladybugs eat 40–50 insects per day and their larvae eat even more.

Praying Mantids—are predators which should only be used in infestation emergencies, since they eat beneficial as well as harmful insects. They are not selective and even eat each other.

Trichogramma Wasps—lay their eggs in hosts such as moth and butterfly larvae which eat leaves. When they hatch, the wasp larvae parasitize the host larvae, which fail to reach maturity. Up to 98 percent of the hosts are rendered useless in this way.

Tachinid Flies—are parasites which help control caterpillars, Japanese beetles, earwigs, gypsy moths, brown tail moths, tomato worms, and grasshoppers.

Syrphid Flies—are parasites that prey upon aphids and help pollinate crops.[63]

After you have done everything possible to provide a healthy, balanced garden for your plants, you may still have insect problems. If so, you should approach the insects involved with the idea of *living control* rather than elimination. Minimization of the pest allows dynamic living control to occur: beneficial predators need the harmful insects as a food source. Total elimination of the insect would disrupt nature's balances.

If there is a problem, identify the pest and try to determine if an *environmental change* can solve the problem. In our research garden, we have minimized (not eliminated though!) gophers by introducing gopher snakes.

The pocket Golden Guides on *Insects and Insect Pests* are invaluable guides for getting to know the creatures that inhabit your garden with you. Out of the 86,000 species of insect in the United States, 76,000 are considered beneficial or friendly.[64] So be careful! An insect which looks ugly or malicious may be a friend. If you can't seem to find an obvious culprit, try exploring at night with a flashlight. Many are active then.

---

63. Beatrice Trum Hunter, *Gardening Without Poisons*, Berkeley Publishing Corp., New York, 1971, pp. 31, 37, 42, 43, 48. The Berkeley Edition was published by arrangement with the Houghton Mifflin Company, who are the original publishers of *Gardening Without Poisons*.

64. Ibid., p. 28.

Ask yourself if the *damage* is *extensive* enough to warrant a "policing" effort. During 1972 bush beans were grown in one of our test beds. The primary leaves were almost entirely destroyed by the 12-spotted cucumber beetle. But in most cases the damage was not so rapid as to prevent the development of healthy secondary leaves. The less tender secondary leaves were ultimately attacked and became quite heavily eaten. About 80% of the secondary leaf area remained, however, and very tasty, unblemished beans were harvested. The yield in pounds was still 3.9 times the United States average! Recent tests have shown that leaf damage of up to 30% by insects can actually increase the yield of some crops. At another extreme you may wish to sacrifice some yield for beauty: many destructive caterpillars become beautiful butterflies. To get the yield you want and/or to encourage the presence of butterflies, you can plant extra plants of the crop they like.

We often underestimate the ability of plants to take care of themselves. The damage done by insects often affects a very small percentage of the edible crop. Because of this, many biointensive gardeners plant a little extra for the insect world to eat. This practice is beautiful, mellow, and in keeping with life-giving forms of insect control. Furthermore, extensive research has shown that beneficial organisms found in soil and ocean environments can withstand stress, in the form of temperature, pressure, pH, and nutrient fluctuations, to a much greater degree in an organically fertilized medium than in a synthetically fertilized medium. I suspect researchers will come to a similar conclusion about plant resistance to insect attack.

Any time an insect or other pest invades your garden, there is an opportunity to learn more about nature's cycles and balances. Learn why they are there and find a *living control.* Look for controls that will affect only the one harmful insect. Protect new seedlings from birds and squirrels with netting or chicken wire, trap earwigs in dry dark places, wash aphids off with a strong spray of water, or block ants with a sticky barrier of vaseline, Tanglefoot, or tack trap. While you are doing this, continue to strive for a long-term natural balance in your growing area.

At our Common Ground Research Garden the only three pest problems we have had to put a lot of energy into are snails, slugs, and gophers. The first few years we primarily trapped gophers. A lot of time was spent checking and resetting traps and worrying about them, yet the damage the gophers did was probably only about 5%. We later found that, in addition to gopher snakes, they really do not like certain things placed in their holes (sardines, garlic juice, fish heads, male urine, and dead gophers). Here a combination of approaches and gentle persistence has paid off. Gopher snakes are, of course, the preventers of a population explosion. Finally, gophers may be blocked with strips of daffodils. Daffodils contain arsenic in their bulbs and thereby can discourage these animals.

We have a simple routine for snails and slugs. At the end of the spring rains we go out at night with flashlights and collect gallons of them. The snails are then dropped in buckets of soapy water, which will kill them. If you use soap that is quick to degrade, they can be dumped on the compost pile the next day. Most of them are caught in the first 3 nights. Going out occasionally over the next 2 weeks will allow you to catch new ones that were too small in the first sweep or that have just hatched from eggs laid in the soil. Such a concentrated cleanup can be effective for several months. There is also the red-bellied snake (*Storeria occipitomaculata*) in Canada, which eats large numbers of slugs. A sorghum mulch is reported to repel slugs as well.

Another kind of problem has been solved through observation. For example, one year a cherry tomato bed was wilting. Several people, including a graduate student studying insects, told us it was caused by nematodes. When we dug down into the soil to look for the damage, we discovered the real source. The soil was bone dry below the upper 8 inches. A good soaking took care of the problem and we learned not to take gardening advice on faith, but to always check it out for ourselves—as we hope you will.

Some other living control approaches to try are:

Hand-picking the insects from the plants once you are certain the insect involved is *harmful* and the source of the problem. Consult a book such as *Insect Pests* (see Bibliography), which has color drawings of insects in their several stages (nymph, larva, adult). Some insects are harmful in only one stage and can even be beneficial in others.

Spraying. In general, insects may be divided into two categories—those which chew and bite plants and those which suck juices from them. *Chewing or biting insects* include caterpillars, flea beetles, potato bugs, cankerworms, cutworms, and grasshoppers. *Aromatic and distasteful* substances such as garlic, onion, and pepper sprays can discourage them. *Sucking insects* include aphids, thrips, nymphs of the squash bug, flies, and scale insects. Soap solutions (not detergents, which would damage the plant and soil as well as the insects), clear miscible oil solutions, and other solutions which asphyxiate the insects by coating their tender bodies and preventing respiration through body spiracles or breathing holes help control these insects.

Traps, such as shredded newspaper in clay pots turned upside down on sticks in the garden, will attract earwigs during daylight hours. Snails and slugs can be trapped under damp boards. They retreat to these places in the heat and light of the day.

Barriers, such as the sticky commercial Tanglefoot substance, will catch some insects crawling along tree trunks during part of their life cycle. When insects are caught in this manner, infestation of the tree in a later season is often prevented. (Tanglefoot barriers must be applied to apple tree trunks in July to catch codling moth larvae leaving the tree. This will minimize codling moth infestation the following spring. Plan ahead!) Plant barriers and decoys can also be used. Grow a vegetable or flower preferred by a particular insect away from the garden to attract it to another location. Place repellant plants near a vegetable or flower that needs protection.

Companion Plants. You may also wish to plant some herbs in your beds for insect control. The age and number of plants used per 100 square feet determine the herb's effectiveness. A young plant does not have an aroma or root exudate strong enough to discourage harmful insects or to attract beneficial ones. Similarly, too few herbs will not control a pest or attract a needed predator. Too many herbs may retard vegetable growth and yield. Composite flowers, such as pot marigolds (calendulas) and sunflowers, are excellent attractants for predatory insects because their large supplies of pollen serve as predator food sources. A few (2–4) plants per 100-square-foot bed will probably suffice. We have not done many experiments with them yet, however, since accurate testing can take 2 to 3 years for one herb grown with one food plant to control one insect. This requires more time and funding than we have. You may wish to try some of these biodynamic observations, though. It's a lot of fun to try and see for yourself!

Probably the most important form of insect control with plants is just diverse cropping. The biointensive method uses diverse cropping and we have only experienced 5% to 10% crop loss due to pests when we are performing "the method" properly. Biodynamic gardeners and farmers also use diverse cropping and have suggested planting 10% more area to make up for crop losses. In contrast, the monocropped acreage of today's commercial agriculture provides an ideal uniform habitat for widespread attack by pests which favor a single crop. Pesticides have been recommended to counteract the problem inherent in monocropping. Yet the Environmental Protection Agency estimates "that thirty years ago American farmers used 50 million pounds of pesticides and lost 7 percent of their crop before harvest. Today, farmers use twelve times more pesticides yet the percentage of the crops lost before harvest has almost doubled."[65] In fact, many pesticides targeted for one pest species actually cause increases in

65. See James S. Turner, *A Chemical Feast: Report on the Food and Drug Administration* (Ralph Nader Study Group Reports) Grossman, New York, 1970. Cited in Frances Moore Lappe and Joseph Collins, *Food First,* Houghton Mifflin Company, Boston, 1977, p. 49.

INSECT PESTS AND PLANT CONTROLS[66]

Insect Pest	Plant Control
Ants	— Spearmint, Tansy, Pennyroyal
Aphids	— Nasturtium, Spearmint, Stinging Nettle, Southernwood, Garlic
Mexican Bean Beetle	— Potatoes
Black Fly	— Intercropping, Stinging Nettle
Cabbage Worm Butterfly	— Sage, Rosemary, Hyssop, Thyme, Mint, Wormwood, Southernwood
Striped Cucumber Beetle	— Radish
Cutworm	— Oak leaf mulch, Tanbark
Black Flea Beetle	— Wormwood, Mint
Flies	— Nut Trees, Rue, Tansy, spray of Wormwood and/or Tomato
June Bug Grub	— Oak leaf mulch, Tanbark
Japanese Beetle	— White Geranium, Datura
Plant Lice	— Castor Bean, Sassafras, Pennyroyal
Mosquito	— Legumes
Malaria Mosquito	— Wormwood, Southernwood, Rosemary
Moths	— Sage, Santolina, Lavender, Mint, Stinging Nettle, Herbs
Colorado Potato Beetle	— Eggplant, Flax, Green Beans
Potato Bugs	— Flax, Eggplant
Slugs	— Oak leaf mulch, Tanbark
Squash Bugs	— Nasturtium
Weevils	— Garlic
Wooly Aphis	— Nasturtium
Worms in Goats	— Carrots
Worms in Horses	— Tansy leaves, Mulberry leaves

the numbers of non-targeted pests. By their action on the physiology of the plant, pesticides can make a plant more nutritionally favorable to insects, thereby increasing the fertility and longevity of feeding pests.[67]

66. Helen Philbrick and Richard B. Gregg, *Companion Plants and How to Use Them,* Devin-Adair Company, Old Greenwich, CT, 1966, pp. 52–53. This book and others should be consulted for the proper use and application rates of these plant remedies. Improper use or application can cause problems and could be harmful to you, your plants, and animals.

67. Francis Chaboussou, "The Role of Potassium and of Cation Equilibrium in the Resistance of the Plant." Chaboussou is the Director of Research at the French National Institute for Agricultural Research, Agricultural Zoology Station of the South-West, 22 Pont de la Maye, France.

It is becoming more evident that pesticides are not an effective solution for crop loss due to pests. It seems that *diverse* cropping without pesticides may be able to reduce total pest losses more than monocropping with pesticides, even in large-scale agriculture. Using standard agricultural practices, Cornell University researchers, in a five-year study completed in 1970, found that without pesticides the insect population could be cut in half when only two crops were grown together.[68] You will make this, and even more, possible when you grow a diversity of plants in your backyard with life-giving techniques!

Only a brief introduction to insect control has been given here. An emphasis has been placed on philosophy and general approaches. *The Bug Book, Companion Plants,* and *Gardening Without Poisons* (see Bibliography) have already vigorously explored in detail the spectrum of organic insect control. These books give companion planting combinations, recipes for insect control solutions, and addresses from which predatory insects can be obtained.

I hope each person who reads this book will try at least one small, 3-foot-by-3-foot biointensive growing bed. You should find the experience fun and exciting beyond your wildest expectations!

68. See Jeff Cox, "The Technique That Halves Your Insect Population," *Organic Gardening and Farming,* May 1973, pp. 103–104.

Bibliography

Many key books are available from Ecology Action's Bountiful Gardens Mail Order Service. Write 19550 Walker Road, Willits, CA 95490 for a free catalog, for current prices, and to inquire about other titles. Ecology Action publishes several research papers on the biodynamic/French intensive method and has books, booklets, and information on beekeeping, mini-farming, homesteading, and related topics. Use the books listed here to make up your own mini-course(s) for study of those areas which interest you most.

Animals

Bement, C. U. *The American Poulterer's Companion.* New York: Harper & Brothers, 1871. 304 pp.

Craig, John A., and Marshall, F. R. *Sheep Farming.* New York: Macmillan.

Cuthbertson, Sir David (Chairman). *The Nutrient Requirements of Farm Livestock—No. 2 Ruminants.* London: Agricultural Research Council, 1965. 264 pp.

de Baïracle Levi, Juliette. *Herbal Handbook for Farm and Stable.* Emmaus, PA: Rodale Press, 1976. 320 pp.

Devendra, C., and Burns, Marca. *Goat Production in the Tropics.* Commonwealth Agricultural Bureaux, Farnham Royal, Bucks, England, 1970. 177 pp.

Jordan, Whitman H. *The Feeding of Animals.* New York: Macmillan, 1903. 450 pp.

Mackenzie, David. *Goat Husbandry.* London: Faber & Faber, 1970. 336 pp.

McKay, G. L., and Larsen, C. *Principles and Practice of Butter-Making.* New York: John Wiley & Sons, 1908. 351 pp.

Morrison, Frank B. *Feeds and Feeding.* 21st ed. Ithaca, NY: Morrison Publishing, 1949. 1,207 pp.

Watson, George C. *Farm Poultry.* New York: Macmillan.

Arid

Appropriate Technology Development Association. "Water Harvesting." *ApTech Newsletter* (Box 311, Gandhi Bhawan, Lucknow–226001 U.P. India).

Arnon, I. *Crop Production in Dry Regions.* Vols. 1 and 2. London: Leonard Hill, 1972. Vol. 1: 649 pp.; Vol. 2: 682 pp.

Bailey, L. H. *Dry Farming.* The Rural Science Series. New York: Macmillan, 1911. 416 pp.

Bainbridge, David A. *Drylander.* Newsletter, Vol. I, No. 2, "Using Trees to Maintain Groundwater," p. 3. Riverside, CA: University of California, 1987. 12 pp.

————. *Drylander.* Newsletter, Vol. II, No. 1, "Pitcher Irrigation," p. 3. Riverside, CA: University of California, 1988.

Bromfield, Louis. *Malabar Farm,* pp. 10–17, 252, 257–261. New York: Harper & Row, 1948. 405 pp.

Brookbank, George. *Desert Gardening.* Tucson, AZ: Fisher Books, 1988. 271 pp. Out of print.

"Cross Ridging Holds Precious Rainwater on the Land." *Developing Countries Farm Radio,* Package No. 14. DCFR (c/o Massey Ferguson, 595 Bay Street, Toronto, Canada), 1988. 5 pp.

Ebeling, Walter. *Handbook of Indian Foods and Fiber of Arid America.* Berkeley, CA: University of California Press, 1986. 971 pp.

Fargher, John. "Arid Landwater Harvesting." Orange, MA: John Fargher, 1985. 8 pp.

Friends of the Arboretum. "Desert Plants." Friends of the Arboretum (P.O. Box 3607, Tucson, AZ 85722).

Goldstein, W. *Alternative Crops, Rotations and Management Systems for the Palouse.* Pullman, WA: Washington State University, 1986. 333 pp.

Gore, Rick. "No Way to Run a Desert." *National Geographic,* June 1985, 694–719.

The Green Deserts Project. "Green Deserts." The Green Deserts Project (Rougham, Bury St. Edmunds, Suffolk IP30 9LY, England). Information sheet. A key group doing work to help revitalize desert areas. You can learn and help by becoming a member. Periodic informational newsletters.

Hall, A. E. *Agriculture in Semi-Arid Environments.* New York: Springer-Verlag, 1979. 340 pp.

Harsch, Johnathon. "Dryland Farming May Return As

Ground Water Levels Drop." *Christian Science Monitor,* 29 July 1980, 10.

Hugalle, N. R. "Tied Ridges Improve Semi-Arid Crop Yields." *International Ag-Sieve* 1, No. 2 (1988): 4.

Indian Agricultural Research Institute. *A New Technology for Dryland Farming.* New Delhi: Indian Agricultural Research Institute, 1970. 189 pp.

International Federation of Organic Agricultural Movements. "Trench Composting for Arid Regions." IFOAM (R.D. 1, Box 323, Kutztown, PA 19530), June 1976. Newsletter.

International Institute of Rural Reconstruction, Siland, Cauite, Philippines and Indian Rural Reconstruction Movement. "Crop Management in the Semi-Arid Tropics." Bangalore, India. 14 pp.

Nehrling, Arno, et al. *Easy Gardening with Drought-Resistant Plants.* New York: Dover, 1968. 320 pp.

Nyhuis, Jane. *Desert Harvest.* Meals for Millions (Box 42622, Tucson, AZ 85733), 1982. 63 pp.

Riddle, R. "Drought-Resistant Fruit and Nuts for the Water-Efficient Landscape." *CFRG Journal,* 1989, 8–19.

Sunset Editors. *Desert Gardening.* Menlo Park, CA: Sunset-Lane, 1967. 96 pp.

_____. *Waterwise Gardening: Landscaping Ideas, Watering Systems and Unthirsty Plants.* Menlo Park, CA: Sunset-Lane, 1989. 96 pp.

Tonge, Peter. "Twice the Yield, Half the Work." *Christian Science Monitor,* 12 January 1988, 23.

UNICEF. "Some Sources of Nutrition from the Dry Season Garden." New York: UNICEF. 1 p.

United Nations Environmental Program. *Desertification Control.* UNEP (P.O. Box 30552, Nairobi, Kenya). Magazine published twice a year.

"What an Inch of Rain Is Worth." *Successful Farming,* January 1974, 79.

Widtsoe, John A. *Dry Farming.* New York: Macmillan, 1919. 445 pp. An important basic work.

Bed Preparation

Sunset Editors. "Getting Started with the French Intensive Method." *Sunset,* September 1972, 168.

Companion Planting

Carr, Anna. *Good Neighbors: Companion Planting for Gardeners.* Emmaus, PA: Rodale Press, 1985. 379 pp. A useful compilation of tradition, research, and practical gardening advice. Out of print.

Cocannouer, Joseph A. *Weeds: Guardians of the Soil.* New York: Devin-Adair, 1948. 179 pp. How weeds help your garden.

Crowhurst, Adrienne. *The Weed Cookbook.* New York: Lancer Books, 1973. 198 pp.

de Baïracle Levi, Juliette. *The Herbal Handbook for Farm and Stable.* Emmaus, PA: Rodale Press, 1976. 320 pp.

Epstein, Emanuel. "Roots." *Scientific American,* May 1973, 48–58.

Franck, Gertrud. *Companion Planting—Successful Gardening the Organic Way.* Wellingborough, Northamptonshire, England: Thorsons Publishers, 1983. 128 pp. Interesting systematic approach.

Gregg, Evelyn S. *Herb Chart.* Biodynamic Farming and Gardening Association, Wyoming, RI. Detailed cultural notes.

Hatfield, Audrey W. *How to Enjoy Your Weeds.* New York: Sterling, 1971. 192 pp. Delightful. Includes an herbal lawn, flower salads, and other charming ideas.

Howes, F. N. *Plants and Beekeeping.* London: Faber & Faber, 1945. 224 pp.

Hylton, William H., ed. *The Rodale Herb Book.* Emmaus, PA: Rodale Press, 1974. 653 pp.

Maeterlinck, Maurice. *The Life of the Bee.* New York: Dodd, Mead & Co., 1916. 427 pp.

Martin, Alexander C. *Weeds.* New York: Golden Press. 160 pp. Inexpensive identification guide.

Muenscher, Walter C., and Hyypio, Peter A. *Weeds.* Ithaca, NY: Cornell University Press, 1980. 586 pp.

Newman, L. Hugh. *Create a Butterfly Garden.* World's Work Ltd. (Kingswood, Fodworth, Surrey, England), 1969. 115 pp.

Philbrick, Helen, and Gregg, Richard B. *Companion Plants and How to Use Them.* Old Greenwich, CT: Devin-Adair, 1966. 113 pp.

Pfeiffer, Ehrenfried. *Sensitive Crystallization Processes.* Spring Valley, NY: Anthroposophic Press, 1936. 59 pp.

_____. *Weeds and What They Tell.* Wyoming, RI: Biodynamic Farming and Gardening Association, 1970. 96 pp. Reading soil conditions by the weeds.

_____. *Chromotography Applied to Quality Testing.* Biodynamic Literature (Box 253, Wyoming, RI 12898), 1984. 44 pp.

Sunset Editors. *Attracting Birds to Your Garden.* Menlo Park, CA: Sunset-Lane, 1974. 96 pp.

_____. *How to Grow Herbs.* Menlo Park, CA: Sunset-Lane, 1974. 80 pp.

Tomkins, Peter. *The Secret Life of Plants.* New York: Harper & Row, 1972. 402 pp. Fascinating.

Tomkins, Peter, and Bird, Christopher. "Love Among the Cabbages." *Harper's,* November 1972, 90ff.

Watts, Mag T. *Reading the Landscape of America.* New York: Collin Books, 1975. 354 pp.

Weaver, John E. *Prairie Plants and Their Environment.* Lincoln, NE: University of Nebraska

Press, 1968. 276 pp.

_____. *Root Development of Field Crops.* New York: McGraw-Hill, 1926. 291 pp.

_____. *Root Development of Vegetable Crops.* New York, McGraw-Hill, 1927. 351 pp. Excellent diagrams of root systems.

White, John T. *Hedgerow.* New York: William Morrow & Co., 1980. 46 pp.

Wilson, Charles M. *Roots: Miracles Below.* New York: Doubleday, 1968. 234 pp.

Composting

Alther, Richard, and Raymond, Richard O. *Improving Garden Soil with Green Manures.* Charlotte, VT: Garden Way Publishing, 1974. 44 pp. Contains good 2-page chart.

Cox, Jeff. "What You Should Know About Nitrogen." *Organic Gardening and Farming,* June 1972, 69–74. See also insert on page 68.

Denison, William C. "Life in Tall Trees." *Scientific American,* June 1973, 75–80.

Donelan, Peter. "Roots in the Soil." Ecology Action (Willits, CA 95490). Information sheet.

Golueke, Clarence G. *Composting: A Study of the Process and Its Principles.* Emmaus, PA: Rodale Press, 1972. 110 pp. For those with an advanced interest.

Griffin, J. M., et al. *Growing and Gathering Your Own Fertilizers.* Ecology Action (Willits, CA 95490), 1988. 140 pp. See Appendix D for information on night soil composting.

Jeavons, John. "Mulching," in "Mulching and Double Digging." Ecology Action (Willits, CA 95490). Information sheet.

Koepf, H. H. *Compost.* Wyoming, RI: Biodynamic Farming and Gardening Association, 1966. 18 pp. Short, detailed pamphlet.

McGarey, Michael G., and Stainforth, Jill, eds. *Compost, Fertilizer, and Biogas Production from Human and Farm Wastes in the People's Republic of China.* Ottawa, Canada: International Development Research Centre, 1978. 94 pp.

Minnich, Jerry, et al. *The Rodale Guide to Composting.* Emmaus, PA: Rodale Press, 1979. 405 pp.

Raabe, Robert D. *The Rapid Composting Method.* Berkeley, CA: California Cooperative Extension Service, 1981. 4 pp.

Rather, Howard C. *Field Crops.* New York: McGraw-Hill, 1942. 454 pp.

Shuval, H. I., et al. *Night-Soil Composting.* Washington, DC: World Bank, 1981. 81 pp.

Soucie, Gary. "How You Gonna Keep It Down on the Farm." *Audubon,* September 1972, 112–115.

Stoner, Carol Hupping, ed. *Goodbye to the Flush Toilet.* Emmaus, PA: Rodale Press, 1977. 285 pp.

University of California, Berkeley, Division of Agricultural Sciences. "The Rapid Composting Method." Leaflet No. 21251. Berkeley: University of California, September 1981. 4 pp.

Van Der Ryn, Sim. *The Toilet Papers.* Santa Barbara, CA: Capra Press, 1978. 124 pp.

Cover/Fodder/Organic Matter Crops

Ahlgren, Gilbert H. *Forage Crops.* New York: McGraw-Hill, 1942. 418 pp.

Coburn, F. D. *The Book of Alfalfa.* New York: Orange Judd Co., 1907. 344 pp.

Hills, Lawrence D. *Comfrey.* New York: Universe Books, 1976. 253 pp.

Hitchcock, A. S. *Manual of the Grasses of the United States.* Washington, DC: U.S. Dept. of Agriculture, Government Printing Office, 1935. 1,040 pp.

Hodgson, Harlow J. "Forage Crops." *Scientific American,* February 1976, 60–75.

Hunter, Peter J. P. *Hunters Guide to Grasses, Clovers, and Weeds.* Chester, England: James Hunter Ltd.

Jeavons, John, and Bruneau, Bill. "Green Manure Crops." *Mother Earth News,* September/ October 1986, 42–45.

Lewis, Rebecca, et al. *Making Pastures Produce.* Emmaus, PA: Rodale Press, 1980. 43 pp.

McLeod, Edwin. *Feed the Soil.* Organic Agriculture Research Institute (P.O. Box 475, Graton, CA 95444), 1982. 209 pp.

Morris, Frank B. *Feeds and Feeding.* 22d ed. Ithaca, NY: Morrison Publishing Co., 1957. 1,165 pp.

Piper, Charles V. *Forage Plants and Their Culture.* New York: Macmillan, 1924. 671 pp.

Schmid, Otto, et al. *Green Manuring, Principles and Practice.* Woods End Agricultural Institute (RFD 1, Box 4050, Mt. Vernon, ME 04357), 1984. 50 pp.

Shaw, Thomas. *Clovers and How to Grow Them.* New York: Orange Judd, 1922. 349 pp.

_____. *Grasses and How to Grow Them.*

Shurtleff, William, and Aoyogi, Akiko. *Kudzu.* Autumn Press (7 Littell Road, Brookline, MA 02146), 1977. 102 pp.

Staten, Hi W. *Grasses and Grassland Farming.* New York: Devin-Adair, 1958. 319 pp.

U.S. Department of Agriculture. *Grass—The Yearbook of Agriculture 1948.* Washington, DC: U.S. Government Printing Office, 1948. 892 pp.

Voisin, Andre. *Better Grassland Sward.* Crosby Lockwood & Son Ltd. (26 Old Brompton Road, London SW7, England), 1960. 341 pp. A unique approach to greatly increased fodder production.

_____. *Grass Productivity.* Philosophical Library (15 East 40th Street, New York, NY 10016), 1959. 353 pp.

Development

Bor, Wout van den. *The Art of Beginning.* Pudoc Wageningen,

The Netherlands: Centre for Agricultural Publications and Documentation, 1983. 174 pp.

Brown, Lester R. *State of the World—1990*. New York: W. W. Norton, 1990. 253 pp. Excellent resource tool. Also see 1984–1989 editions.

Buell, Beck, ed. *Alternatives to the Peace Corps*. Institute for Food and Development Policy (145 Ninth Street, San Francisco, CA 94103), 1988. 47 pp.

Bunch, Roland. *Two Ears of Corn*. World Neighbors (5116 N. Portland, Oklahoma City, OK 73112), 1982. 250 pp.

Darrow, Ken, et al. *Trans-Cultural Study Guide*. Volunteers in Asia (Box 4543, Stanford, CA 94305), 1981. 155 pp.

_____. *Appropriate Technology Source Book*. Volunteers in Asia (Box 4543, Stanford, CA 94305), 1986. 799 pp.

Dickson, Murray. *Where There Is No Dentist*. The Hesperian Foundation (Box 1692, Palo Alto, CA 94302), 1983. 188 pp.

Edwards, Michael. *Arriving Where We Started*. Voluntary Service Overseas (9 Belgrave Square, London, England), 1983. 208 pp.

Fantini, Alvino E., ed. *Cross-Cultural Orientation*. The Experiment in International Living (P.O. Box 676, Battleboro, VT 05301), 1984. 115 pp.

Food and Agriculture Organization of the United Nations. *FAO Production Yearbook—1988*. Rome: FAO, 1989.

Information for Low External Input Agriculture. *Understanding Traditional Agriculture*. Bibliography. ILEIA (P.O. Box 64, 3830 AB Leusden, The Netherlands), 1987. 114 pp.

Slider, Ronald J. *Rich Christians in an Age of Hunger,* pp. 151–160. Downers Grove, IL: Inter-Varsity Press, 1980. 249 pp.

United Nations Development Programme. *Human Development Report—1990*. New York: Oxford University Press, 1990. 189 pp.

Vickery, Deborah and James. *Intensive Vegetable Gardening for Profit and Self-Sufficiency*. Washington, DC: U.S. Peace Corps, Information Collection and Exchange, 1981. 158 pp. In English and Spanish.

Wade, Isabel. *City Food-Crop Selection in Third World Cities*. Urban Resource Systems (783 Buena Vista W., San Francisco, CA 94117), 1986. 54 pp.

Werner, David. *Where There Is No Doctor*. The Hesperian Foundation (Box 1692, Palo Alto, CA 94302), 1977. 403 pp. Also available in Spanish.

_____. *Helping Health Workers Learn*. The Hesperian Foundation (Box 1692, Palo Alto, CA 94302), 1982. 573 pp.

World Resources Institute. *World Resources—1990–91*. New York: Oxford University Press, 1990. 383 pp. Also see this publication for other years.

Experiences

Bromfield, Louis. *Malabar Farm*. New York: Ballantine Books, 1970. 470 pp.

Brown, Lester R. *The Twenty-Ninth Day*. New York: W. W. Norton, 1978. 363 pp.

Burns, Scott. *The Household Economy*. Boston: Beacon Press, 1974.

Dorf, P. *Liberty Hyde Bailey: An Informal Biography*. Ithaca, NY: Cornell University Press, 1956. 257 pp.

Faulkner, Edward H. *Plowman's Folly*. Norman, OK: University of Oklahoma Press, 1943. 155 pp.

King, F. H. *Farmers of Forty Centuries*. Emmaus, PA: Rodale Press, 1972. 441 pp.

McRobie, George. *Small Is Possible*. New York: Harper & Row, 1980.

Nearing, Helen, and Nearing, Scott. *Continuing the Good Life*. New York: Schocken Books, 1979. 194 pp.

_____. *Living the Good Life*. New York: Schocken Books, 1970. 213 pp.

Rifkin, Jeremy. *Entropy*. New York: Bantam Books, 1981. 302 pp.

Schumacher, E. F. *Small Is Beautiful*. New York: Harper & Row, 1973. 305 pp.

_____. *Good Work*. New York: Harper & Row, 1979. 223 pp.

Seshadri, C. V. *Biodynamic Gardening: Monograph Series on Engineering of Photosynthetic Systems*. Vol. 4. Shri AMM Murugappa Chettier Research Centre (Tharamani, Madras, India), 1980. 38 pp.

Seymour, John. *I'm a Stranger Here Myself*. London: Faber & Faber, 1978. 140 pp. Absorbing personal account.

Smith, Marney. *Growing Your Own Food*. Save the Children Federation (48 Wilton Road, Westport, CT 06880), 1980. 35 pp.

Teale, Edwin Way, ed. *The Wilderness World of John Muir*. Boston: Houghton Mifflin, 1964. 332 pp.

Thomas, William L., Jr. *Man's Role in Changing the Face of the Earth*. Vols. 1 and 2. Chicago: University of Chicago Press, 1956. 1,193 pp.

Wells, Kenneth McNeil. *The Owl Pen Reader*. New York: Doubleday, 1969. 445 pp.

Zwinger, Ann. *Beyond the Aspen Grove*. New York: Random House, 1970. 368 pp.

Fertilizer

Norman, Cynthia. "Dung Ho." *National Gardening*. National Gardening Association (180 Flynn Avenue, Burlington, VT 05401), May 1987, 28–30.

Parnes, Robert. *Fertile Soil—A Grower's Guide to Organic and Inorganic Fertilizers*. agAccess (P.O. Box 2008, Davis, CA 95617), 1990. 194 pp.

Films and Video Tapes

Bullfrog Films, Dept. F., Oley, PA 19547. Good selection of films on food, farming, land use, and the environment, including "Gardensong," a

PBS special on Alan Chadwick and the biointensive method, and *Circle of Plenty,* a PBS–TV special on Ecology Action's work and a key biointensive mini-farming project in Mexico. Send 2 stamps for catalog.

Man of the Trees. Music for Little People (P.O. Box 1460, Redway, CA 95560). Video.

The Man Who Planted Trees (Academy Award, 1987). Distributed by Direct Cinema (P.O. Box 69799, Los Angeles, CA 90069). Excellent animated adaptation of Jean Giono's classic story.

National Video Portrait Library, 1869 Kirby Rd., McLean, VA 22101. 55-minute, B&W, ¾" video cassette of a spontaneous philosophical interview with the late Alan Chadwick. Send 2 stamps when inquiring.

On the Edge of the Forest. Bullfrog Films (Oley, PA 19547). Excellent video of Dr. E. F. Schumacher, author of *Small Is Beautiful.* A key perception about agro-forestry and trees.

Stopping the Coming Ice Age. Distributed by Institute for a Future (2000 Center Street, Berkeley, CA 94704). A 60-minute video.

The Vanishing Soil. Available from Biodynamic Farming and Gardening Association (165 West Street, Duxbury, MA 02332). Video.

Flowers

Anderson, E. B., et al. *The Oxford Book of Garden Flowers.* New York: Oxford University Press, 1963. 207 pp.

Arranging Cut Flowers. San Francisco: Ortho Books, 1985. 96 pp.

Black, Penny. *The Book of Pressed Flowers.* New York: Simon & Schuster, 1988. 120 pp. Excellent ideas, plants and colors. Good information on tools, equipment, and how to press flowers.

Blamey, Marjorie. *Flowers of the Countryside.* New York: William Morrow, 1980. 224 pp.

Cavagnaro, David. "A Seed Savers Guide to Flowers." *National Gardening,* August 1988, 39–45.

Crockett, James U. *Crockett's Flower Garden.* New York: Little, Brown, 1981. 311 pp.

Crowhurst, Adrienne. *The Flower Cookbook.* New York: Lancer Books, 1973. 198 pp.

Foster, Catharine O. *Organic Flower Gardening.* Emmaus, PA: Rodale Press, 1975. 305 pp. Excellent!

Hatfield, Audrey W. *Flowers to Know and Grow.* New York: Scribner's, 1950. 174 pp.

Hillier, Malcolm. *The Book of Fresh Flowers.* New York: Simon & Schuster, 1986. 252 pp.

Hillier, Malcolm, et al. *The Book of Dried Flowers.* New York: Simon & Schuster, 1986. 192 pp.

Huxley, Anthony, ed. *Garden Annuals and Bulbs.* New York: Macmillan, 1971. 208 pp.

_____. *Garden Perennials and Water Plants.* New York: Macmillan, 1971. 216 pp.

Ichikawa, Satomi. *Rosy's Garden— A Child's Keepsake of Flowers.* New York: Putnam and Grosset, 1990. 48 pp. Excellent.

James, Theodore, Jr. *The Potpourri Gardener.* New York: Macmillan, 1990. 148 pp.

Karel, Leonard. *Dried Flowers: From Antiquity to the Present.* Metuchen, NJ: Scarecrow Press, 1973.

Kasperski, Victoria R. *How to Make Cut Flowers Last.* New York: William Morrow, 1975. 191 pp.

Kramer, Jack. *The Old-Fashioned Cutting Garden.* New York: Macmillan, 1979. 160 pp.

MacNicol, Mary. *Flower Cookery.* New York: Collier Books, 1967. 262 pp.

Schneider, Alfred F. *Parks Success with Bulbs.* Greenwood, SC: George W. Park Seed Co.,

1981. 173 pp.

Squires, M. *The Art of Drying Plants and Flowers.* New York: Bonanza, 1958. 258 pp.

Sunset Editors. *Garden Colors: Annuals and Perennials.* Menlo Park, CA: Sunset-Lane, 1981. 96 pp.

Thorpe, Patricia. *Everlastings: The Complete Book of Dried Flowers.* New York: Facts on File Publications, 1985. 144 pp.

White, Edward A. *The Principles of Floriculture.* New York: Macmillan, 1931. 467 pp.

Wilder, Louise B. *The Fragrant Garden.* New York: Dover, 1974. 407 pp.

Food & Nutrition

Agricultural Research Service, U.S. Department of Agriculture. *Composition of Foods.* Agriculture Handbook No. 8. Washington, DC: U.S. Government Printing Office, 1963. 190 pp.

Board of Directors. "Position Paper on the Vegetarian Approach to Eating." *The American Dietetic Association Reports,* July 1980, 61–69.

Brown, Edward. *The Tassajara Bread Book.* Boulder, CO: Shambhala Books, 1971. 145 pp.

Bubel, Nancy, et al. *Root Cellaring.* Emmaus, PA: Rodale Press, 1979. 297 pp. Out of print.

Burton, W. G. *The Potato.* 3d ed. New York: Halsted Press, 1989. 724 pp.

Church, Charles F., and Church, Helen W. *Food Values of Portions Commonly Used.* Philadelphia: Lippincott, 1970. 180 pp.

Comité Interdepartmental de Nutrición para la Defensa Nacional, et al. *Tabla de Composicion de Alimentos Para Uso en America Latina.* Bethesda, MD: National Institutes of Health, 1961. 157 pp. Also available in English.

Creasy, Rosalind. *Cooking from the Garden.* San Francisco: Sierra Club Books, 1988. 547 pp.

De Long, Deanna. *How to Dry*

Foods. H. P. Books (P.O. Box 5367, Tucson, AZ 85703), 1979. 160 pp.

Duhon, David and Gebhard, Cindy. *One Circle: How to Grow a Complete Diet in Less Than 1000 Square Feet.* Willits, CA. Ecology Action, 1984. 200 pp. Excellent.

Evans, Ianto. *Lorena Stoves.* Volunteers in Asia (Box 4543, Stanford, CA 94305), 1978. 144 pp.

Flores, Marina, et al. *Valor Nutritivo de los Alimentos Para Centro America y Panama.* Guatemala: Investigaciones Dieteticas—Nutrición Aplicada, 1971. 15 pp.

Food and Agriculture Organization of the United Nations. *Food Composition Table for Use in Africa.* Rome: FAO, 1968. 306 pp.

Food and Agriculture Organization of the United Nations. *Amino-Acid Contents of Food.* Rome: FAO, 1970. 285 pp.

Food and Agriculture Organization of the United Nations. *Food Composition Table for Use in East Asia.* Rome: FAO, 1972. 334 pp.

Freeman, John A. *Survival Gardening.* John's Press (Mt. Gallant Road, P.O. Box 3405 CRS, Rock Hill, SC 29731), 1982. 84 pp.

Glen, E., et al. *Sustainable Food Production for a Complete Diet.* Tucson, AZ: Environmental Research Laboratory, 1989. 25 pp.

Greene, Bert. *The Grains Cookbook.* New York: Workman Publishing, 1988. 410 pp.

Gussow, John. *The Feeding Web.* Palo Alto, CA: Bull Publishing, 1978. 457 pp.

Hagler, Louise. *The Farm Vegetarian Cookbook.* Summertown, TN: The Book Publishing Company, 1978. 219 pp.

Heritage, Ford. *Composition and Facts about Foods.* Health Research (70 La Fayette Street, Mokelumne Hill, CA 95245), 1971. 121 pp.

Hertzberg, Ruth, et al. *Putting Food By.* New York: Bantam Books, 1973. 565 pp.

Hewitt, Jean. *The New York Times Natural Foods Cookbook.* New York: Avon Books, 1971. 434 pp.

Higginbotham, Pearl, and Pinkham, Mary Ellen. *Mary Ellen's Best of Helpful Hints—Fast/Easy/Fun Ways of Solving Household Problems.* New York: Warner Books, 1979. 119 pp.

Hur, Robin. *Food Reform: Our Desperate Need.* Heidelberg Publishers (3707 Kerbey Lane, Austin, TX 78731), 1975. 260 pp.

Hurd, Frank J. *Ten Talents.* Collegedale, TN: College Press, 1985. 368 pp.

Katzen, Mollie. *The Moosewood Cookbook.* Berkeley, CA: Ten Speed Press, 1977. 240 pp. Tasty recipes for lots of fresh vegetables.

_____. *The Enchanted Broccoli Forest.* Berkeley, CA: Ten Speed Press, 1982. 320 pp.

_____. *Still Life with Menu.* Berkeley, CA: Ten Speed Press, 1988. 350 pp.

Kirschmann, John D. *Nutrition Almanac.* New York: McGraw-Hill, 1979. 313 pp.

Kline, Jeff. *How to Sun Dry Your Food.* Self-Reliance Foundation (Box 1, Las Trampas, NM 87576), 1983. 100 pp.

Lappé, Frances M. *Diet for a Small Planet.* New York: Friends of the Earth/Ballantine Books, 1971. 301 pp.

_____. *Diet for a Small Planet.* New York: Ballantine Books, 1984. 496 pp.

Linder, Maria C. "A Review of the Evidence for Food Quality." *Biodynamics,* Summer 1973, 1–11.

Macmaniman, Gen. *Dry It.* Fall City, WA: Living Food Dehydrators, 1973. 58 pp.

Moosewood Staff. *New Recipes from Moosewood Restaurant.* Berkeley, CA: Ten Speed Press, 1987. 302 pp.

Morash, Marian. *The Victory Garden Cookbook.* New York: Knopf, 1982.

National Academy of Sciences. *Recommended Dietary Allowances.* 8th ed. Washington, DC: NAS, 1974. 129 pp.

Pennington, Jean. *Food Values of Portions Commonly Used.* 15th ed. New York: Harper & Row, 1989.

Robertson, Laurel, et al. *New Laurel's Kitchen.* Berkeley, CA: Ten Speed Press, 1986. 512 pp.

_____. *The Laurel's Kitchen Bread Book.* New York: Random House, 1984. 447 pp.

Root, Waverly. *Food—An Authoritative and Visual History and Dictionary of the Foods of the World.* New York: Simon & Schuster, 1980. 602 pp.

Santa Clara County California Planned Parenthood. *Zucchini Cookbook.* Planned Parenthood (421 Ocean Street, Santa Cruz, CA 95060).

Simmons, Paula. *Zucchini Cookbook.* Seattle, WA: Pacific Search, 1974. 127 pp.

Solar Box Cookers International, 1724-11th Street, Sacramento, CA 95814. Excellent solar oven plans, recipes, and cooking information. Write for publications list.

Stoner, Carol. *Stocking Up.* Emmaus, PA: Rodale Press, 1973. 351 pp.

Stowe, Sally and Martin. *The Brilliant Bean.* New York: Bantam, 1988. 276 pp.

Thomas, Anna. *The Vegetarian Epicure.* New York: Vintage Books, 1972. 305 pp.

Twelve Months Harvest. Ortho Book Division (Chevron Chemical Co., San Francisco, CA), 1975. 96 pp. Covers canning, freezing, smoking, drying, cheese, cider, soap, and grinding grain. Many good tips.

Volunteers in Technical Assistance. *Wood Conserving Cook Stoves.* Volunteers in Technical Assistance (3706 Rhode Island Avenue, Mt. Rainier, MD 20822), 1980. 111 pp.

Yepsen, Roger B., Jr., ed. *Home*

Food Systems. Emmaus, PA: Rodale Press, 1981. 475 pp.

General

Bailey, L. H. *Cyclopedia of American Agriculture.* Vol. II, Crops. London, England: Macmillan & Co., 1907. 699 pp. Excellent.

————. *The Farm and Garden Rule-Book.* New York: Macmillan, 1915. 586 pp.

————. *The Horticulturalist's Rule-Book.* New York: Macmillan, 1909. 312 pp.

————. *Principles of Agriculture.* New York: Macmillan, 1909. 336 pp.

————. *Manual of Gardening.* New York: Macmillan, 1914. 541 pp.

Bennett, Charles F., Jr. *Man and Earth's Ecosystems.* New York: Wiley, 1975. 331 pp.

Berry, Wendell. *The Unsettling of America: Culture and Agriculture.* San Francisco: Sierra Club Books, 1977. 226 pp. Eloquent and passionate view of the sociological aspects of farming.

Biodynamics Journal. Richmond Townhouse Road, Wyoming, RI 02898.

Bronson, William. "The Lesson of a Garden." *Cry California,* Winter 1970–71.

Cocannouer, Joseph A. *Farming With Nature.* Norman, OK: University of Oklahoma Press, 1954. 147 pp.

Creasy, Rosalind. *The Complete Book of Edible Landscaping.* San Francisco: Sierra Club Books, 1982. 379 pp.

Cuthbertson, Tom. *Alan Chadwick's Enchanted Garden.* New York: Dutton, 1978. 199 pp. Captures the flavor of working under the originator of the biointensive method.

Foster, Catharine O. *The Organic Gardener.* New York: Random House, 1972. 234 pp. Excellent, chatty, experienced. New England area especially.

Fukuoka, Masanobu. *The One-Straw Revolution.* Emmaus, PA: Rodale Press, 1978. 181 pp.

Natural farming from a Japanese philosopher/farmer. One of the few to address a sustainable grain culture.

Heckel, Alice, ed. *The Pfeiffer Garden Book—Biodynamics in the Home Garden.* Wyoming, RI: Biodynamic Farming and Gardening Association, 1967. 199 pp.

Hill, Lewis. *Successful Cold Climate Gardening.* Brattleboro, VT: Stephen Greene Press, 1981. 308 pp.

Huxley, Anthony. *An Illustrated History of Gardening.* New York: Paddington Press, 1978. 352 pp.

Jeavons, John C. "New Ways from Old." *Cry California,* Winter 1973–74.

Jobb, Jamie. *My Garden Companion.* San Francisco: Sierra Club Books, 1977. 350 pp. Especially for beginners.

King, F. H. *Farmers of Forty Centuries.* Emmaus, PA: Rodale Press, 1972. 441 pp. First-hand observations of Chinese agriculture.

Koepf, Herbert H., Peterson, B. D., and Schauman, Wolfgang. *Biodynamic Agriculture: An Introduction.* Spring Valley, NY: Anthroposophic Press, 1976. 429 pp.

Kraft, Ken, and Kraft, Pat. *Growing Food the Natural Way.* New York: Doubleday, 1973. 292 pp. California-area orientation.

Martinez Valdez, Juan Manuel, and Alarcón Navarro, Dr. Francisco. *Huertos Familiares.* Academia de Investigacion en Demografía Médica (Apartado Postal 27–486, Mexico City, D.F., Mexico), 1988. 116 pp., plus 24 slides. Very good.

Merrill, Richard, ed. *Radical Agriculture.* New York: Harper & Row, 1976. 459 pp. Philosophical and political aspects of food production.

O'Brien, R. Dalziel. *Intensive Gardening.* London: Faber & Faber, 1956. 183 pp. Useful for potential mini-farmers.

Ocone, Lynn. *Guide to Kids' Gardening.* New York: John Wiley & Sons. 148 pp.

Perelman, Michael J. "Farming With Petroleum." *Environment,* October 1972, 8–13.

————, and Shea, Kevin P. "The Big Farm." *Environment,* December 1972, 10–15.

Perry, Robert L. *Basic Gardening in Florida Sand.* Florida Gardening Companion (P.O. Box 896, Largo, FL 33540), 1977.

Pfeiffer, Dr. Ehrenfried. *Biodynamic Farming and Gardening—Soil Fertility Renewal and Preservation.* New York: Anthroposophic Press, 1938. 240 pp.

————. *Biodynamic Farming—Articles 1942–1962.* Wyoming, RI: Biodynamic Farming and Gardening Association. 150 pp.

Philbrick, John, and Philbrick, Helen. *Gardening for Health and Nutrition.* Blauvelt, NY: Rudolf Steiner Publications, 1971. 93 pp.

Raftery, Kevin, and Gilbert, Kim. *Kids Gardening.* Palo Alto, CA: Klutz Press. 88 pp., plus seeds for 13 kinds of crops.

Rateaver, Bargyla, and Rateaver, Gylver. *The Organic Method Primer.* Published by the authors (Pauma Valley, CA 92061), 1973. 257 pp. Packed with detailed information.

Rodale, J. I., ed. *The Encyclopedia of Organic Gardening.* Emmaus, PA: Rodale Press, 1959. 1,145 pp. *and*

————. *How to Grow Fruits and Vegetables by the Organic Method.* Emmaus, PA: Rodale Press, 1961. 926 pp. Two excellent references. Many prefer the encyclopedia format, but we find the second to be more complete.

Rodale, Robert, ed. *The Basic Book of Organic Gardening.* New York: Ballantine Books, 1971. 377 pp. Condensed information includes 14-day compost and nationwide planting dates.

Salisbury, E. J. *The Living Garden (or The How and Why of Garden*

Life). London: G. Bell & Sons, 1946. 232 pp. An excellent book.

Seymour, John. *The Complete Book of Self Sufficiency.* London: Faber & Faber, 1976. 256 pp. Coffee-table size. *and*

_____. *John Seymour's Gardening Book (for Children).* G. Whizzard Publications Ltd. (105 Great Russell Street, London WC1, England), 1978. 61 pp. *and*

_____. *The Self-Sufficient Gardener.* London: Faber & Faber, 1978. 256 pp. Coffee-table size. Seymour has long been a popular back-to-the-land advocate in England, both doing it and writing about it in his own humorous style. His new "productions" are gorgeously illustrated, accurate, and uncluttered. The first includes grains, livestock, energy, and skills such as spinning, metalwork, and thatching, as well as raising fruits and vegetables. The third listed concentrates on smaller-scale food production.

Smith, Marney. *Gardening With Conscience.* New York: Seabury Press, 1981. 86 pp.

Soper, John. *Studying the Agriculture Course.* Bio-Dynamic Agricultural Association (35 Park Road, London NW1 6XT, England), 1976. 88 pp.

Steiner, Rudolf. *Agriculture—A Course of Eight Lectures.* London: Bio-Dynamic Agricultural Association, 1958. 175 pp. The basis of the biodynamic movement. Advanced reading.

Storl, Wolf. *Culture and Horticulture.* Wyoming, RI: Biodynamic Farming and Gardening Association, 1979. Biodynamics and organic agricultural history explained simply.

Sunset Editors. *Sunset's New Western Garden Book.* Menlo Park, CA: Sunset-Lane, 1979. 512 pp. Indispensable descriptions and cultural directions for flowering plants, trees, and landscaping. For West Coast gardeners. Not organic.

Tiedjens, Victor A. *The Vegetable Encyclopedia and Gardener's Guide.* New York: New Home Library, 1943. 215 pp. Important cultural detailings.

U.S. Department of Agriculture. *Report and Recommendations on Organic Farming.* Office of Governmental and Public Affairs USDA (Washington, DC 20205), 1980. 94 pp.

Walters, Charles, Jr., and Fenzau, C. J. *An Acres U.S.A. Primer.* Raytown, MO: Acres U.S.A., 1979. 449 pp.

Grains

Cole, John N. *Amaranth.* Emmaus, PA: Rodale Press, 1979. 311 pp.

Creasy, Rosalind. "The Bread Garden." *Harrowsmith,* September/October 1986, 89–90, 92–96.

Gorman, Marion. "Gardener's Bread." *Organic Gardening.* Emmaus, PA: Rodale Press, December 1988, 53–54.

Hunt, Thomas F. *The Cereals in America.* New York: Orange Judd, 1912. 421 pp.

Leonard, Thom. "Staff of Life." *Organic Gardening.* Emmaus, PA: Rodale Press, December 1988, 46–51.

Leonard, Warren H., and Martin, John H. *Cereal Crops.* New York: Macmillan, 1963. 824 pp.

Logsdon, Gene. *Small-Scale Grain Raising.* Emmaus, PA: Rodale Press, 1977. 305 pp.

Montgomery, E. G. *The Corn Crops.* New York: Macmillan, 1916. 347 pp.

Rodale, Robert. *Amaranth Round-up.* Emmaus, PA: Rodale Press, 1977. 48 pp.

Greenhouse Culture

Abrahams, Doc, and Abrahams, Katy. *Organic Gardening Under Glass.* Emmaus, PA: Rodale Press, 1975. 308 pp.

Anderson, Phyllis. "Gardening Under a Roomy Tent You Make with Shadecloth or Plastic Over PVC Pipe." *Sunset,* Southern California edition, March 1980, 200–1.

Antill, David. *Gardening Under Protection.* EP Publishing Ltd. (East Ardsley, Wakefield, West Yorkshire WF3 2JN, England), 1978. 72 pp.

Aquatias, A. *Intensive Culture of Vegetables.* Solar Survival Press (Harrisville, NH 03450), 1978. 192 pp. Reprint from 1913 on raising food under glass.

Bailey, L. H. *The Forcing Book.* New York: Macmillan, 1903. 259 pp.

_____. *The Nursery-Manual.* New York: Macmillan, 1923. 456 pp.

Chase, J. L. H. *Cloche Gardening.* London: Faber & Faber, 1948. 195 pp.

Colebrook, Binda. *Winter Gardening in the Maritime Northwest.* Tilth Association (Rt. 2, Box 190-A, Arlington, WA 98223), 1977. 128 pp.

Dosher, Paul, et al. History chapter in *Intensive Gardening Round the Year.* Brattleboro, VT: Stephen Greene Press, 1981. 144 pp.

Fisher, Rick, and Yanda, Bill. *The Food and Heat Producing Solar Greenhouse.* John Muir Publications (Santa Fe, NM 87501), 1976. 161 pp. Detailed.

Hill, Lewis. *Successful Cold-Climate Gardening.* Brattleboro, VT: Stephen Greene Press, 1981. 308 pp.

Lawrence, William J. C. *Better Glasshouse Crops.* London: Allen & Unwin.

_____. *Science and the Glasshouse.* Oliver & Boyd (98 Great Russell Street, London WC1, England), 1950. 175 pp.

Lawrence, William J. C., and Newell, J. *Seed and Potting Composts.* London: Allen & Unwin, 1941. 136 pp.

McCullagh, James C., ed. *The Solar Greenhouse Book.* Emmaus, PA: Rodale Press, 1978. 328 pp.

Nearing, Helen, and Nearing,

Scott. *Building and Using Our Sun-Heated Greenhouse: Grow Vegetables All Year-Round.* Charlotte, VT: Garden Way, 1977. 148 pp.

Rieke, Dr. Paul E., and Warncke, Dr. Darryl D. *Greenhouse Soils.* Chestertown, MD: LaMotte Chemical Products Co., 1975. 36 pp.

Herbs

De Baggio, Thomas. "Growing Herbs." *The Herb Companion,* October/November 1988, 9–13.

Foster, Gertrude B., et al. *Parks Success with Herbs.* Greenwood, SC: George W. Park Seed Co., 1980. 192 pp.

Grieve, M. *A Modern Herbal.* Vols. 1 and 2. Ed. by Mrs. C. F. Leyel. New York: Dover, 1971. 474 pp. each volume.

Hoffmann, David L. *The Herb User's Guide.* Rochester, VT: Thorsons Publishing Group, 1987. 240 pp.

————. *The Holistic Herbal.* Longmead, Shaftesbury, Dorset, England: Element Books, 1988. 280 pp.

Keville, Kathy. "A Guide to Harvesting." Part 2 in *The Herbal Craftsman.* Herb Farm (14648 Pear Tree Lane, Nevada City, CA 95959). 3 pp.

————. "Herbal Tinctures, Everything You Wanted to Know . . ." *Vegetarian Times— Well Being,* No. 49.

————. "Salves—Making and Keeping Your Own." *Vegetarian Times—Well Being,* Issue No. 47. (Or write to Herb Farm, 14648 Pear Tree Lane, Nevada City, CA 95959.)

Kowalchick, Claire, et al. *Rodale's Encyclopedia of Herbs.* Emmaus, PA: Rodale Press, 1987. 545 pp.

Lima, Patrick. *Harrowsmith's Illustrated Book of Herbs.* Ontario, Canada: Camden House, 1986. 175 pp.

Tierra, Michael. *Planetary Herbology.* Santa Fe, NM: Lotus Press, 1988. 485 pp.

————. *The Way of Herbs.* New York: Washington Square Press, 1983. 288 pp.

Tolley, Emelie, et al. *Herbs, Gardens, Decorations and Recipes.* New York: Crown Publishers, 1985. 244 pp.

High-Altitude Food Raising

Allen, Judy. "Mountain Top Gardening." *National Gardening,* September 1985, 14–18.

————. "Undercover Report." *National Gardening,* September 1986, 18–19.

————. "Seedlings Under Snow." *National Gardening,* November 1986, 12–13.

————. "A Mountain Legend." *National Gardening,* November 1987, 24–27.

————. "Endless Summer." *National Gardening,* October 1989, 36–39, 50–51.

Information for Low External Input Agriculture. *Mountain Agriculture,* Vol. 4, No. 1 (March 1988). ILEIA (P.O. Box 64, 3830 AB Leusden, The Netherlands). An excellent magazine. 24 pp.

Weinberg, Julie. *Growing Food in the High Desert.* Santa Fe, NM: Sunstone Press, 1985. 91 pp.

History and Philosophy

Aquatias, A. *Intensive Culture of Vegetables—French System.* Harrisville, NH: Solar Survival Press, 1978. 192 pp.

Bonnefons, Nicholas de. *The French Gardiner: Instructing How to Cultivate All Sorts of Fruit Trees, and Herbs for the Garden: Together With Directions to Dry and Conserve Them in Their Natural.* St. Paul's Church-Yard, England: John Crooke, 1658. 294 pp.

Buchanan, Keith. *Transformation of the Chinese Earth.* New York: Praeger, 1970. 335 pp.

Christensen, Carl. *The Green Bible.* Johnny Publishing (P.O. Box 624, Ben Lomand, CA 95005). $11 postpaid. Excellent.

Clark, Robert, ed. *Our Sustainable Table.* San Francisco: North Point Press, 1990. 176 pp.

Coe, Michael D. "The Chinampas of Mexico." *Scientific American,* July 1964, 90–98.

Courtois, Gerald M. *Manuel pratique de culture maraichere.* Paris: J. Hetzeletcie, 1845. 336 pp. Excellent book on the detailed techniques of the French intensive market gardeners.

Doherty, Catherine de Hueck. *Apostolic Farming.* Madonna House Publications (Combermere, Ontario, Canada K0J 1L0). 22 pp.

Duhon, David. *A History of Intensive Food Gardening.* Distributed by Ecology Action (Willits, CA 95490), 1984. 136 pp.

King, F. H. *Farmers of Forty Centuries.* Emmaus, PA: Rodale Press, 1911. 441 pp. Out of print.

Malself, A. J. *French Intensive Gardening.* London, England: W. H. and L. Collingridge, [1932?]. 128 pp. Out of print.

Marx, Gary. "Bolivia Sows Ancient Fruits." *Chicago Tribune,* 2 September 1990, 1:5.

Matheny, Ray T., and Gurr, Deanne L. "Variation in Prehistoric Agricultural Systems of the New World." *Annual Review of Anthropology* 12 (1983): 79–103.

Reed, Charles A., ed. *Origins of Agriculture.* The Hague, The Netherlands: Mouton Publishers, 1977. 1,013 pp.

Smith, Thomas. *French Gardening.* London: Utopia Press, 1909. 128 pp.

Stevens, William. "Scientists Revive a Lost Secret of Farming." *New York Times,* 22 November 1988, C-1, C-15.

Struevur, Stuart. *Prehistoric Agriculture.* Garden City, NY: Natural History Press, 1971. 733 pp.

Weathers, John. *French Market Gardening.* London: John Murray Co., 1909. 225 pp. Out of print.

————. *Commercial Gardening.* Vols. I–IV. London: Gresham

Publishing Co., 1913. Out of print.

Wittwer, Sylvan, et al. *Feeding a Billion—Frontiers of Chinese Agriculture.* East Lansing, MI: Michigan State University Press, 1987. 462 pp.

Homesteading

"The American Agriculturist" editors. *Broom-Corn and Brooms.* New York: Orange Judd, 1906. 59 pp.

Cary, Mara. *Useful Baskets.* Boston: Houghton Mifflin, 1977. 132 pp.

Income

DeVault, George. "City Farm Grosses $238,000 on ½ Acre." *The New Farm.* Emmaus, PA: Rodale Press, July/August 1990, 12–15.

Gibson, Eric. "Big Bucks From Small Acres." *Income Opportunities,* July/August 1988, 54–56.

Jeavons, John. *The Complete 21-Bed Biointensive Mini-Farm,* pp. 23–26. Ecology Action (Willits, CA 95490), 1986. 39 pp.

Kona Kai Farms. Spring Newsletter, March 1988. Kona Kai Farms (1824 5th Street, Berkeley, CA 94710). 4 pp.

Quarrell, C. P. *Intensive Salad Production.* London: Crosby Lockwood & Sons, 1945. 250 pp.

"Salad: Fresh From 4th Street." *Berkeley Ecology Center Newsletter,* p. 2. Berkeley, CA: Ecology Center, March 1986.

Insect Life

Ball, Jeff. *Rodale's Garden Problem Solver.* Emmaus, PA: Rodale Press, 1988. 556 pp.

Barclay, Leslie W., et al. *Insect and Disease Management in the Home Orchard.* Berkeley, CA: California Cooperative Extension Service, 1981. 39 pp.

Carlson, Rachel. *Silent Spring.* Boston: Houghton Mifflin, 1962.

Carr, Anna. *Rodale's Color Handbook of Garden Insects.* Emmaus, PA: Rodale Press, 1979. 241

pp.

Fichter, George S. *Insect Pests.* New York: Golden Press, 1966. 160 pp.

Fish and Wildlife Service, U.S. Department of the Interior. *Attracting and Feeding Birds.* Conservation Bulletin No. 1, U.S. Government Printing Office, Washington, DC, revised 1973. 10 pp.

Flint, Mary Louise. *Pests of the Garden and Small Farm: A Grower's Guide.* Davis, CA: University of California, 1990. 288 pp.

Hunter, Beatrice Trum. *Gardening Without Poisons.* New York: Berkeley Publishing, 1971. 352 pp. Comprehensive survey of insect control methods.

Levi, Herbert W. *Spiders.* New York: Golden Press, 1968. 160 pp.

McGregor, S. E. *Insect Pollination of Cultivated Crop Plants.* Washington, DC: Agricultural Research Service, U.S. Department of Agriculture, 1976. 411 pp. Excellent.

Milne, Lorus, and Milne, Margery. *The Audubon Society Field Guide to North American Insects and Spiders.* New York: Knopf, 1980. 1,008 pp. Small format. Excellent color photographs!

Mitchell, Robert T. *Butterflies and Moths.* New York: Golden Press, 1962. 160 pp.

Pesticide Action Network, 965 Mission Street, #514, San Francisco, CA 94103. Worldwide information clearinghouse on pesticide dangers.

Philbrick, John, and Philbrick, Helen, eds. *The Bug Book.* Charlotte, VT: Garden Way, 1974. 126 pp.

Rincon-Vitova Insectories, P.O. Box 95, Oak View, CA 93022. Predatory insect source.

Schwartz, P. H., Jr. *Control of Insects on Deciduous Fruits and Tree Gnats in the Home Orchard—Without Insecticides.* Hyattsville, MD: U.S. Department of Agriculture Research

Service, 1975. 36 pp.

Smith, Miranda, et al. *Rodale's Garden Insect, Disease and Weed Identification Guide.* Emmaus, PA: Rodale Press, 1979. 328 pp.

Tanem, Bob. "Deer List: 1982 Update." Santa Venetia Nursery (273 N. San Pedro Road, San Rafael, CA 94903). 2 pp.

Yepson, Roger B., Jr. *Organic Plant Protection.* Emmaus, PA: Rodale Press, 1976. 688 pp.

_____. *The Encyclopedia of Natural Insects and Disease Control.* Emmaus, PA: Rodale Press, 1984. 490 pp.

Zim, Herbert S. *Insects.* New York: Golden Press, 1956. 160 pp.

Language and Travel

Amery, Heather, et al. *The First 1,000 Words in Spanish.* London: Usborne Publishing, 1979. 62 pp.

Hamilton, Gervase. *A Health Handbook for the Tropics.* Voluntary Service Overseas (9 Belgrave Square, London SW1X 8PW, England), 1982. 111 pp.

Harpstrite, Pat, and Montrouil, Georgia. *Spanish/English Glossary of Terms Used in "How to Grow More Vegetables."* Ecology Action (Willits, CA 95490), 1987. 30 pp.

Pavick, Alan M., M.D. *First Travel—Meds for Injuries and Illness.* Publishing Corporation of America (15 West Aylesbury Road, Timonium, MD 21093), 1986. 138 pp. compact.

Peace Corps. *A Glossary of Agricultural Terms—Spanish/English–English/Spanish.* Washington, DC: American Language Center, The American University, 1976. 107 pp.

The Sybervision Foreign Language Series, 7133 Koll Center Parkway, Pleasanton, CA 94566. Excellent audio learning tapes with manual. 647 pp.

Wilkes, Angela. *Spanish for Beginners.* Lincolnwood, IL:

National Textbook Company, 1988. 50 pp.

Learning/Teaching

Bailey, L. H., ed. *Cornell Nature Study Leaflets.* Albany, NY: J. B. Lyon Co., Printers, 1904. 607 pp.

————. *Cyclopedia of American Agriculture in Four Volumes.* New York: Macmillan, 1907. 2,675 pp., including many illustrations.

————. *The Standard Cyclopedia of Horticulture in Three Volumes.* New York: Macmillan, 1944. 4,056 pp. including 4,000+ engravings and other illustrations.

————. *The Training of Farmers.* New York: Macmillan, 1909. 263 pp.

Bieny, D. R. *The Why and How of Home Horticulture.* San Francisco: W. H. Freeman, 1980. 513 pp.

Chittenden, Fred J., ed. *Dictionary of Gardening in Three Volumes.* 2d ed. Oxford, England: Royal Horticulture Society, Clarendon Press, 1977. 2,316 pp.

Dorf, Phillip. *Liberty Hyde Bailey— An Informal Biography.* Ithaca, NY: Cornell University Press, 1956. 259 pp.

Gibson, William G. *Eye Spy.* New York: Harper & Brothers, 1899. 264 pp.

Hilgard, E. W., and Osterhout, W. J. V. *Agriculture for Schools of the Pacific Slope.* New York: Macmillan, 1927. 428 pp.

Jeetze, Hartmut von. "In Defense of Old Fashioned Training." *Bio Dynamics.* Bio-Dynamic Farming and Gardening Association (P.O. Box 550, Kimberton, PA 19442). Vol. 122 (Spring 1977): 7–11; Vol. 123 (Summer 1977): 23–26.

Osterhout, W. J. V. *Experiments With Plants.* New York: Macmillan, 1911. 492 pp.

Synge, Patrick M., ed. *Dictionary of Gardening—Second Edition Supplement.* Oxford, England:
Royal Horticultural Society, Clarendon Press, 1979. 554 pp.

Magazines

Back Home. P.O. Box 370, Mountain Home, NC 28758. Excellent new urban and rural "homesteading" skills periodical.

Fine Gardening. Rodale Press, 33 E. Minor Street, Emmaus, PA 18049.

Harrowsmith/Country Life. Camden House Publishing, Telemedia Communications, Ferry Road, Charlotte, VT 05445.

Herb Companion. Interweave Press, 306 N. Washington Avenue, Loveland, CO 80537.

Horticulture. Horticulture Association, 755 Boyleston Street, Boston, MA 02116.

Mountain Agriculture. Information for Low External Input Agriculture, P.O. Box 64, 3830 AB Leusden, The Netherlands. An excellent magazine.

National Gardening. National Gardening Association, 180 Flynn Avenue, Burlington, VT 05401.

Organic Gardening. Rodale Press, 33 E. Minor Street, Emmaus, PA 18049.

Other Crops

Arora, David. *Mushrooms Demystified.* Berkeley, CA: Ten Speed Press, 1979. 668 pp.

Bailey, L. H. *The Garden of Gourds.* New York: Macmillan, 1937. 134 pp.

Beard, Benjamin H. "The Sunflower Crop." *Scientific American,* May 1981, 150–161.

Cox, Jeff. "The Sunflower Seed Huller and Oil Press." *Organic Gardening,* April 1979, 58–61.

Erickson-Brown, Charlotte. *Use of Plants for the Past Five Hundred Years.* Breezy Creeks Press (Box 104, Aurora, Ontario, Canada L4G 3H1), 1979. 510 pp.

Fraser, Samuel. *The Strawberry.* New York: Orange Judd, 1926. 120 pp.

Hand, F. E., and Cockerham,
K. L. *The Sweet Potato.* New York: Macmillan, 1921. 261 pp.

Harris. *The Sugar Beet in America.* New York: Macmillan.

Knowles, Paul F., and Miller, Milton D. *Safflower.* Circular 532. Davis, CA: California Agricultural Experiment Station Extension Service, 1965. 51 pp.

Meeker, John. "Backyard Bamboo." *Organic Gardening,* October 1980, 88–99.

Pratt, Anne. *Flowering Plants, Grasses, Sedges and Ferns of Great Britain.* 4 vols. London: Frederick Warne & Co., 1905.

van den Heuvel, Kick. *Wood and Bamboo for Rural Water Supply.* Delft, The Netherlands: Delft University Press, 1981. 76 pp.

Wicherley, W. *The Whole Art of Rubber-Growing.* Philadelphia: Lippincott, 1911. 151 pp.

Seed Catalogs

Abundant Life Catalog, P.O. Box 772, Port Townsend, WA 98368. Seeds and books.

American Bamboo Co., 345 West Second Street, Dayton, OH 45402.

American Willow Growers Network, RFD Box 124-A, S. New Berlin, NY 13843. Books.

Anderson Valley Nursery, P.O. Box 504, Boonville, CA 95415. Perennials, shrubs, and trees.

Applesource, Route 1, Chapin, IL 62628. Apple trees.

Archia's Seed, 106–108 E. Main Street, Sedalia, MO 65301. Seeds; garden and greenhouse supplies.

Bakker of Holland, U.S. Bulb Reservation Center, Louisiana, MO 63350. Bulbs and perennials.

Bear Creek Nursery, P.O. Box 411, Northport, WA 99157. Trees, tools, and books.

Biologische Tuinzaden 83, De Bolster, 9605 PL, Kielwindeweer, Germany. Vegetable seeds.

Bonanza Seed International, P.O. Box V, Gilroy, CA 95020. Vegetable seeds.

Bountiful Gardens, 19550 Walker Road, Willits, CA 95490. Ecology Action's international mail order service for vegetable, grain, compost-crop, flower, and herb seeds in growing-area-sized packets; key gardening books and supplies; and all Ecology Action publications.

Breck's, 6523 N. Galena Road, Peoria, IL 61632. Bulbs, wildflowers and lilies.

Brittingham's Plant Farms, P.O. Box 2538, Salisbury, MD 21801. Berries, grapes, and asparagus.

Burgess Seed and Plant Co., 905 Four Seasons Road, Bloomington, IL 61701. Seeds, bulbs, plants, and supplies.

Burpee Seed Co., 300 Park Ave., Warminster, PA 18991. Large, well-known company with wide selection of vegetables and flowers.

California Conservation Corps, P.O. Box 329, Yountville Center, Yountville, CA 94599. Trees.

California Gardener's Seed Co., 904 Silver Spur Road, Suite 414, Rolling Hills Estates, CA 90274. Seeds and garden supplies.

Caprilands Herb Farm, 534 Silver Street, Coventry, CT 06238. Herb plants and books.

Carroll Gardens, P.O. Box 310, Westminster, MD 21157. Roses, vines, woody plants, perennials, herbs, books and supplies.

Catnip Acres Farm, Christian Street, Oxford, CT 06483. Herbs and flowers.

Charles H. Mueller, River Road, New Hope, PA 18938. Flowers, lilies, and bulbs.

Clyde Robin Seed Co., P.O. Box 2366, Castro Valley, CA 94546. Wildflower seeds.

Companion Plants, 7247 N. Coolville Ridge Road, Athens, OH 45701. Plants.

Comstock, Ferre and Co., 236 Main Street, Wethersfield, CT 06109. Seeds and supplies.

Cook's Garden, P.O. Box 65, Londonderry, VT 05148. Seeds and supplies.

Country Hills Greenhouse, Route 2, Corning, OH 43710. Plants.

Crockett Seed Co., P.O. Box 237, Metamora, OH 43540. Seeds.

Cruickshank's, 1015 Mount Pleasant Road, Toronto, Ontario M4P 2M1, Canada. Seeds, bulbs, books and supplies.

Davidson-Wilson Greenhouses, R.R. 2, Crawfordsville, IN 47933. Familiar, flowering, and exotic tropical house plants, mini and standard violets.

Dean Foster's Nursery, Hartford, MI 49057. Berries, grapes, roots, hedges; fruit, nut, ornamental, shade, and evergreen trees.

Dean Swift Seed Co., P.O. Box 8, Jaroso, CO 81138. Bulk tree seeds.

P. de Jager and Sons, P.O. Box 100, Brewster, NY 10509. Bulbs and lilies.

J. A. Demonchaux Seeds Co., 827 N. Kansas, Topeka, KS 66608. Vegetable and herb seeds.

Di Giorgi Co., 1411 Third St., Council Bluffs, IA 51501. Forage crops, old-fashioned lettuce and other vegetables, open-pollinated corn.

Dr. Yoo Farm, P.O. Box 90, College Park, MD 20740. Oriental vegetable seeds.

Earl May Seed and Nursery, Shenandoah, IA 51603. Fertilizers, berries, grapes, vines, hedges, shrubs, roses, seeds; fruit and nut trees.

Early Seed and Feed, Ltd., P.O. Box 3024, Saskatoon, Saskatchewan S7K 3S9, Canada. Grain, fodder, and cover crops.

Ed Hume Seeds, P.O. Box 1450, Kent, WA 98035. Seeds and tools.

Edible Landscapes, P.O. Box 77, Afton, VA 22920. Trees, berries, grapes, and vines.

Environmental Seed, P.O. Box 5904, El Monte, CA 91734. Wildflower seeds.

Epicure Seeds, Avon, NY 14414. Choice varieties from gourmet seed houses of Europe.

Essence of Old Gardeners, P.O. Box 407, Redkey, IN 47373. Seeds.

Exotica Seed Company and Rare Fruit Nursery, P.O. Box 160, Vista, CA 92083. Rare fruits and vegetables, vines; nuts, palms, and flowering trees.

Farmer's Seed and Nursery, 2207 E. Oakland Avenue, Bloomington, IL 61701. Seeds, cover crops, potatoes, berries, vines, grapes, hedges, shrubs, roses; fruit and nut trees, supplies.

Forest Farm, 990 Tetherow Road, Williams, OR 97544. Plants, trees, and books.

Fox Hill Farm, 440 W. Michigan Avenue, Box 9, Parma, MI 49269. Flowers and herbs.

Frey Nurseries, 14000 Tomki Road, Redwood Valley, CA 95470. Plants.

Friends of the Trees Society, P.O. Box 1064, Tonasket, WA 98855. Books. Excellent.

Fungi Perfecti, P.O. Box 7634, Olympia, WA 98507. Mushroom growing supplies and books.

Garden City Seeds, 1324 Red Crow Road, Victor, MT 59875. Seeds, herbs, roots, fertilizers, supplies and books.

Gleckler's Seedman, Metamora, OH 43540. Unusual seeds.

Grain Exchange, 2440 E. Water Well Road, Salina, KS 67401. Key grains.

Great Northern Botanical Association, P.O. Box 362, Helena, MT 59624. Northern Rockies specialty crops and plant information.

G. S. Grimes Seeds, 201 W. Main Street, Smethport, PA 16749. Seeds, bulbs, and perennials.

Gurney's Seed & Nursery, Yankton, SD 57079. Seeds, vines, berries, ground covers, hedges, shrubs, bulbs, perennials, roses, house plants; fruit, nut, shade, and flowering trees; supplies.

Hansen New Plants, Fremont Exchange Building #555, Fremont, NE 68025. Specialized fruit trees and bushes.

Harmony Farm Supply, P.O. Box 451, Graton, CA 95444. Plants, berries, fruit and nut trees.

Harris Seeds, 3670 Buffalo Road, Rochester, NY 14624. Seeds, tools and supplies.

Hart Seed Co., P.O. Box 9169, Wethersfield, CT 06109. Largest selection of old-fashioned and non-hybrid vegetables. Many hard-to-find varieties available on request.

Henry Doubleday Research Association—Ryton Gardens—The National Centre for Organic Gardening, Ryton-on-Dunsmore, Coventry CV8 3LG, England. Vegetable, flower, herb, and green manure seeds, organic fertilizer, safe pesticides, comfrey products, educational materials, books, and attractant plants. Excellent group.

Henry Field's Seed and Nursery, Shenandoah, IA 51602. Seeds, ground cover, vines, berries, roses, lilies, perennials, and oriental grasses; fruit, nut, and flowering trees; supplies.

Herb Gathering Catalog, 4000 W. 126th Street, Leawood, KS 66209. French gourmet vegetable seeds, herbs, strawberries, potpourri, and books.

Herbst Brothers, 1000 N. Main Street, Brewster, NY 10509. Seeds, annuals, perennials, trees, and bulbs; greenhouse and nursery supplies.

Heritage Roses, 40340 Wilderness Road, Branscomb, CA 95417. Roses.

Hidden Springs Nursery, Rt. 14, Box 159, Cookeville, TN 38501. Edible landscaping plants, herbs and tree crops.

High Altitude Gardens, P.O. Box 4238, Ketchum, ID 83340. Vegetable, wildflower, and herb seeds; native grasses and supplies.

Hillier Nurseries Ltd., Ampfield, Ramsey, Hants S05 9PA, England. Excellent tree and plant supplier.

Hilltop Herb Farm, Box 866, Cleveland, TX 77327. Herb plants.

Holland Bulb Farms, P.O. Box 127, Westwood, NJ 07675. Bulbs.

Horticultural Enterprises, P.O. Box 340082, Dallas, TX 75234. Mexican vegetable and pepper seeds.

J. L. Hudson Seedman, P.O. Box 1058, Redwood City, CA 94064. Vegetable, flower, and herb seeds, books. Excellent selection.

Hurov's Tropical Seeds, P.O. Box 1596, Chula Vista, CA 92012. Tropical seeds and indoor exotics.

Johnny's Selected Seeds, Foss Hill Road, Albion, ME 04910. Small seed company with integrity. Carries native American crops, select oriental vegetables, grains, short-maturing soybeans, and supplies.

J. H. Judkins and Sons Tree Nursery, Route 4, Smithville, TN 37166. Hedges, shrubs, ground cover, vines, and fruit trees.

Kester's Wild Game Nurseries, Box V, Omro, WI 54963. Grain, vegetable, and grass seeds, publications.

KUSA, Box 761, Ojai, CA 93023. Key seed crop seeds and literature. Excellent.

Larner Seeds, P.O. Box 60143, 445 Monroe Drive, Palo Alto, CA 94306. Vegetable, flower, grass, shrub, vine, and tree seeds. Specializes in California and New England native seeds.

Le Marche Seeds International, P.O. Box 190, Dixon, CA 95620. Vegetable seeds and books.

Henry Leuthardt, Montauk Highway, East Moriches, Long Island, NY 11940. Specializes in old-fashioned varieties of apple trees, pear trees, and grapes.

Living Tree Center, P.O. Box 797, Volinas, CA 94924. Seeds and trees.

Lockhart Seeds, 3 N. Wilson Way, Stockton, CA 95201. Vegetable seeds.

Lost Prairie Herb Farm, 805 Kienas Road, Kalispell, MT 59901.

Plants, supplies, and books.

McClure and Zimmerman, P.O. Box 368, 108 W. Winnebago, Friesland, WI 53935. Bulbs and books.

Meadowbrook Herb Garden, Route 138, Wyoming, RI 02898. Biodynamically grown herbs, seasonings, teas, seeds, cosmetics, and books.

Mellinger's, 2310 W. South Range Road, North Lima, OH 44452. Unusual imported vegetable, herb, flower, and grass seeds; berries, vines. Wide variety of familiar and unusual trees, plants and roses. Mushrooms, tools, supplies, books, and greenhouse equipment.

Merry Gardens, Camden, ME 04843. Good herbal plant selection, including fruit-scented sage.

Messelaar Bulb Co., P.O. Box 269, Ipswich, MA 01938. Bulbs.

Michigan Bulb Co., 1950 Waldorf, Grand Rapids, MI 49550. Grapes, berries, roses, plants, flowers, and fruit trees.

Susan and Rex Mongold, HCR 15, Dyer, NV 89010. Seed potatoes.

Moon Mountain, P.O. Box 34, Morro Bay, CA 93442. Wildflower seeds.

Native Seeds/Search, 2509 N. Campbell Ave. #325, Tucson, AZ 85719. Herbs, books, dyes, and baskets. Excellent cotton and tobacco seeds, drought-tolerant corn, beans, and vegetables.

New England Strawberry Nursery, S. Deerfield, MA 01373. Strawberries.

Nichols Garden Nursery, 1190 North Pacific Highway, Albany, OR 97321. Unusual specialties: elephant garlic, luffa sponge, winemaking supplies, herbs.

North Central Comfrey Products, P.O. Box 195, Glidden, WI 54527. Comfrey and comfrey products.

North Star Gardens, 19060 Manning Trail N, Marine-on-St. Croix, MN 55047. Raspberries—northern, western and southern stock.

Northwood Nursery, 28696 S. Cramer Road, Molalla, OR 97038. Trees, shrubs, roses, exotic edibles, books and tools.

Nource Farms, Inc., P.O. Box 485, R.F.D., South Deerfield, MA 01373. Strawberry, raspberry, asparagus, rhubarb starts source.

George W. Park Seed Co., Cokesbury Road, Greenwood, SC 29647. The best selection of flowers. Gorgeous, full-color catalog available free.

Peace Seeds—"A Planetary Gene Pool Resource & Service," 2385 SE Thompson Street, Corvallis, OR 97333. Wide variety of organically grown seeds and publications. Excellent.

Phoenix Seeds, P.O. Box 9, Stanley, Tasmania 7331. Organic seed varieties.

Raintree Nursery, 391 Butts Road, Morton, WA 98356. Berries, plants, fruit and nut trees, books, supplies.

Ramsey Seed, P.O. Box 352, 205 Stockton Street, Manteca, CA 95336. Wide variety of seeds, including those for compost crops.

Redwood City Seed Co., P.O. Box 361, Redwood City, CA 94064. Basic selection of non-hybrid, untreated vegetable and herb seeds. Expert at locating various tree seeds, including redwoods.

Reliable Seeds, 3862 Carlsbad Boulevard, Carlsbad, CA 92008. Seeds.

Richter's—Canada's Herb Specialist, Goodwood, Ontario, Canada L0C 1A0. Vegetable, herb, plant, and flower seeds, supplies, potpourri, natural medicines, books, and insects.

Rocky Mountain Seed Service, Box 215, Golden, British Columbia, Canada V0A 1H0. British Columbia native seeds, including hard-to-find varieties.

P. L. Rohrer and Brothers, P.O. Box 25, Smoketown, PA 17576. Vegetable and flower seeds plus some cover crops and grains.

Ronniger's Seed Potatoes, Star Route 1, Moyie Springs, ID 83845. Sixty varieties of organically grown potatoes; cover crops and books.

Roses of Yesterday and Today, 802 Brown's Valley Road, Watsonville, CA 95076. Old, rare, unusual, and modern roses.

Russell Graham, 4030 Eagle Crest Road NW, Salem, OR 97304. Bulbs, flowers, perennials, ferns, and oriental grasses.

St. Lawrence Nurseries, R.D. 2, Potsdam, NY 13676. Berries, vines; fruit and nut trees.

Salt Springs Seeds, Box 33, Ganges, British Columbia, Canada V0S 1E0. Seeds.

Sanctuary Seeds, 1913 Yew Street, Vancouver, British Columbia, Canada V6K 3G3. Seeds, companion plants, and medicinals.

Sandy Mush Herb Nursery, Rt. 2, Surrett Cove Road, Leicester, NC 28748. Seeds, plants, herbs, and books.

Sassafras Farms, P.O. Box 1007, Topanga, CA 90290. Two dozen organically grown vegetable varieties and miscellaneous roots.

"Seeds of Change," P.O. Box 280, Gila, NM 88038. Organic vegetable, flower, herb, and bean.

Seed Savers Exchange, Kent Whealy, Rural Rt. 3, Box 239, Decorah, IA 52101. Exchange listings published yearly for $2. Good source of heirloom varieties. Listing includes seed saving guide. Excellent.

Seed Saving Project, LAWR, University of California, Davis, CA 95616. Rare and endangered vegetable varieties and unique heritage seeds.

Seeds Blum, Idaho City Stage, Boise, ID 83706. Heirloom varieties plus good information on seed collection.

Self Reliance Seed Co., P.O. Box 96, Stanley, Tasmania 7331. Vegetable, annual, herb, and tree seeds.

Shepard's Garden Seeds, 30 Irene Street, Torrington, CT 06790. Special vegetable, flower, and herb seeds; supplies and books.

R. H. Shumway, P.O. Box 1, Graniteville, SC 29829. Vegetable, flower, herb, grass, grain, fodder, and cover crop seeds; roses, berries, fruit trees, and supplies.

Sonoma Antique Apple Nursery, 4395 Westside Road, Healdsburg, CA 95448. Fruit trees.

Southern Exposure Seed Exchange, P.O. Box 158, North Garden, VA 22959. Apple, vegetable, and flower seeds; supplies and books.

Southmeadow Fruit Gardens, Lakeside, MI 49116. Large selection of fruit trees.

Spring Hill Nurseries, 110 W. Elm Street, Tipp City, OH 45371. Perennial plants and flowers.

Stark Brothers Nurseries and Orchards Co., Louisiana, MO 63353. Hedges, shrubs, vines, berries, ground cover, roses; fruit, nut, shade, and ornamental trees; supplies and books. Specializes in fruit trees, especially dwarf and semi-dwarf varieties, including many developed by Luther Burbank.

Steel Plant Co., Gleason, TN 38229. Sweet potato starts; onion, cauliflower, cabbage, brussels sprouts, and broccoli seeds.

Stokes Seeds, P.O. Box 548, Buffalo, NY 14240. Carries excellent varieties of many vegetables, especially carrots.

Suffolk Herbs, Sawyer's Farm, Little Cornard, Sudbury, Suffolk C010 0NY, England. Wide variety of seeds and herbs.

Sunnybrook Farms Nursery, 9448 Mayfield Road, Chesterland, OH 44026. Scented geranium source.

Suttons Seeds, London Road, Earley, Reading, Berkshire RG6 1AB, England. For gourmet gardeners. Excellent, tasty varieties, hot-house vegetables.

Synergy Seeds, P.O. Box 5, Rumsey, CA 95679. Seeds.

Talavaya Seeds, P.O. Box 707, Santa Cruz Station, Santa Cruz, NM 87507. Drought-tolerant heritage seeds; books and research information.

Taylor Herb Gardens, 1535 Lone Oak Road, Vista, CA 92084. Herb seeds and plants by mail.

Territorial Seed Co., P.O. Box 27, Lorane, OR 97451. Seeds, tools, and supplies.

Thompson and Morgan, P.O. Box 1308, Jackson, NJ 08527. Wide variety of seeds.

Tolowa Nursery, P.O. Box 509, Talent, OR 97540. Berries, grapes; fruit, nut, woodlot, and ornamental trees.

Tomato Growers Supply, P.O. Box 2237, Fort Myers, FL 33902. Tomato and pepper seeds, books, supplies, and cooking equipment.

Tradewinds Bamboo, P.O. Box 70, Calpella, CA 95418. Bamboo.

Tree Crops Nursery, Rt. 1, Box 44B, Covelo, CA 95428. Excellent fruit tree stock—known and rare.

True Seed Exchange, R.R. 1, Princeton, MO 64673. Exchange for home-grown seed. To join (i.e., to list your own or to receive listings), send $2.

Tsang and Ma Good Earth Seed Co., P.O. Box 5644, Redwood City, CA 94063. Oriental vegetable seeds and cooking utensils.

Valley Seed Service, P.O. Box 9335, Fresno, CA 93791. Specialty seeds for research.

Van Bourgondien, P.O. Box A, 245 Farmingdale Road, Babylon, NY 11702. Bulbs, ground cover seeds, and rare perennials.

Vandenberg, Black Meadow Road, Chester, NY 10918. Bulbs, indoor plants, lilies, perennials, and wildflowers.

Van Engelon, 313 Maple Street, Litchfield, CT 06759. Bulbs and lilies.

Vermont Bean Seed Co., P.O. Box 308, Bomoseen, VT 05732. All kinds of beans for those who want to start growing more protein crops.

Vesey's Seeds for Short Seasons, P.O. Box 9000, Calais, ME 04619. Vegetable and flower seeds, supplies, tools, books, and natural pest control.

Victory Gardens Plants, P.O. Box 867, Mendocino, CA 95460. Landscaping plants.

Vilmorin Andrieux, 4, quai de la Megisserie, 75001 Paris, France. Old, respected seed house specializing in high-quality gourmet vegetables. Catalog in French. Expensive minimum order.

Volkman/North Coast Seed Co., P.O. Box 5875, Portland, OR 97228. Grass, pasture and bird seed.

Wayside Gardens, 1 Garden Lane, Hodges, SC 29695. Trees, vines, shrubs, plants, supplies, and books.

Well-Sweep Herb Farm, 317 Mountain Bethel Road, Port Murray, NJ 09865. Herbs, supplies, and books.

White Flower Farm, Litchfield, CT 06759. Plants, flowers, tools, books, and supplies.

Willhite Seeds Co., P.O. Box 23, Poolville, TX 76076. Vegetable seeds.

Wilson Brothers Floral Co., Roachdale, IN 46172. Scented geranium source.

Dave Wilson Nursery, Hughson, CA 95328. Good fruit trees.

Winterthur, Ridgely, MD 21685. Rare plants.

Wolf River Nurseries, Route 67, Buskirk, NY 12028. Vines, berries, and trees.

Yates Vegetable Seed Catalog for Commercial Growers, P.O. Box 616, Toowoomba, Queensland, Australia 4350. Specializes in tropical varieties suitable for the Southern Hemisphere. Free international seed catalog.

Yerba Buena Nursery, 19500 Skyline Boulevard, Woodside, CA 94062. Native California plants. Excellent.

Seed Propagation

Ackland, J. D. East African Crops. London: Longman Group, 1980. 252 pp. Very good.

Bailey, L. H. How Plants Got Their Names. New York: Dover, 1963. 181 pp.

Brickell, Christopher, ed. Plant Propagation. New York: Simon & Schuster, 1979. 96 pp.

_____. Fruit. New York: Simon & Schuster, 1980. 96 pp.

_____. Vegetables. New York: Simon & Schuster, 1980. 96 pp.

Bubel, Nancy. "Saving Seeds." Mother Earth News, September/October 1987, 58–63

Buchanan, Rita. A Weaver's Garden. Loveland, CO: Interweave Press, 1987. 230 pp.

Dremann, Craig. Vegetable Seed Production. Redwood City Seed Co. (P.O. Box 360, Redwood City, CA 94064), 1974. 6 pp. For moderate climates.

Erichsen-Brown, Charlotte. Use of Plants for the Past 500 Years. Breezy Creeks Press (Box 104, Aurora, Ontario, Canada L46 3H1), 1979, 510 pp.

Food and Agriculture Organization of the United Nations. The Planet—The Flower. Rome: FAO, 1976. 29 pp. In the U.S.: UNIPUB, 1180 Avenue of the Americas, New York, NY 10036.

_____. The Planet—The Living Plant and the Root. Rome: FAO, 1976. 29 pp. In the U.S.: UNIPUB, 1180 Avenue of the Americas, New York, NY 10036.

_____. The Planet—The Stem, the Buds, and the Leaves. Rome: FAO, 1976. 30 pp. In the U.S.: UNIPUB, 1180 Avenue of the Americas, New York, NY 10036.

Fowler, Cary, and Mooney, Pat. Shattering—Food, Politics, and the

Loss of Genetic Diversity. Tucson, AZ: University of Arizona Press, 1990. 278 pp.

Fyfe, Agnes. Moon and Planet. Arlesheim, Switzerland: Society for Cancer Research, 1975. 94 pp.

George, Raymond A. T. Vegetable Seed Production. London and New York: Longman, 1985. 318 pp.

Goldberg, Rebecca, et al. Biotechnology's Bitter Harvest. Biotechnology Working Group, 1990. 73 pp.

"Green Revolution." The Elements, pp. 1, 14–16 (1901 Q Street NW, Washington DC 20009), June 1975.

"Green Revolution Hits Double Trouble." U.S. News & World Report, 28 July 1980, 37, 40.

Hartmann, Hudson T., et al. Plant Propagation—Principles and Practices. 5th ed. Englewood Cliffs, NJ: Prentice Hall, 1990. 647 pp.

Hawthorn, Leslie, and Pollard, Leonard H. Seed Production. New York: Blakiston Co., 1954. 626 pp. A classic.

Healey, B. J. A Gardener's Guide to Plant Names. New York: Scribner's, 1972. 284 pp.

Heiser, Charles B., Jr. Seed to Civilization. San Francisco: W. H. Freeman, 1973. 243 pp.

"How Green Is the Green Revolution?" Enfo. (Box 761, Berkeley, CA 94701), September 1973, 1–2.

Johnson, A. F., and Smith, H. A. Plant Names Simplified. Landsmans Bookshop Ltd. (Buckenhill, Bromyard, Herefordshire, England), 1972. 120 pp.

Johnston, Robert, Jr. Growing Garden Seeds. Johnny's Selected Seeds (Albion, ME 04910), 1976. 32 pp. Culture of plants for saving seed.

Kann, Peter R. "The Food Crisis." The Wall Street Journal, 18 November 1974, 1, 14.

Knott, James E. Handbook for Vegetable Growers. New York: John Wiley, 1957. 245 pp. Useful charts for small farmers.

Heavy chemical orientation.

Lorenz, Oscar A., and Maynard, Donald N. Knott's Handbook for Vegetable Growers. 3d ed. New York: Wiley & Sons, 1988.

Manual Seed Cleaning Screens available in the following mesh sizes (in fractions of inches): $1/4$, $1/8$, $1/12$, $1/16$, $1/30$. Made of stainless steel for long use. Screen mesh and framed screens available at a per-square-foot price. Write for current prices: Abundant Life Seed Co., P.O. Box 772, Port Townsend, WA 98368.

Merrill, Richard. "Ecology of the Green Counter-Revolution," pp. 24–32. Santa Barbara, CA: Community Environmental Council, 1973.

Miller, Douglas C. Vegetable and Herb Seed Growing for the Gardener and Small Farmer. Bullkill Creek Publishing (Hersey, MI 49639), 1977. 46 pp. A good book to start with.

Mullen, William. "The Green Revolution: Can the World Salvage It?" San Francisco Examiner and Chronicle, 14 December 1975, A-13.

Nabham, Gary Paul. Enduring Seeds. San Francisco: North Point Press, 1989. 225 pp.

Reilly, Ann. Park's Success With Seeds. George W. Park Seed Co. (Greenwood, SC 29647), 1978. 364 pp.

Rickett, Harold W. Botany for Gardeners. New York: Macmillan Co., 1957. 236 pp.

Rogers, Marc. Growing and Saving Vegetable Seeds. Charlotte, VT: Garden Way, 1978. 140 pp.

Seed Saver's Exchange. Garden Seed Inventory. 2d ed. Seed Saver's Exchange (R.R. 3, Box 239, Decorah, IA 52101), 1988. Excellent listing of all open-pollinated vegetable seed varieties in the United States.

————. Fruit, Berry and Nut Inventory. Seed Saver's Exchange (R.R. 3, Box 239, Decorah, IA 52101), 1989. 366 pp.

U.S. Department of Agriculture. Seeds—The Yearbook of Agriculture, 1961. Washington, DC: U.S. Government Printing Office, 1961. 591 pp.

Wallace, James N. "Is the Green Revolution Over?" San Francisco Examiner and Chronicle, 17 August 1980.

Wilkes, H. Garrison, and Wilkes, Susan. "The Green Revolution." Environment, October 1972, 32–39.

"The Withering Green Revolution." Natural History, March 1973, 20–21.

Yamaguchii, Mas. World Vegetables: Principles, Production and Nutritive Value. New York: Van Nostrand Reinhold Co., 1983. 413 pp. Very good.

Soil

Albrecht, William A. The Albrecht Papers. Raytown, MI: Acres USA, 1975. 515 pp.

Balfour, Lady E. B. The Living Soil and The Haughley Experiment. London: Faber & Faber, 1943, 1975. 383 pp.

Brady, Nyle C. The Nature and Properties of Soils. 9th ed. New York: Macmillan, 1984. 750 pp.

Carter, Vernon G., and Dale, Tom. Topsoil and Civilization. Norman, OK: University of Oklahoma Press, 1955. 292 pp. Describes how flourishing civilizations have fallen into decay by not maintaining their agricultural health and soil.

"The Effect on Soil Conditions of Mechanized Cultivation at High Moisture Content and of Loosening by Hand Digging." Journal of Agricultural Science, No. 976, 567–571.

Farb, Peter. Living Earth. New York: Harper Colophon, 1959. 175 pp. Easy-to-read peek at the life under the soil.

Faulkner, Edward H. Plowman's Folly. Norman, OK: University of Oklahoma Press, 1943. 155 pp. Classic.

Fenzau, C. J. An Acres U.S.A. Primer, pp. 81–83, 94–95. Raytown, MO: Acres U.S.A.,

1979. 435 pp.

Hall, Sir A. D. *The Soil—An Introduction to the Scientific Study of the Growth of Crops.* New York: E. P. Dutton, 1920. 352 pp.

Handbook on Soils. Brooklyn, NY: Brooklyn Botanic Garden, 1956. 81 pp. Some photos of root systems in the soil.

Howard, Sir Albert. *The Soil and Health.* New York: Devin-Adair, 1956. 307 pp. A cornerstone of the organic movement.

Hyams, Edward. *Soil and Civilization.* New York: Harper & Row, 1976. 312 pp. Reprint from 1952.

Jackson, Wes. *New Roots for Agriculture.* San Francisco: Friends of the Earth, 1980. 155 pp. Addresses the importance of developing sustainable agricultural systems including perennial seed-producing plants.

Jenny, Hans, *The Soil Resource: Origin and Behavior.* New York: Springer-Verlag, 1980. 377 pp.

King, F. H. *The Soil.* New York: Macmillan, 1895. 303 pp.

Larkcom, Joy. "Deep Cultivation." Subsection of "Soil and Soil Pests." *Journal of the Royal Horticultural Society* 104, part 6 (June 1979), 252–255.

Lowdermilk, W. C. "Conquest of the Land through Seven Thousand Years." *Agricultural Information Bulletin,* No. 99. Washington, DC: U.S. Government Printing Office, 1975. 30 pp.

Lyon, T. Littleton, and Buckman, Harry O. *The Nature and Properties of Soils.* New York: Macmillan, 1929. 428 pp. 1st ed. only for more organic treatment.

————. *The Nature and Properties of Soils.* 4th ed. New York: Macmillan, 1943. 499 pp.

Pauli, F. W. *Soil Fertility: A Biodynamic Approach.* Adam Hilger Ltd. (98 St. Pancras Way, London NW1, England), 1976. 204 pp.

Perry, Robert L. *Basic Gardening in Florida Sand.* Robert Perry (4007 Elrod Avenue, Tampa FL 33616), 1977. 72 pp.

Pfeiffer, Ehrenfried. *Biodynamic Farming and Gardening—Soil Fertility Renewal and Preservation.* Spring Valley, NY: Anthroposophic Press, 1943. 240 pp.

Sanchez, Pedro A. *Properties and Management of Soils in the Tropics.* New York: John Wiley & Sons, 1976. 618 pp.

"Trench Composting: A Model for Africa." *Organic Gardening and Farming,* January 1976, 149–150.

U.S. Department of Agriculture. *Soils and Men—The Yearbook of Agriculture, 1938.* Washington, DC: U.S. Government Printing Office, 1938. 1,232 pp.

Waksman, Selam A. *Humus.* Baitimore, MD: Williams and Wilkins Co., 1938. 526 pp.

Watkins, Norma. "How to Grow More Vegetables Organically in South Florida." Environmental Demonstration Center, Life Lab Division (Miami Dade Community College, 300 NE 2nd Avenue, Miami, FL 33132), 1979. 8 pp.

Wildman, William E., et al. "Soil: Physical Environment and How It Affects Plant Growth." Leaflet No. 2280. University of California, Division of Agricultural Sciences, June 1975. 10 pp.

Supply Catalogs

agAccess, P.O. Box 2008, Davis, CA 95617. Excellent books.

Catalog for Cooks, Williams-Sonoma, P.O. Box 7456, San Francisco, CA 94120. Cooking utensils.

Coast Dry Flowers and Baskets, Box 10, San Francisco, CA 94101. Dry flowers, bouquets, baskets and floral supplies.

Cotton Clouds, Rt. 2, Desert Hills #16, Safford, AZ 85546. Cotton yarn.

Dramm, P.O. Box 528, Manitowoc, WI 54220. Professional watering tools.

Earth Care Paper, P.O. Box 3335, Madison, WI 53704. Recycled paper products.

Environmental Concerns, 9051-E Mill Station Road, Sebastopol, CA 95472. Products for a safer, cleaner world, including biodegradable soaps and recycled paper.

Florist Products Horticultural Supplies, 2242 N. Palmer Drive, Schaumburg, IL 60195. Supplies and tools.

Gardener's Supply, 128 Intervale Road, Burlington, VA 05401. Garden tools, greenhouses, and supplies.

Magic Garden Supply, P.O. Box 68, Redway, CA 95560. Supplies.

Nasco Farm and Ranch, P.O. Box 901, Fort Atkinson, WI 53538. Farm and ranch supplies.

Necessary Trading Co., P.O. Box 3050, New Castle, VA 24127. Organic solutions and books.

New England Cheesemaking Co., 85 Main St., Ashfield, MA 01330. Supplies and books.

Peaceful Valley Farm Supply, P.O. Box 2209, Grass Valley, CA 95945. Fertilizers, supplies, seeds, and books. Excellent source.

SelfCare Catalog, 349 Healdsburg Avenue, Healdsburg, CA 95448. Products for self-help health care, including key books.

Smith and Hawken, 25 Corte Madera, Mill Valley, CA 94941. Tools, clothes, bulbs, and books.

Timber Press, 9999 Southwest Wilshire, Portland, OR 97225. Books.

Walt Nicke's Garden Talk, P.O. Box 433, Topsfield, MA 01983. Supplies and tools. Good catalog.

Wild Weeds, P.O. Box 88, Redway, CA 95560. Herbal solutions for all purposes, seeds and books.

Terracing

Copijn, A. N. *A-Frames and Other Levelling Instruments.* ETC Foundation, AME Programne (P.O. Box 64, 3830 AB Leusden, The Netherlands), December 1986. 13 pp.

————. *Soil Protection.* ETC

Foundation, AME Programne (P.O. Box 64, 3830 AB Leusden, The Netherlands), September 1987. 16 pp.

How to Farm Hilly Lands. Forestry for People Series. The Philippines: Bureau of Forest Development. 15 pp.

"Kenyans Shore Up Hopes and Topsoil with Terraces." *Christian Science Monitor,* 9 May 1988.

Wenner, Carl G. *Trees in Erosion and Soil Conservation.* Nairobi: Ministry of Agriculture, Farm Management Branch Project and Evaluation Division, 11 August 1980. 26 pp.

_____. *An Outline of Soil Conservation in Kenya.* Kenya: Ministry of Agriculture, Soil Conservation Extension Unit. 57 pp.

World Bank. *Vetiver Grass—The Hedge Against Erosion.* Washington, DC: World Bank, 1990. 78 pp.

Testing

Soil Testing Service. Timberleaf Farm, 5569 State Street, Albany, OH 45710. Excellent. Send for information on services and prices. The basic and trace mineral tests are highly recommended.

Watercheck. 893 Ecorse Road, Ypsilanti, MI 48197. Excellent water testing laboratory. Write for information.

Tools

Arts Machine Shop, Harrison at Oregon Trail, American Falls, ID 83211. Good quality soil corers.

The C. S. Bell Co., 170 W. Davis St., Tiffin, OH 44883. Grain mills and shellers.

Blackburn, Graham. *Woodworking Handtools.* New York: Simon & Schuster, 1974. 238 pp.

Branch, Diana S. *Tools for Homesteaders, Gardeners, and Small-Scale Farmers.* Emmaus, PA: Rodale Press, 1978. 512 pp.

Carruthers, Ian. *Tools for Agriculture.* London: Intermediate

Technology Publications, 1985. 264 pp.

J. A. Cissell Co., Squnkum-Yellowbrook Road, Farmingdale, NJ 07727. Five-to-ten-year bird netting.

Composite Growing Systems, P.O. Box 343, Skyline Boulevard, La Honda, CA 94020. Learning Boxes (4-tiered microcosm of garden bed for teachers).

Countryside General Store, 103 N. Monroe Street, Waterloo, WI 53595.

Cumberland General Store, Rt. 3, Box 479, Crossville, TN 38555.

Dry Stone Walling. British Trust for Conservation Volunteers Ltd. (Zoological Gardens, Regents Park, London NW1 4RY, England), 1977. 120 pp.

Ecology Action, 2225 El Camino Real, Palo Alto, CA 94306. Mail-order La Motte soil test kits.

Growth Point Magazine, from Horticultural Therapy, Goulds Ground, Vallis Way, Frome, Somerset BA11 3DW, England. £8 surface overseas, £10 airmail overseas. Gardening magazine for the physically handicapped.

Hand and Food Ltd., P.O. Box 611, Brattleboro, VT 05301. Grain harvesting, other hand tools, and relevant publications.

Happy Valley Ranch, P.O. Box 9153, Yakima, WA 98909. Cider, fruit, and wine presses.

Hersey Products, Inc., 250 Elm Street, Dedham, MA 02026. Moderately priced water meter that measures in tenths of gallons. Order number: QOH 0201-MVR-30A-COMPACT-10-SCG-B-L/ CONN-RZ-BOTTOM.

Intermediate Technology, 556 Santa Cruz Avenue, No. 6, Menlo Park, CA 94025. An excellent "Small Is Beautiful/Small Is Possible" networking and information group. Membership consulting service and publications discount. This group is especially interested in small scale, locally financed, and controlled industry,

particularly in rural areas—such as small paper mills using kenaf and other alternatives to pulpwood, smaller scale wool processing technology, and so on. They are also interested in helping individuals and groups establish county-level local resources information, action centers, and marketplaces.

Jackson, Albert, and Day, David. *Tools and How to Use Them.* New York: Knopf, 1979. 252 pp.

Jacobs Brothers Co., 8928 Sepulveda Boulevard, Sepulveda, CA 91343. Fifteen-year shade and pest (3%) netting in various percentages of shading capacity.

Jones, Bernard E., ed. *The Complete Woodworker.* Berkeley, CA: Ten Speed Press, 1980. 408 pp.

Joseph, Stephen, et al. *Wood Conserving Cookstoves: A Design Guide.* MD: Volunteers in Technical Assistance (3706 Rhode Island Avenue, Mount Rainier, MD 20822), 1981.

Kerr Enterprises, P.O. Box 27417, Tempe, AZ 85281. A *very* good solar box cooker. Send $4 for plans and other material.

McCullagh, James C. *Pedal Power—In Work, Leisure and Transportation.* Emmaus, PA: Rodale Press, 1977. 133 pp.

Mack, Norman, ed. *Back to Basics—How to Learn and Enjoy Traditional American Skills.* Pleasantville, NY: Reader's Digest, 1981. 456 pp.

McRobie, George, ed. *Tools for Organic Farming.* London: Intermediate Technology Publications, 1990. 77 pp.

Martin Processing, Inc., Film Division, P.O. Box 5068, Martinsville, VA 24112. Fifteen-year Llumar plastic film for constructing mini-greenhouses.

Necessary Trading Company, Box 3050, 328 Main Street, New Castle, VA 24127. Mail order form and garden supplies, including organic fertilizers.

Nitragin, Inc., 3101 West Custer Avenue, Milwaukee, WI 53209. Source of many kinds of inocula for seeds, so you can maximize the fixing of nitrogen in the soil by legumes, and obtain higher yields and higher protein contents.

Northeast Carry Trading Company, 110 Water Street, Hallowell, ME 04347.

Ohio Earth Food, 13737 Duquette Avenue NE, Hartville, OH 44632. Mail-order organic fertilizers.

Organic Farm and Garden Center, 840 Potter Street, Berkeley, CA 94710. Mail-order fertilizers, including "clodbuster."

Rahn, James J. *Making the Weather Work for You—A Practical Guide for Gardener and Farmer.* Charlotte, VT: Garden Way, 1979. 205 pp.

Smith and Hawken, 68 Homer Lane, Drawer 52, Palo Alto, CA 94301. Superbly crafted D-handled spades and forks from England.

Stratoflex, Inc., 220 Roberts Cut-Off, P.O. Box 10398, Fort Worth, TX 76114. Excellent heavy-duty water hoses. (We like the #230-12.)

Tresemer, David. *The Scythe Book—Mowing Hay, Cutting Weeds, and Harvesting Small Grains With Hand Tools.* Brattleboro, VT: Hand and Foot Ltd., 1981. 120 pp.

Vivian, John. *Building Stone Walls.* Charlotte, VT: Garden Way, 1978. 109 pp.

VJ Growers Supply, 500 W. Orange Blossom Trail, Apopka, FL 32703. Six-year clear vinyl 6-mil plastic film for constructing mini-greenhouses. Available in 54-inch-wide, 100-foot-long rolls only.

Walt Nicke's Garden Talk, P.O. Box 433, Topsfield, MA 01983. Catalog of Haws watering cans and other high-quality small tools. Also carries Spyn-gydes which guide hoses *easily* around corners of growing areas.

Trees

Ayensu, Edward S., et al. *Firewood Crops.* Washington, DC: National Academy of Sciences, 1980. 237 pp.

Bailey, L. H. *The Principles of Fruit-Growing.* New York: Macmillan, 1897. 516 pp.

_____. *The Apple Tree.* New York: Macmillan, 1922. 117 pp.

_____. *The Cultivated Conifers in North America.* New York: Macmillan, 1933. 404 pp.

_____. *The Pruning Manual.* New York: Macmillan, 1954. 320 pp. Constantly revised for 50 years and now out of print.

Baker, Richard St. Barbe. *Men of the Trees.* New York: Dial Press, 1931. 283 pp.

_____. *Among the Trees.* London: Man of the Trees, 1935. 96 pp.

_____. *Trees—A Book of the Seasons.* London: Lindsay Drummond, 1940. 113 pp.

_____. *The Redwoods.* Lindsay Drummond Ltd. (2 Guilford Place, London WC1, England), 1945. 95 pp.

_____. *Green Glory.* New York: A. A. Wyn, Inc., 1949. 253 pp.

_____. *I Planted Trees.* London: Lutterworth Press, 1952. 262 pp.

_____. *Sahara Challenge.* London: Lutterworth Press, 1954. 152 pp. Important book.

_____. *Kabongo—The Story of a Kikuyu Chief.* New York: A. S. Barnes and Co., 1955. 127 pp.

_____. *Dance of the Trees.* Oldbourne Press (121/128 Fleet Street, London EC4, England), 1956. 192 pp.

_____. *Kamiti.* New York: Duell, Sloan and Pearce, 1958. 117 pp.

_____. *Famous Trees of New Zealand.* Wellington, New Zealand: A. H. and A. W. Reed, 1965. 150 pp.

_____. *Caravan Story and Country Notebook.* Wolverton, Bucks, England: McCorquodale & Co., 1969. 71 pp.

_____. *My Life—My Trees.*

Findhorn Publications (The Park, Forres IV36 0TZ, Scotland), 1970. 167 pp.

_____. *The Brotherhood of the Trees.* London: Adelphi. 64 pp.

_____. *Trees in the Environment—Selected Writings of Richard St. Barbe Baker.* Saskatchewan, Canada: University of Saskatchewan Archives. 153 pp. Unpublished manuscript.

Brickell, Christopher. *Pruning.* New York: Simon & Schuster, 1980. 96 pp.

British Trust for Conservation Volunteers. *Hedging—A Practical Handbook.* Reading, Berkshire, England: Wembly Press, 1988. 119 pp. Excellent book on the practical techniques needed to establish living fences.

Brockman, Frank. *Trees of North America.* Racine, WI: Golden Press, 1979. 280 pp.

Brooks, Reid, and Hesse, Claron. *Western Fruit Gardening.* Berkeley, CA: University of California Press, 1953. 287 pp. Old but still good.

Cheyney, E. G. *Farm Forestry.* New York: Macmillan.

Cheyney, E. G., and Wentling, J. P. *The Farm Woodlot.* New York: Macmillan, 1919. 343 pp.

Clark, F. B. *Planting Black Walnut for Timber.* Washington, DC: U.S. Department of Agricultural Forest Service, 1976. 10 pp.

Coit, J. Eliot. *Citrus Fruits.* New York: Macmillan, 1917. 520 pp.

Collingwood, G. H., and Brush, Warren D. *Knowing Your Trees.* American Forestry Association, 1978. 389 pp.

Commission on International Relations. *Firewood Crops.* Washington, DC: National Academy of Sciences, 1980. 237 pp.

Cord, Fred W. *Bush Fruits.* New York: Macmillan, 1909. 537 pp.

Douglas, J. S., and Hart, Robert A. de J. *Forest Farming.* London: Intermediate Technology Publications, 1984. 207 pp. Excellent.

Downing, A. J. *The Fruits and Fruit Trees of America.* New York: John Wiley, 1862. 760 pp.

Food and Agriculture Organization of the United Nations (FAO-UN). *Forest Tree Seed Directory.* New York: United Nations, 1975. 283 pp.

Foster, Ruth. *Landscaping That Saves Energy Dollars.* New York: David McKay, 1978.

Friends of the Trees Society, Star Route, Box 74, Oroville, WA 98844. Good tree information.

Garner, R. J. *The Grafter's Handbook.* New York: Oxford University Press, 1979. 319 pp.

Giono, Jean. *The Man Who Planted Hope and Grew Happiness.* Friends of Nature (Winchester, MA 01890), 1967. 17 pp. True account of a one-man tree planting program. Inspirational.

Green Deserts, Ltd. Rougham, Bury St. Edmunds, Suffolk IP30 9LY, England. Subscription includes an annual membership magazine, periodic updates and a living tree held in trust. £7.50 overseas. Life membership £100. A Registered Charity doing research and practical work in reclaiming deserts.

Gridley, Karen, ed. *Man of the Trees—Selected Writings of Richard St. Barbe Baker.* Ecology Action (Willits, CA 95490), October 1989. 144 pp.

Hart, Edward. *Hedge Laying and Fencing—The Countryman's Art Explained.* Wellingborough, Northamptonshire, England: Thorsons Publishers, 1981. 128 pp.

Hartmann, Hudson T., and Opitiz, Karl W. *Olive Production in California.* University of California Agricultural Publications (207 University Hall, Berkeley, CA 94720), 1966. 63 pp.

Hartmann, Hudson T., et al. *Propagation of Temperate-Zone Fruit Plants.* Davis, CA: University of California Cooperative Extension Service, 1979. 63 pp.

The Harvard Forest Models. Cambridge, MA: Harvard College, 1941. 48 pp.

Hillier Nurseries. *Manual of Trees and Shrubs.* London: David and Charles Publishers. A key publication.

Hudson, Roy L. *Sunset Pruning Handbook.* Menlo Park, CA: Lane, 1952. 80 pp.

Hume, H. H. *The Cultivation of Citrus Fruits.* New York: Macmillan, 1954. 561 pp.

Hutchinson, F. *A Guide to the Richard St. Barbe Baker Papers.* Saskatchewan, Canada: University of Saskatchewan Archives, September 1988. 26 pp.

Huxley, Anthony, ed. *Deciduous Garden Trees and Shrubs.* New York: Macmillan, 1973. 216 pp.

_____. *Evergreen Garden Trees and Shrubs.* New York: Macmillan, 1973. 216 pp.

James, Theodore, Jr. *How to Select, Grow and Enjoy Fruit, Berries & Nuts in the East and Midwest.* Tucson, AZ: H. P. Books, 1983. 144 pp. Out of print.

Johnson, Hugh. *The International Book of Trees.* New York: Bonanza Books, 1980. 288 pp. Good background.

Kang, B. T., et al. *Alley Cropping—A Stable Alternative to Shifting Cultivations.* International Institute of Tropical Agriculture (Oyo Road, PMB 5320 Ibadan, Nigeria), 1984. 22 pp.

Koch, Frank D. *Avocado Grower's Handbook.* Bonsall, CA: Bon Sall Publications, 1983. 273 pp.

Kraft, Ken, and Kraft, Pat. *Fruits for the Home Garden.* New York: Morrow, 1968. 287 pp.

_____. *Grow Your Own Dwarf Fruit Trees.* New York: Walker, 1974. 218 pp.

Kyle, H. R., et al. *CCC Forestry.* Washington, DC: U.S. Department of the Interior, Office of Education, 1937. 334 pp.

Leucaena Based Farming. World Neighbors (5116 N. Portland, Oklahoma City, OK 73112), 1986. 29 pp.

Lorette, Louis. *The Lorette System of Pruning.* London: Martin Hopkinson & Co., Ltd., 1925. 164 pp. Practiced by Chadwick. Fruit trees are gently pinched and trained during summer.

MacDicken, K., and Vergara, N. *Agroforestry: Classification and Management.* New York: Wiley & Sons, 1990. 382 pp.

Mann, Rink. *Backyard Sugarin'.* Woodstock, VT: Countryman Press, 1978. 78 pp.

Martin, R. Sanford. *How to Prune Fruit Trees.* Published by author (10535 Las Lunitas Avenue, Tujunga, CA 91042), 1978. 90 pp. Best and simplest book on pruning for West Coast gardeners.

Men of the Trees. *Richard St. Barbe Baker 1889–1972: A Keepsake Book for All Ages and Generations.* Perth, Australia: Men of the Trees, 1989. 72 pp.

Mollison, Bill, and Holmgren, David. *Permaculture One.* Corgi Books (Trans-World Publishers Ltd., Century House, 61–61 Uxbridge Road, Ealing W5 5SA, England), 1978. 128 pp.

_____. *Permaculture Two.* Tagari Books (P.O. Box 96, Stanley, Tasmania 7331, Australia).

Moore, S. W. *Practical Orcharding On Rough Lands.* Akron, OH: New Werner Company, 1911. 289 pp.

North American Fruit Explorer's Quarterly. Henry Converse, 2317 Seneca Lane, Paducah, KY 42001.

Paddock, Whipple. *Fruit Growing in Arid Regions.* New York: Macmillan, 1913. 395 pp.

Rivers, Thomas. *The Miniature Fruit Garden.* New York: Orange Judd, 1866. 133 pp.

Sheat, W. G. *Propagation of Trees, Shrubs, and Conifers.* New York: Macmillan, 1957.

Smith, J. Russell. *Tree Crops, Key to a Permanent Agriculture.* Old Greenwich, CT: Devin-Adair,

1953. 408 pp. Classic work on an important concept.

Sommers, Paul. *Low Cost Farming in the Humid Tropics: An Illustrated Handbook.* Island Publishing House (STA. Mesa P.O. Box 406, Metro Manila, Philippines), 1984. 38 pp.

Sunset Editors. *Garden Trees.* Menlo Park, CA: Sunset-Lane, 1975. 96 pp.

_____. *Pruning Handbook.* Menlo Park, CA: Sunset-Lane, 1976. 96 pp.

Thomas, Eric. *Hedgerows.* New York: William Morrow Co., 1980. 46 pp.

Thompson, Bruce. *Black Walnuts for Fun & Profit.* Beaverton, OR: Timber Press, 1976. 285 pp.

Titmuss, F. H. *A Concise Encyclopedia of World Timbers.* New York: Philosophical Library, 1949. 156 pp.

Tukey, Harold Bradford. *Dwarfed Fruit Trees.* Ithaca, NY: Cornell University Press, 1964. 562 pp. Definitive work on the subject.

U.S. Department of Agriculture. *Trees—The Yearbook of Agriculture, 1949.* Washington, DC: U.S. Government Printing Office, 1949. 944 pp.

University of California Extension Service. *Avocado Care in the Home Orchard.* 1975. 3 pp.

Walheim, Lance, and Stebbins, Robert L. *Western Fruit, Berries and Nuts—How to Select, Grow and Enjoy.* H. P. Books (P.O. Box 5367, Tucson, AZ 85703), 1981. 192 pp. Excellent. Worth several lifetimes of experience. Good for all tree raisers—not just Western ones.

Walheim, Richard R. L. *Citrus—How to Select, Grow, and Enjoy.* H. P. Books (P.O. Box 5367, Tucson, AZ 85703), 1980. 176 pp.

Waugh, F. A. *Plums and Plum Culture.* New York: Orange Judd, 1910. 371 pp.

Weiner, M. A. *Plant a Tree.* New York: Macmillan, 1975. 277 pp. Excellent.

Wijewardene, Ray, et al. *Conservation Farming.* Marga Publica-

tions (61, Isipathana Mawatha, Colombo 5, Sri Lanka).

Williams, S. R. *Compost Fruit Growing.* London: W. Foulsham & Co. Ltd., 1961. 126 pp.

Yepsen, Roger B., Jr. *Trees for the Yard, Orchard, and Woodlot.* Emmaus, PA: Rodale Press, 1976. 305 pp.

Tropics/Publications

Bernhardt, Ed. *Home Gardening in Costa Rica.* The Tico Times (P.O. Box 4632, San Jose, Costa Rica), 1985. 88 pp.

The Bio-Intensive Approach to Family Food Gardens. International Institute of Rural Reconstruction (1775 Broadway, New York, NY 10019). Information packet.

Composting for the Tropics. Bocking, England: Henry Doubleday Research Association, 1963. 28 pp. Useful pamphlet for humid areas.

Ecology Action staff. *A Preliminary Guide to Tropical Biointensive Food Raising.* Palo Alto, CA: Ecology Action, 1982. 31 pp. Includes large bibliography.

Goeltenboth, Friedhelm, ed. *Subsistence Agriculture Improvement: Manual for the Humid Tropics.* In *Tropical Agroecology,* No. 4. Lanham, MD: Unipub, 1990. 228 pp.

Hodges, R. D., ed. *Composting in Tropical Agriculture.* Ipswich, England: International Institute of Biological Husbandry, 1979. 32 pp.

International Institute of Rural Reconstruction. *Regenerative Agricultural Technologies.* IIRR (1775 Broadway, New York, NY 10019). Information packet.

Irvine, F. R. *West African Crops.* Oxford, England: Oxford University Press, 1969. 272 pp.

Schwartz, H., and Pastor-Corrales. *Bean Production Problems in the Tropics.* 2d ed. Centro Internacional de Agricultura Tropical (Apartado Aeréo 6713, Cali, Colombia),

1989. 725 pp.

Steiner, Kurt G. *Intercropping in Tropical Smallholder Agriculture with Special Reference to West Africa.* Deutsche Gesellschaft fur Technische Zusammenarbeith (Postfach 5180, D–6236 Eschborn/Ts. 1, Germany), 1984. 304 pp.

Stoll, Gaby. *Natural Crop Protection—Based on Local Farm Resources in the Tropics and Subtropics.* TRIOPS (Raoffeisenstrasse 24, D–6070 Lagen, Germany), 1986. 188 pp.

UNICEF. *The UNICEF Home Gardens Book.* New York: UNICEF.

Tropics/Groups to Contact for Further Information:

Asian Vegetable Research and Development Center, P.O. Box 42, Shanhua, Tainan 741, Taiwan ROC.

Biointensive Mini Farming Information—Mexico. Av. Centenario, Edif. H10–1–2 Col., Lomas de Plateros, Mexico D.F. 01480 C.P. Specializes in training. Excellent.

Educational Concerns for Hunger Organization, R.R. 2, Box 852, Fort Myers, FL 33903.

Institute for Tropical Agriculture, University of Florida, Box 13533, Gainesville, FL 32604.

International Institute of Rural Reconstruction, 1775 Broadway, New York, NY 10019.

International Institute of Rural Reconstruction, Silang, Cavite, Philippines. Specializes in biointensive mini-farming.

International Institute of Tropical Agriculture, 133 Dharmapala Mawatha, Columbo 7, Sri Lanka.

League for International Food Education, 915 15th Street NW, Suite 915, Washington, DC 20005.

Manor House Agricultural Centre, Private Bag, Kitale, Kenya, East Africa. Specializes in biointensive mini-farming. Training.

Mayaquez Institute of Tropical Agriculture, SEA, Box 70, Mayaquez, Puerto Rico 00708.

Volunteers in Asia, Box 4543, Stanford, CA 94305.

Volunteers in Technical Assistance, 3706 Rhode Island Avenue, Mt. Rainier, MD 20822.

Water

Cocannouer, Joseph A. *Water and the Cycle of Life*. Old Greenwich, CT: Devin-Adair, 1962. 142 pp. All his books are fascinating and easy to read.

James, I. C., et al. "How Much Water in a 12-Ounce Can?" Washington, DC: U.S. Geological Survey, 1976. 18 pp.

_____. *Principles of Irrigation Practice*. New York: Macmillan, 1920. 496 pp.

Vegetables

Bailey, L. H. *Principles of Vegetable Gardening*. New York: Macmillan, 1901. 450 pp.

Burrage, Albert C. *Burrage on Vegetables*. Boston: Houghton-Mifflin, 1975. 224 pp. Good notes on scheduling for continuous harvest.

Harrison, S. G., et al. *The Oxford Book of Food Plants*. New York: Oxford University Press, 1969. 207 pp.

Sanders, T. W. *Vegetables and Their Cultivation*. Many eds. London: Q. H. & L.

Collingridge, 1928. 508 pp.

Sutton & Sons. *The Culture of Vegetables and Flowers from Seeds and Roots*. London: Simpkin, Marshall, Hamilton, Kent & Co., 1898. 427 pp. Excellent. Out of print.

Vilmorin-Andrieux, M. M. *The Vegetable Garden*. Softcover edition: Berkeley, CA: Ten Speed Press, 1981. 620 pp. Hardcover edition: The Jeavons-Leler Press (5798 Ridgewood Rd., Willits, CA 95490), 1976. 620 pp. Very detailed reprint of the excellent 1885 English edition by John Murray. This classic is still one of the most useful works on cultural directions in existence today.

Who is Ecology Action?

Ecology Action of the Midpeninsula is a local, non-profit, tax-exempt, environmental research and education organization located at 5798 Ridgewood Road, Willits, California 95490 U.S.A. Formed in the early 1970's, it acted as a catalyst in the recycling of glass and metal wastes in the city of Palo Alto. This project, for which Ecology Action won three awards, was taken over by the city to be run as an ongoing service.

Currently, Ecology Action consists of four self-supporting projects: (1) *An organic garden supply store and educational center* offering inexpensive seeds, tools, books, fertilizers, and gardening advice. Store sales pay for two full-time staff persons and support periodic free classes on the biointensive method and other topics. (2) *Urban and rural homesteading information and supplies.* Adjoining the store is a library on topics such as cheesemaking, blacksmithing, raising chickens and bees, tending goats, and other skills. Ecology Action maintains files on experienced people, publishes a newsletter of local information (about four issues a year), and offers periodic classes. Membership fees ($30 per year) support its ongoing work, library, newsletter, and mini-farming work. (3) *A mini-farming demonstration and research garden area.* Currently the mini-farming staff includes two paid staff positions and two apprentices. Salaries and stipends are paid out of sales of this book and other publications, supporting memberships, and contributions from foundations, corporations, and individuals. (4) *A mail order service,* Bountiful Gardens, which offers biointensive and key food-raising publications, open-pollinated seeds, and supplies to gardeners around the world.

One project of Ecology Action is a non-profit story and educational center, where seeds are sold like penny candy. Start a bulk seed buying group in your community. The savings are tremendous when you "package" your own. Our store, Common Ground, is located at 2225 El Camino Real, Palo Alto, CA 94306. It is open 10–5, Tuesday–Sunday, 415-328-6752.

Ecology Action Offerings

(1) Periodic class series on the biointensive method and urban homesteading topics, on Saturday mornings.

(2) Periodic tours of the research site.

(3) Short mini-farming workshops, plus a few long-term apprenticeships to those who are sincere, committed, and responsible. The two key questions asked of interested workers are: "Can you make a 3- to 5-year commitment?" and "How do you expect to be using the skills and knowledge when you leave?"

(4) We will answer short questions by mail if a stamped self-addressed envelope is enclosed. We continue to develop information sheets covering the most common questions.

Our main work is the continued testing of the biointensive method yields, spacings, timing, varieties, resource consumption, economic viability, and sustainability. You can become a garden supporter for $30 a year. This support is tax deductible.

Perhaps it is unfair to compare the yields we obtain in our hard clay subsoil with commercial agricultural yields. Stunted broccoli plant on the *left* was grown using *normal backyard techniques:* loosening the soil and adding chemical fertilizer. Broccoli shown in the *middle* was obtained by loosening the soil *12 inches deep* and incorporating a 3-inch layer of aged manure with some compost. Broccoli on the *right* demonstrates the superiority of *the biointensive method.*

Biointensive Applications

The biointensive method, with its high yields, low water and fertilizer consumption, and soil-building techniques is eminently practical for serious small-scale food production. Some possible applications are:

☐ One mini-farmer may be able to net $5,000 to $20,000 a year on a 1/8-acre mini-farm. He or she might work a 40-hour week and take a 4-month vacation each year. (For more details see Ecology Action's *Backyard Homestead, Mini-Farm and Garden Log Book* and *Cucumber Bonanza,* a Self-Teaching Mini-Series booklet.)

☐ A backyard gardener in the United States could grow a

Biointensive techniques are being used to improve people's diets in over 50 countries around the world. Here a raised bed garden is planted in India.

year's supply of vegetables and soft fruits (322 pounds) on 100 square feet in a 6-month growing season. This food would be worth more than $200 and could eventually be grown in 5-10 minutes a day, making the gardener's time worth $6.50–$13.00+ per hour.

☐ An entire balanced diet can possibly be grown on as little as 1,000 square feet per person in an 8-month growing season. (See David Duhon and Cindy Gebhard's *One Circle,* published by Ecology Action.) Using commercial agricultural techniques, it takes approximately 32,000 square feet per person in India, 10,100 square feet in the United States, and 4,800 square feet in Japan to grow similar diets.

☐ Eventually we hope to be producing as much food per hour by hand as commercial agriculture produces with machines.

Key points such as low start-up cost, low water usage, and diversity of crops make the biointensive approach especially viable for small farmers in the developing world. This decentralized, self-sufficient approach is consistent with current emphasis on enabling countries and communities to provide their own food.

Sustainability

The most important element in assessing agricultural systems is whether or not the yields are sustainable in an environmentally balanced way. For thousands of years the Chinese practiced a manual, organic form of intensive farming using only fertilizers grown or produced on the farmstead. They were able to feed 1.5 to 2 times more people per acre than the United States presently does with mechanized chemical techniques (assuming similar non-meat diets). In addition, chemical techniques deplete the soil's capacity to produce. Wilson Clark, in the January 1975 issue of *Smithsonian,* noted: "Even though more corn was produced per acre in 1968 than in the 1940's, the efficiency with which crops used available [nitrogen] fertilizer actually declined fivefold."

Chemical agriculture requires ever-increasing fertilizer at an increasing cost as petroleum supplies dwindle. Use of chemical fertilizers depletes beneficial microbial life, breaks down soil structure, and adds to soil salinity. Impoverished soil makes crops more vulnerable to disease and insect attack and requires larger energy output in the form of pesticides to sustain production. "A modern agriculture, racing one step ahead of the apocalypse, is not ecologically sane, no matter

POTENTIAL OF SMALL-SCALE BIOINTENSIVE FOOD-RAISING AS INDICATED BY ECOLOGY ACTION'S RESEARCH TO DATE

Production as compared to U.S. commercial averages, per unit area

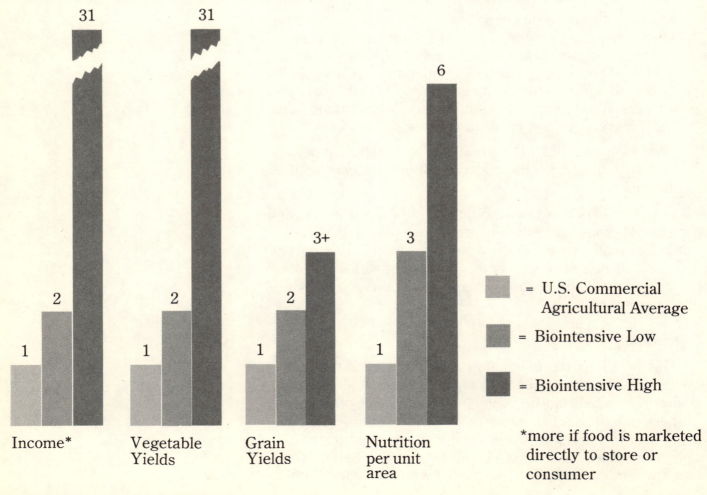

Income*   Vegetable Yields   Grain Yields   Nutrition per unit area

= U.S. Commercial Agricultural Average

= Biointensive Low

= Biointensive High

*more if food is marketed directly to store or consumer

Pounds of food produced per hour

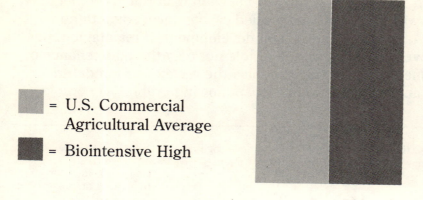

Potentially can reach the same as with machines as soil improves, practitioner's skills and yields increase, and through the use of new, simple, labor-saving hand devices.

= U.S. Commercial Agricultural Average

= Biointensive High

Resource use as compared with U.S. commercial average, per pound of food produced

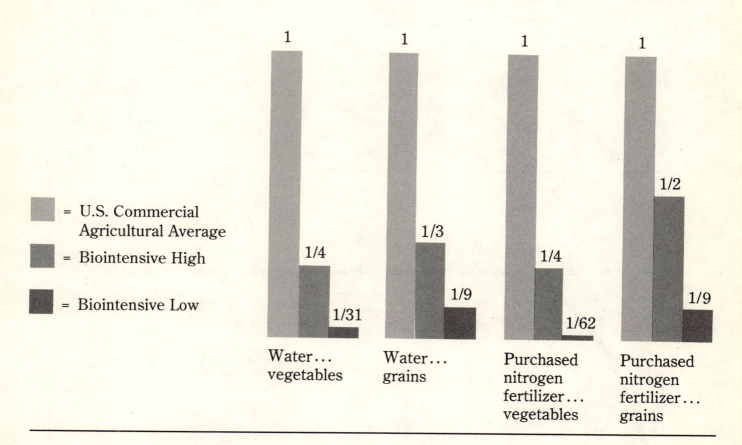

= U.S. Commercial Agricultural Average

= Biointensive High

= Biointensive Low

	Water... vegetables	Water... grains	Purchased nitrogen fertilizer... vegetables	Purchased nitrogen fertilizer... grains
U.S. Commercial Agricultural Average	1	1	1	1
Biointensive High	1/4	1/3	1/4	1/2
Biointensive Low	1/31	1/9	1/62	1/9

how productive, efficient, or economically sound it may seem" (John Todd in *The New Alchemy Institute Bulletin,* No. 2).

Biological agriculture can sustain yields because it puts back into the soil those elements needed to sustain fertility. A small-scale personal agriculture recycles the nutrients and humus so important to the microbial life forms that fix atmospheric nitrogen and produce disease-preventing antibiotics.

Preliminary studies by soil scientists at the University of California, Berkeley, indicate that in as little as a 6-month period (and as many as 8 years) the soil involved in our tests (which was only a "C-horizon" subsoil material at the beginning) was built up to a humified carbon level equal to hundreds of years of natural soil development! If maintained, this improvement may make possible not only the maintenance of sustainable soil fertility, but also the reclamation of deteriorated and marginal lands. (See following graph.) The

---

A ■ ■ ■ ■ ■ ■ ■

Observed increase (build-up) in carbon at Ecology Action Research Test Site (tentative figures) in soil (which was sub-soil to begin with). Program began June, 1972.

Question: What would be the fate of the carbon curve (or nitrogen curve) if the bed were now left fallow after the normal "intense" organic matter input?

1 □ □ □ □ □ □ □ □ □

Remains at "natural" steady state level?

—*Unlikely*

2 ● ● ● ● ● ● ● ● ●

Substantial drop, but leveling off, then rising again under "natural development?"

—*Most likely.* Accelerated gain of hundreds of years of soil development (in as little as six months' or as much as eight years' time with Ecology Action-type cultivation).

3 ○ ○ ○ ○ ○ ○ ○ ○ ○

Drastic drop back down to initial zero?

—*Unlikely*

B ▬▬▬▬

Normal build-up of soil by natural processes.

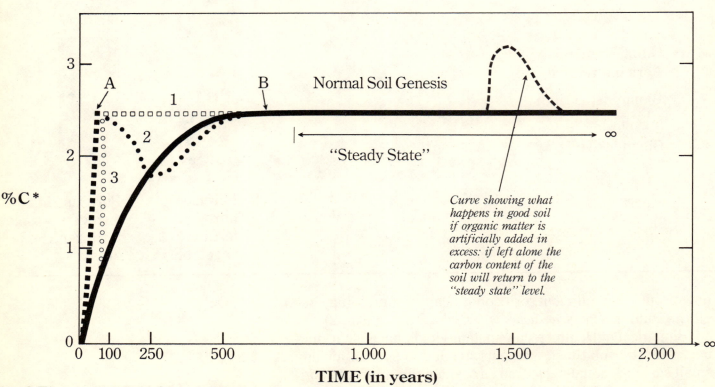

Normal Soil Genesis

"Steady State"

Curve showing what happens in good soil if organic matter is artificially added in excess: if left alone the carbon content of the soil will return to the "steady state" level.

%C *

TIME (in years)

*% C Times ∼ 1.7 ≅ % Organic Matter

biointensive method also nurtures the soil life and structure, utilizes renewable resources, can be productive economically on a small manual scale, and provides higher yields.

For more background on ways to practically approach sustainable soil fertility, also see Ecology Action's Self-Teaching Mini-Series Booklets: *Biointensive Mini-Farming—A Rational Use of Natural Resources; Biointensive Micro-Farming—A Seventeen Year Perspective; Micro-Farming as a Key to the Revitalization of the World's Agriculture and Environment; Ecology Action's Comprehensive Definition of Sustainability; The Complete 21-Bed Biointensive Mini-Farm: Fertility, Nutrition and Income; One Basic Mexican Diet;* and *One Complete Kenyan Mini-Farm.*

EA Publications:

(Send self-addressed, stamped envelope for mail-order information.)

David Duhon and Cindy Gebhard. *One Circle: How to Grow a Complete Diet in Less Than 1,000 Square Feet.* Willits, CA: Ecology Action of the Midpeninsula, 1984. 200 pp. This book helps you to explore your nutritional needs and to design and produce a smallest-scale complete diet.

John Jeavons. *How to Grow More Vegetables Than You Ever Thought Possible On Less Land Than You Can Imagine.* Berkeley, CA: Ten Speed Press, revised 1991. 208 pp. Ecology Action's popular primer giving basic instructions for the biointensive method.

————. *Cultivo Biointensivo de Alimentos.* Palo Alto, CA: Ecology Action of the Midpeninsula, 1991. Spanish translation of the *fourth* edition of *How to Grow More Vegetables . . .*

————. *Comment faire pousser . . .* Berkeley, CA: Ten Speed Press, 1982. 192 pp. French translation of the *second* edition of *How to Grow More Vegetables . . .* with updated data in metric units.

————. *Mehr Gemuse Im Eingenen Garten.* Palo Alto, CA: Ecology Action of the Midpeninsula, 1981. 82 pp. German translation of the *first* edition of *How to Grow More Vegetables . . .*

Miniature greenhouses fit right over the growing beds. Plans for this one are available in one of Ecology Action's *Backyard Homestead, Mini-Farm and Garden Log Book.* Send for a current publications list.

————. Hindi translation of the *first* edition of *How to Grow More Vegetables . . .* Palo Alto, CA: Ecology Action of the Midpeninsula, 1987. 70 pp.

————. *1972 Preliminary Research Report.* Palo Alto, CA: Ecology Action of the Midpeninsula, 1973. 22 pp. Ecology Action's first data report on the biointensive method and implications for small farmers.

————. *1972–1975 Research Report Summary.* Palo Alto, CA: Ecology Action of the Midpeninsula, 1976. 19 pp. Summary of data and projections of Ecology Action's first 4 years of research with intensive techniques.

John Jeavons, J. Mogador Griffin, and Robin Leler. *The Backyard Homestead, Mini-Farm, and Garden Log Book.* Berkeley, CA: Ten Speed Press, 1983. 224 pp. A handbook for everyday use in developing greater self-sufficiency in a backyard homestead or in actually earning an income from a small farm. There is material covering tools and crop testing, as well as calendars, graphs, charts, and plenty of space for record keeping. It also includes updated information on creating your own self-fertilizing herbal lawn.

Michael Shepard and John Jeavons. *Appropriate Agriculture.* Menlo Park, CA: Intermediate Technology, 1977. 14 pp. Paper given by Peter N. Gillingham at a "Small Is Beautiful" conference featuring Dr. E. F. Schumacher at the University of California at Davis.

John Jeavons. "Quantitative Research on the Biodynamic/French Intensive Method." In *Small Scale Intensive Food Production—Improving the Nutrition of the Most Economically Disadvantaged Families,* pp. 32–38. Workshop proceedings prepared on behalf of the Office of Nutrition, Bureau for Technical Assistance, U.S. Agency of International Development. Published by League for International Food Education, Washington, DC, 1977.

Hugh Roberts, ed. *Intensive Food Production On A Human Scale—Proceedings of the 3rd International Conference on Small Scale and Intensive Food Production.* Palo Alto, CA: Ecology Action of the Midpeninsula, 1982. 224 pp. The result of a gathering of 100 people from projects in sixteen countries.

Man of the Trees: Selected Writings of Richard St. Barbe Baker. Edited by Karen Gridley. Palo Alto, CA: Ecology Action of the Midpininsula, 1989. 120 pp. This collection of excerpts from Richard St. Barbe Baker's most important writings provides a fascinating glimpse of one of this century's most farsighted individuals. Beyond mere human interest, however, the book carries an urgent message about the vital role of trees in planetary survival.

Use of a U-bar digging tool cuts digging time and helps make bio intensive mini-farming competitive with mechanized techniques.

Self-Teaching Mini-Series Booklets:

Biointensive Mini-Farming: A Rational Use of Natural Resources. 15 pp. Explains what Ecology Action is doing and why.

Cucumber Bonanza. 24 pp. Takes cucumbers as an example of a crop history and goes through 7 years of work, bringing the 1973 yield of 140 pounds of marketable cucumbers per 100 square feet to over 400 pounds in 1979. An excellent introduction to mini-farming and the variables which can be examined in obtaining improved yields.

One Crop Test Booklet: Soybeans. 24 pp., plus Data Sheet & Log Form. Contains step-by-step instructions for conducting comparative tests for spacing and yield (with optional water monitoring) for soybeans—an important protein crop throughout the world. This booklet enables one to participate in Ecology Action's research or to simply grow better soybeans for oneself.

Progress Since the League for International Food Education Conference of 1976. Speech given by John Jeavons at the Second International Conference on Small-Scale Intensive Food Production, October 1981.

Grow Your Compost Materials at Home. 17 pp. An approach to sustainable organic matter production and soil fertility on a "closed system" basis.

A Preliminary Guide to Tropical Biointensive Food Raising. 31 pp.

Growing and Gathering Your Own Fertilizers. 125 pp.

Growing to Seed. 80 pp. How to grow your own seed in the smallest possible area while preserving genetic diversity.

The Complete 21-Bed Biointensive Mini-Farm: Fertility, Nutrition and Income. 39 pp. Explores sustainably growing all your own food, some to make a small income, and compost crops, in as little as 2,100 square feet.

One Basic Mexican Diet. 32 pp. In English and Spanish. Explores complete nutritional self-sufficiency in a small area with one Mexican diet as a focal point.

Foliar Feeding. 9 pp.

Backyard Garden Research. 32 pp. Improving your garden's performance through observation.

Dried, Cut, and Edible Flowers for Pleasure, Food and Income. 61 pp.

Biointensive Micro-Farming: A Seventeen Year Perspective. 20 pp.

An Ecology Action Reading Guide. 36 pp. Design your own curriculum.

Micro-Farming as a Key to the Revitalization of the World's Agriculture and Environment. 13 pp.

Grow Your Manure for Free. 32 pp. Summary of compost crops to grow for improving your soil's fertility.

Biointensive Composting. 12 pp.

Ecology Action's Comprehensive Definition of Sustainability. 4 pp.
One Complete Kenyan Mini-Farm. 48 pp.

One-Page Information Sheets and Booklets:

Backyard Gardening. Intensive techniques for home food production.

Mini-Farming. Brief outline of advantages and applications of Ecology Action's small-farming approach; in English, Spanish, French, German, Portuguese, Hungarian, Czech, Russian, and Mandarin Chinese.

Intensive Gardening—Less Water and Higher Yields. Reprint from *Organic Gardening and Farming* magazine, July 1977.

Homesteader's Bibliography.

Suggestions to Minimize Insect Pests in Your Garden.

Slug and Snail Control.

Gopher Control.

Whiteflies.

Biological Controls.

Beekeeper's Bibliography.

Roots in the Soil.

Mazibuko Trench Method.

Mulching and Double-digging.

Triple-digging.

Double-digging vs. Rototilling.

Double-digging vs. U-barring.

More about Amaranth and Quinoa.

Tree Collards.

Water Rationing and Home Gardening.

A Slide Show: 65 slides and written script describing Ecology Action's many years of research with biointensive food-raising techniques. Briefly covers: basics of the method, impact upon backyard food production, potential for truck farming, water, fertilizer and resource use, new tools such as mini-greenhouses and the U-bar, the herbal lawn, and more.

Related Publications by Other Organizations:

C. V. Seshadri, et al. *Bio-Dynamic Gardening.* Vol. 4. Shri A. M., M. Murugappa Chettiar Research Centre, Tharamani, Madras, 600 113, India, 1980. 38 pp.

———. *Bio-Dynamic Horticulture-Improvements & Extension.* Vol. 15. Shri A. M., M. Murugappa Chettiar Research Centre, Tharamani, Madras, 600 113, India, 1983. 43 pp.

Intensive Small Farms and the Urban Fringe. Sausalito, CA: Landal Institute for Small Farm Research, 1976. 93 pp. Based in part on Ecology Action's research.

A Preliminary Assessment of the Applicability of French Intensive/ Biodynamic Gardening Techniques in Tropical Settings. Santa Barbara, CA: Direct International Development/Direct Relief Foundation, 1978. 47 pp. Report from on-site visits to four

intensive demonstration gardens in Central America.
Y. H. Yang. "Home Gardens as a Nutrition Intervention." *Small Scale Intensive Food Production—Improving the Nutrition of the Most Economically Disadvantaged Families,* pp. 60–80. Washington, DC: League for International Food Education, 1977.

Accredited Classes in Biointensive Mini-Farming:

Ohio University, Attention: Steve Rioch, 5569 State Street, Albany, OH 45710. Ohio University has also approved (subject to full funding) a 4-year college program in biointensive agriculture.

Videotapes of Our Work:

Two award-winning PBS specials documenting our work have been televised nationally. They are available for rental or purchase from Bullfrog Films, Oley, PA 19547. *Gardensong* (1983) is a beautiful film about Alan Chadwick's work, our own, and that of others. *Circle of Plenty* (1987) is about our Willits garden and the *Menos y Mejores* project in northern Mexico. *Circle of Plenty* addresses some serious problems in world agriculture and shows that the biointensive method is a viable solution even under Third World conditions with poor soil.

Bountiful Gardens

For a select list of mail-order gardening books, fertilizers, and seeds, send a stamped, self-addressed envelope to Bountiful Gardens, 19550 Walker Road, Willits, California 95490.
—A Project of Ecology Action

NOTES

NOTES

NOTES

NOTES

NOTES

NOTES

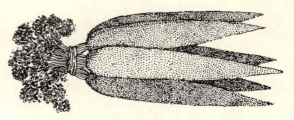